BREAKFAST AT KÜSNACHT

Conversations on C.G. Jung and Beyond

Stefano Carpani

Preface by Verena Kast

CHIRON PUBLICATIONS • ASHEVILLE, NORTH CAROLINA

www.ChironPublications.com

Interior design by Danijela Mijailovic
Cover design by Andrea Scurati
Printed primarily in the United States of America.

ISBN 978-1-63051-804-2 paperback
ISBN 978-1-63051-805-9 hardcover
ISBN 978-1-63051-806-6 electronic
ISBN 978-1-63051-807-3 limited edition paperback

Library of Congress Cataloging-in-Publication Data

Names: Carpani, Stefano, author. | Kast, Verena, 1943- writer of preface.
Title: Breakfast at Küsnacht : conversations on C.G. Jung and beyond / Stefano Carpani ; preface by Verena Kast.
Description: Asheville, North Carolina : Chiron Publications, [2020] | Includes bibliographical references. | Summary: "Breakfast at Küsnacht: Conversations on C.G. Jung and Beyond comprises a series of interviews with 10 Jungians and a special guest, Susie Orbach, feminist and relational psychotherapist. Each interview begins by asking them about the central steps of their intellectual biography/journey and which authors (or research arcas) they consider essential for their own development and work (also beyond psychoanalysis). Therefore, when interviewing the Jungians, three basic questions were asked: (1) Who is Jung? Or, who is your Jung? (2) What is Jung's relevance today? (3) What are dreams? These questions preceded a look into their own work and contributions. Themes contained within the book include: C.G. Jung's work and his validity today; HIV and AIDS; Anima/Animus and Homosexuality; Alchemy; Dreams; Marie-Louise von Franz; Wolfgang Giegerich and Hegel; Otto Gross, the Personal and the Political; Individuation; Painting, Drawing and the Unconscious; the Red Book; Relational Psychoanalysis; Women, Feminism, Love and Revolution; The application of the I-Ching in therapy; Becoming and Analyst. Contributors are: Paul Attinello, Ph.D. John Beebe, Ph.D. Ursula Brasch, M.A. Stefano Carpani, M.A., M.Phil. Gottfried M. Heuer, Ph.D. George Hogenson, Ph.D. Philip Kime, Ph.D. Marianne Meister-Notter, Dr. Phil. Susie Orbach, Ph.D. Alfred Ribi, M.D. Murray Stein, Ph.D. Mark Winborn, Ph.D"— Provided by publisher.
Identifiers: LCCN 2020016267 (print) | LCCN 2020016268 (ebook) | ISBN 9781630518042 (paperback) | ISBN 9781630518059 (hardcover) | ISBN 9781630518066 (ebook)
Subjects: LCSH: Psychoanalysis. | Jung, C. G. (Carl Gustav), 1875-1961.
Classification: LCC BF173.J85 C38 2020 (print) | LCC BF173.J85 (ebook) | DDC 150.19/54—dc23
LC record available at https://lccn.loc.gov/2020016267
LC ebook record available at https://lccn.loc.gov/2020016268

"The hour of departure has arrived, and we go our ways—I to die, and you to live. Which is better, God only knows."

Plato (Apology of Socrates)

"All beginnings are difficult."

Talmud

"Why were you searching for me? Didn't you know I had to be in my Father's house?"

Luke (2:49)

To the memory of my training-analyst

Dr. Med. Günter Langwieler,

and to my daughters, Bianca, Olivia, and Carlotta,

this book is dedicated.

CONTENTS

ACKNOWLEDGEMENTS

"Socrates, whose mother was a midwife, used to say that his art[1] was like the art of the midwife. She does not herself give birth to the child, but she is there to help during the delivery. Similarly, Socrates saw his task as helping people "give birth" to the correct insight, since real understanding must come from within. It cannot be imparted by someone else. And only the understanding that comes from within can lead to true insight" (Gaarder, 1994: p.66).

Similarly, psychoanalysis—especially Jungian—can be compared to the art of midwifery. To me, psychoanalysis—which Jung and von Franz described as an art and craft—is the absolute metaphor for what midwifery is: to accompany an individual to birth (anew) and to become who she/he really is. To become who she/he really is has never been before.

This book has many midwives who I want to thank here for their accompaniment, friendships, guidance, and for helping to finance its publication. They are Paul Attinello, John Beebe, Ursula Brasch, Heather Formaini, Verena Kast, Elizabeth Leuenberger-Kais, Marianne Meister, Andrew Samuels, and Andrea Scurati. I owe them my respect and gratitude.

A particular word of thanks goes to my friends Elizabeth and Andrea. Elizabeth transcribed the interviews from the original YouTube videos, and later edited them all. Andrea edited all the videos and designed the cover of this book. This book and series, without their dedication, precision,

[1] Philosophy

knowledge, and friendship, would not have been possible. Thank you!

I also want to thank all contributors who generously accepted my request for an interview, beginning in 2017, for my YouTube series, titled, "Breakfast at Küsnacht." At the same time, I would also like to thank those I interviewed who—for one reason or another—did not appear in this book.

In particular, I would like to express my gratitude to Murray Stein, who supported my idea to create such a book, was the first one to work on the interview transcripts with me, and put me in contact with Chiron. And of course, many thanks go to Chiron´s team—Steve Buser, Leonard Cruz, and Jennifer Fitzgerald—who decided to publish this book.

Alina and Andrea Mondini, my *Züricher* friends and hosts, have to be thanked dearly. Their hospitality and generosity during my training at the C.G. Jung Institute in Küsnacht made my stay in Switzerland warmer and pleasurable.

Unfortunately, there are only four women featured here. Along with Verena Kast's preface, three of those interviewed were women (Ursula Brasch, Marianne Meister, and Susie Orbach). I am particularly thankful to them all because, although I requested interviews with at least as many women as men, it seems that men are more prone to step forward and join such an initiative. I hope to be able to bring more women into the spotlight in a future book—perhaps Volume 2 will feature even more women than men!

This book is dedicated to the memory of my training-analyst Dr. Med. Günter Langwieler, who died, suddenly, in March 2019. Günter was a lateral thinker, and a generous, warm, and witty man. He was, in my opinion, a true dream catcher; and, above all, he was a good man. He was convinced that C.G. Jung had developed his own "theory of neurosis," and he recently wrote about this in *Jung's Theory of Neurosis between Dissociation and Imagination* (Zeitschrift für Analytische Psychologie, 2018).

A truly compassionate and relational man (although he never defined himself in terms of relational psychoanalysis), Dr. Langwieler (2018) was convinced of the "self-critical, non-dogmatic attitude of the therapist," which means "a permanent attention of the therapist for observations during psychotherapy which contradict his theoretical expectations." I had the honour and pleasure of undergoing training analysis with him between 2015 and 2018, and I am grateful to Günter, who taught me the art and craft of dream interpretation and active imagination with his own gentle approach, kindness, and patience. He accompanied me in my personal development, navigating the troubles of modern life, and he supported me throughout the different stages of my training at the C.G. Jung Institute in Zürich. Above all, he taught me that, "we cannot solve a complex. We can only solve a conflict."

And because life is stronger than death, this book is also dedicated to my daughters Bianca, Olivia, and Carlotta. They, like all children, are the future.

PREFACE

Verena Kast

A young man (born 1978), Stefano Carpani, who at the time was far along in his training to be a Jungian psychoanalyst, conducted interviews with the analysts he met with during his training, and placed the interviews on YouTube. Now they have been transcribed and are made available in print in this volume.

The colleagues with whom he conducted the interviews seem to have been chosen rather randomly, in accordance with Stefano Carpani's interests. What did he do? He talked to men and women who have become Jungian analysts. He asked about their intellectual careers, but above all what C.G. Jung means to them and how C.G. Jung is perceived in the present world. He asked about preferences and how they bring their special knowledge into psychotherapeutic practice. He also asked, among other things, "what is love?"

They are idiosyncratic interviews—and I can't get rid of the thought that Stefano was looking for models of Jung's analysts and continues to look for them, perhaps mentors as well. His hidden question may be: How is it possible to be a successful and satisfied Jungian analyst in this world? Or, let's think of Susie Orbach: How is it possible to be a feminist analyst? Of course, Stefano Carpani justified the interviews on YouTube with the fact that it was important to him that Jung's psychology become visible and audible, that the question of who C.G. Jung was, what meaning he still has, was asked again and again and so gets disseminated on the net. This is an honorable undertaking, possibly due to the fact that among other things, the book is dedicated to our colleague Dr. Günter Langwieler, who died too early, a colleague to whom it was very important that Jungian psychology should remain visible, or become visible again, a colleague who wanted to bring theory and practice into line in Jungian psychology.

But I think the search illustrated in this book has to do with the interviewer's search for his own Jungian identity, in which many Jungian identities are inquired into and depicted. The colleagues who were interviewed were selected according to the interviewer's taste and the randomness and fascination of the encounters, but also according to the willingness of the interviewees to engage in such an undertaking.

Breakfast at Küsnacht: this title is intended to link the various interviews. Why Breakfast at Küsnacht, when some interviews aren't connected with Küsnacht, one even explicitly means: Breakfast beyond Küsnacht? Is Küsnacht connected with Jung, with the source of Jung's psychotherapy, a classical place of memory, or is it about the author's first journalistic activity of this type, with these interviews? Is it his "breakfast"—and can we expect other nourishing activities in the course of time?

It is to the credit of this collection of interviews that readers become familiar and stimulated with various Jungian analysts, with focal points on their narrative biographies, their theoretical preferences, their convictions. As little as there is "the C.G. Jung," there is "the Jungian analyst," and yet I think that if you read these interviews, you can feel and discern a common basic attitude.

I wish for this book many interested readers.

Verena Kast
St. Gallen, December 2019

INTRODUCTION

Stefano Carpani

"Thank God, I'm Jung, and not a Jungian," remarked C.G. Jung (*Memories, Dreams, Reflections*, p.78). Today, more than 60 years after Jung´s death, there are many ways to be a Jungian.

If, as Andrew Samuels claimed in his 1985 book, *Jung and the Post-Jungians*, there are three main post-Jungian traditions—the "classical," "developmental," and "archetypal," which I have underlined somewhere else (*The Plural Turn*, Routledge, forthcoming 2020)—it may now be time for a fourth: the "plural." This approach, encompassing eclecticism and integration, is rooted in Samuels's work, and aims to restore and enhance Jung's work and Analytical Psychology at the core of depth psychology by studying the psyche as plural and, therefore, also political. That being said, I propose that this is, however, not the only new approach.

I call those who use this new approach: *neo-Jungians*.[2] This is a heterogeneous, international, and multicultural group of scholars who, on the one hand base their work on the teachings of Jung (and the post-Jungians), while on the other hand have opened their investigations beyond Analytical Psychology. Therefore, the neo-Jungians are able to balance the teachings of Jung and the post-Jungians with those teachings coming from other schools and traditions

[2] Not to be confused with Robert Moore´s "Neo-Jungian Mapping of the Psyche."

(both within and beyond psychoanalysis) in a mutual and plural, enriching exchange. In fact, contemporary neo-Jungians can be linked (although not limited) to relational (and post-relational) psychoanalysis, feminist psychoanalysis, the intersubjective approach, psychosocial studies, and cultural studies, to name a few.

The neo-Jungians find, in the following features of psychosocial studies, their purpose:

> (1) Psychosocial studies investigate the ways in which psychic and social processes demand to be understood as always implicated in each other, as mutually constitutive, co-produced, or abstracted levels of a single dialectical process.
> (2) Psychosocial studies can be understood as an interdisciplinary field in search of transdisciplinary objects of knowledge.
> (3) Psychosocial studies is also distinguished by its emphasis on affect, the irrational and unconscious process, often, but not necessarily, understood psychoanalytically.
> (4) Psychosocial studies object to the idea of thinking separately about psychological and social processes and then examining the way they intersect with each other.

Thus, there are many ways to be Jungian (or to be a Jungian), and this is very good news. It signifies that Analytical Psychology is alive, and reflects the continuing interest in, as well as perhaps even rejuvenation of, Jung´s theory at the beginning of the 21st century.

The fact that there are many ways to be a Jungian brought about my desire to speak with as many Jungians as possible, as well as from a wide range of different countries and training institutes. I did so with a little bit of courage and, in particular, the wish to capture the voice of senior Jungians. Therefore, the aim of this project is to bring Jung´s theory to a wider audience (beyond those specifically interested in Analytical Psychology), via a series of video interviews published on YouTube. In this way, I sought to give voice to diverse, key figures in the world of Analytical Psychology.

This project, which I titled "Breakfast at Küsnacht," comprises a series of conversations with ten Jungians and a special guest, Susie Orbach, feminist and relational psychotherapist.

I began each interview by asking them about the central steps of their intellectual biography/journey and which authors (or research areas) they consider essential for their own development and work (also beyond psychoanalysis). Therefore, when interviewing the Jungians, I also asked three basic questions: (1) Who is Jung? Or, who is *your* Jung? (2) What is Jung´s relevance today? (3) What are dreams? These questions preceded a look into their own work and contributions.

Paul Attinello was the last person I interviewed before sending the manuscript to the publisher. Although he is not senior in the field, his life story is certainly worth it. That is why I decided to include it here. Paul talked about his life and how and when he contracted HIV, after which he shared how he met Jung´s work and later decided to become a Jungian analyst. This, to me, is the most intimate conversation of the whole book.

John Beebe and I met in Wraklow, Poland, in June 2019, where he was a keynote speaker at a conference titled, "Collective Structures of Imagination – Image – Myth – Society," and where I presented my paper, titled, "The Fall of the Berlin Wall: Complex Theory and the Numinous in the Development of History." This was the first time John and I met. We found ourselves at ease, and our interview is the proof. We discussed his work on intuition, personality types, the father, and integrity. Picking up on a comment of his during the "Jung and Activism" conference in Prague 2017, I asked him to talk about anima and animus as non-gender, binary concepts, homosexuality, and individuation.

Ursula Brasch and I met at her home and praxis near to the Black Forest, Germany, in summer 2018. I asked her what dreams are and how to understand them. We looked at C.G. Jung and Richard Wilhelm's *The Secret of the Golden Flower* and the *I Ching*. We also discuss how the I Ching can be used therapeutically with patients, and later we looked into the concept of meaning and of opposites.

Gottfried M. Heuer is the leading world expert on Otto Gross. We met in summer 2017 in London, England. Rather than discussing the relationship between Gross and Jung, as is usually done, what sets this interview apart is that we look, instead, at Otto Gross´s concept of "The Personal is the Political" and discuss the relevance of Gross´s work today.

George Hogenson underlined Jung's very strong emphasis on the importance of the image for psychological well-being and the fact that, in modern societies, we have replaced this with an absolute wild proliferation of imagery through the media. Therefore, he looks at the fact that we seem to be surrounded by many images, but those images lack substance. Therefore, he claims that Jung had a deeper sense than any of the other psychologists or psychoanalysts, and that modernity, in general, has lost the dimension of depth to human experience. He discusses how images help transformation and lead, if taken into account with depth, to psychological well-being.

Philip Kime, after addressing the three-basic questions, looked beyond Jung and into the work of Wolfgang Giegerich (via Hegel and philosophy). We also talked about theory and practice when working with patients.

Marianne Meister-Notter considers the creative side of Jung´s approach, paying particular attention to painting and drawing. This conversation is a clinical portrait of how Meister-Notter works with unconscious materials employing painting and drawing with her clients.

Susie Orbach and I never actually met in person. Therefore, I am especially thankful to her for having agreed to meet via Skype, and to be part of this book. I wrote to her in the spring of 2018, introducing myself and explaining that I would like to talk to her about feminism, relational psychoanalysis, love, and revolution, and she accepted! She agreed to be interviewed by me without knowing one another personally. We met online: I was in Berlin and she was in London.

Alfred Ribi was the first Jungian I contacted for this project at the beginning of 2017, and was the first to accept my invitation to meet for an interview. We met at his praxis near Zürich (Erlenbach) on February 17, 2017, for what was to be a short interview; but we ultimately spent a very enjoyable two hours together! Our interview focused on C.G. Jung, Marie-Louise von Franz, alchemy, and the relevance of Analytical Psychology today. It was also fascinating to hear him speak of the 73 times he dreamt of Jung, and the book he wrote about these dreams, which allowed him to overcome his inferiority complex.

Murray Stein talked about C.G. Jung, individuation, dreams, Jung's *The Red Book* and its relevance today. We also discussed several passages from the original play Stein wrote with Henry Abramovitch, "The Analyst and the Rabbi."

Mark Winborn focused on who C.G. Jung was, and whether psychoanalysis is about democracy or aristocracy. We also discussed Mark´s latest book, wondering about psychoanalysis and whether interpretation is an art or a technique.

C.G. Jung and Thinking about HIV/AIDS

Paul Attinello

SC: Paul, thank you so much for joining *Breakfast at Küsnacht*, and congratulations. You just defended your thesis, a few days ago. Your thesis was about C.G. Jung and HIV/AIDS. Before we go into this, could you share the central steps in your intellectual biography/journey?

PA: When I was young, I was fascinated with complex things—modernist music, continental philosophers, experimental theatre, unusual approaches to fiction. But I didn't get into the university I wanted, stumbled through a poor undergraduate degree, and so left it all behind to become a resentful wanderer... AIDS crashed into my life and forced me to engage with the emotional world—but through grief and anger, which is not ideal. The '80s and '90s were a slew of failures and successes in San Francisco, Los Angeles, Berlin, Hong Kong, Australia—all rather chaotic in retrospect; I finally landed in northern England, with a Ph.D. and a stable job, though not much of a personal life. I suppose I'm an example of resilience, but on a slow timetable—it took years to put back together my intellectual fascinations, emotional concerns, and creativity; most of that happened around studying at the Jung-Institut, which gave me more purpose and direction than I've had in decades. Of course, there is a certain sadness in, now, focusing my thinking on AIDS—like a Holocaust survivor, I seem to be mostly memory; but perhaps there is also some life left.

SC: Who are the authors and the research areas you consider essential for your own development and work?

PA: The worlds of cultural theory and philosophy, of music and theatre and art, of writing—I've always been a bit of a glass bead game player; though, as in Hesse's novel, that game eventually becomes a bit thin. I can still be passionately moved to action in relation to the big thinkers—Benjamin, Foucault, Deleuze—and Jung makes a good complement to all of those. It's interesting that my research has also pulled me into the more visceral, more physical, more emotional—and so to Meredith Monk, Diamanda Galás. Like many people, I'm fascinated by what is different from me, and it would be fair to say a lot of my research attempts to translate that more physical world into something I can engage with and follow. As for the world of psychoanalysis—it increasingly seems that all the famous thinkers are saying things that can be integrated into a larger, more flexible sense of what the mind does. I'm long past being willing to take sides, but it's heartening that it finally seems easy to think through Jung, Bion, Klein, Freud, without worrying about any boundaries.

SC: Who is Carl Gustav Jung, or even—who is your own Carl Gustav Jung?

PA: I´d known a bit about Jung before 1987 but, strangely enough, my diagnosis of being HIV-positive—or at the time of having AIDS—in April 1987, the social worker who gave me my results was a Jungian analyst in training in Los Angeles—Mitch Walker, who's still an analyst there. I had already known that I would be HIV-positive, but it was still a huge shock, so that entire thing where you think you know something cognitively and, bang!—it hits you like a ton of bricks. We talked a bit afterwards and he said, would I like to be one of his training analysands; so I went to analysis with him for five years, which was wonderful. Mitch is brilliant—interesting, complicated, he had a background with the Radical Faeries and had very strong opinions about what it was to be gay, and how that fit the classic anima/animus structure—fairly radical ideas. And the only interesting problem with that is, because I'm diagnosed HIV-positive in 1987, most of our discussion is: what am I going to do about the fact that I'm going to die soon. So that was, in some ways, kind of strange, but hugely meaningful for me. Mitch allowed me to do some reading during the analysis—he actually said well, I can't stop you anyway—so I was reading Schwartz-Salant and other Jungians about interesting things... So, I had this general impression of—well, over the decades, as a music scholar, a musicologist, I ended up being very tied to the gender studies/cultural studies people, who of course use a lot of Freud and Lacan. I didn't much want to do Freud and I really did not want to do Lacan, so it was interesting to start putting Jung in the place of those.

Jung for me was relativist, flexible, brilliant—but, more than Freud and more than Lacan, he seems to know that we don't quite know what's going on in the mind; it's speculative, we're trying things out. Being experimental is much easier for Jung than it was for them, and that made me happy because I don't think we know what we're doing yet, either. So that ended up being just really alive, sort of more exciting. And then, various decades of doing various things ... and about ten years ago now, I was feeling a bit disaffected, disconnected, teaching in a university in northern England, but didn't feel much in contact with my life; and so I thought I would come here to Küsnacht for the study program that is a sort of a taster program. I came here in 2009, and gradually decided to actually train to be an analyst, finally finishing this week [early July 2019]. So, that very strange story ... it's interlinked with the entire HIV/AIDS story, but it is a sort of parallel track, almost.

SC: Jung is about many things; among them are dreams, symbols... Did you have dreams related to AIDS in the last 40 years?

PA: Well ... yes. [laughter] It's interesting: some of the biggest chunks of dreams are around that. Of course, sexual dreams and chaotic dreams, but some of the big dreams were interestingly... I'd have intermittent dreams with train stations, airports, it was always planes and trains that were leaving, but had people I know leaving on them, or not leaving, and people I didn't know; there would be various structures where somehow the meaning would always come down to all of this death material, people leaving—am I leaving now, am I leaving later; that went on for some years.

And then a series of San Francisco dreams—that was very interesting because that's where it all starts for me. San Francisco... I arrived there in 1979 after a terrible undergraduate degree, and basically sex, drugs, and singing in bars; lots of fun. But in the winter of 1981 or winter of 1982 I had a few illnesses that I think were probably what we now call seroconversion disorders, which are essentially the flu-like illnesses that you'll have when you first get the virus. There's something rather obscure where you're sick for a week or two—it varies from person to person, but they have targeted this—it is something you can see when the virus first enters the body, it explodes for a bit and then goes dormant for a while. So, I had things like that in the winter of 1981, winter of 1982, along with a guy I'd had sex with—a lovely guy, Reid, we were both rather nervous about this at the time and didn't know what it was. Then Reid fell very sick in the summer of 1983, and he took six months to die—grotesquely, really; a very tall, handsome blond man who sort of blew up like a balloon—pancreas problems, Kaposi's sarcoma on his skin. In later years the gay community would get very good at taking care of people in hospitals, but at the time we were kind of incompetent at it and, in fact, he took care of us. At one point in the hospital, I was staring at him, completely freaked out by all of this, and he said: "You have to stop screwing around and get out of San Francisco, apply to go do graduate degrees." He died

December 2, 1983, and I got into UCLA about a week later; so you can see how for me all of those personal stories were all intertwined.

SC: It's very interesting to me that the social worker who told you that you were positive was a Jungian analyst in training. The title of your thesis, which will become a book, is "The Passionate Body: AIDS, Archetype, Cultural Complex."[3] Your work is divided into sections—let's start with "Infection/taint: Revulsion and disgust." What do you mean?

PA: Well ... some of the first things about infection are things that we don't think about much. Infection is very logical, very scientific, it's perfectly normal, we teach kids about it in school. You know that people in some Asian cities do smart things such as wearing masks during cold and flu season, and we know what to touch and what not to touch in order to avoid infection. But the tricky thing that we don't think about very often is that all that logical, scientific world is also kind of illusory: we don't experience infection directly, we are *told* about it—which generates its own strange, incomprehensible complex. Those of us who are educated and who identify with our educations, who believe our educations, would just say, this is a fact. But certainly—and I think any doctor, any hospital, is very aware of this; and in our HIV patient groups, I have one in Newcastle and am a member of a few more—the assumption that everyone believes in what an infection is, completely, that is a little exaggerated. It's a little hallucinatory, it's a little weird, and I think some people don't quite believe what we tell them about infection, about how it is contracted. And of course, they won't believe us when people say: this is safe, that is safe, there's no way you can

[3] Paul Attinello, "The Passionate Body: AIDS, Archetype, Cultural Complex." Küsnacht: C.G. Jung-Institut, 2019.

get it that way. Infection looks like some sort of contact magic, so many people will just not believe that there are *any* behaviors that are safe. You know there are hundreds of stories about this, all through the entire history of HIV/AIDS, and everyone knows many of them; but here is one of the recent ones from one of my patient groups, from a few years ago. One of our members from Africa was having trouble with her leg; she was in a hospital near us, in another small city. Newcastle upon Tyne, where I live now, is really a larger city in the middle of a lot of small cities—things are very dispersed, with different hospitals and sometimes different levels of education. She told us about the hospital orderly who was pushing her along in a wheelchair, and double-gloving himself to do so. Now this makes no sense. And this is a hospital orderly, this is someone who should know better. So that whole hallucinatory bit, that's very much the sort of thing that hangs around AIDS in the way that it hung around plague, cholera, and all those mysterious illnesses, and of course tuberculosis, that would be a big one for the nineteenth century. Everything that *can* be contacted in certain ways but *not* others—but regular, non-medical people will tend not to believe that, will tend to see it everywhere.

SC: So, can we say that, at that time, and even today, infection links to sin? And/or ignorance.

PA: Well, it would link to sin by... We do think of infection as bad. Infection may be quasi-invisible, very scientific, but of course we associate it absolutely with "bad." You have children, you know how we do this—don't touch that, don't eat that, don't pick that up off the ground—so it's all "bad stuff." So there's something about badness, about being touched by the badness of the world. That would lead into the whole discussion of social disease, sex in the world, being in contact with people. Sexuality is, of course, contact, and the world is contact. In the thesis there was a point where I was talking about—I can probably even expand this more—some of the Jungians who talked about AIDS—one of the best is Eugene Monick, he spends a lot of time on this—he will talk about the whole problem. The best counterexample is Kimberly Bergalis.[4] This is a case from 1990, you probably won't know it, it's very American. She was a young woman in Florida, very pretty, very blonde, so very photogenic for the television cameras.

SC: Farrah Fawcett style?

PA: But more innocent, really, so perfect for this kind of trial story. She was infected with HIV by her dentist; she didn't have sex with him—it was apparently carelessness with the bleeding and the sores and the openness around the teeth and that sort of thing. And of course, as there were no useful medications at the time, he was not only HIV-positive, but he probably had fairly high levels of the virus in his bloodstream. One of the things she said in court that was crucial was: "I'm a good person, this shouldn't happen to me." This is one of the very tricky things—Monick will talk about this—and of course this will show up in the discussions in *AION*; this will be core to advanced levels of Jung's thinking, the understanding that fate, and the world and what happens to us—we don't get to control it, it has nothing to do with what we want. We *are* exposed to the world. Sexuality is of course being exposed to the world, but even leaving the house is being exposed to the world, and when Bergalis said, "I'm a good person, this shouldn't happen to me," it's like ... you don't get to make that kind of bargain. That's just not possible. In a realistic life ... it's exposure to the world. So, I think one of the reasons that sin—you like the word "sin" here, that surprised me a bit...

---

[4] Eugene Monick, *Evil, Sexuality, and Disease in Grünewald's Body of Christ*. Dallas: Spring, 1993.

SC: It's not that I like it, it's from my culture, I'm Italian, I grew up in a cultural environment where sin is important. Those that don't comply with morality, with right or wrong, as this story just said, is, well, that is a sin.

PA: Of course, of course, but it works, it works: you must have done something bad.

SC: God is punishing you.

PA: You may or may not remember this but, also in the eighties—this didn't go on for long, it quickly became sort of forbidden—but there was a point when people were using the term "innocent victim," which meant children who had been born to a mother who was HIV+, or someone who was hemophiliac and got HIV through a blood transfusion, someone like that who was "innocent." Now nobody ever pointed out the very obvious opposite term, which would be all the "guilty" victims. So, it is a lot like that strange treatment of tuberculosis in the 19th century, because so often they didn't just think about it as an airborne disease, they'll think about it as: there is something erotic and sexual and infected about it, that sort of thing. And so: "Oh, look, you're sick, you must have been bad."

SC: You write about fear and anger—one part is titled, "Who gave it to you?" and another is titled, "Terror and anxiety," and then, "Structures for handling fear."

PA: I was thinking about that whole section as outlining different emotions, which tend to cluster very strongly. Individual people—well of course, as you know, when you've had people in the room undergoing analysis or counseling of any kind, they'll go through different emotions, shift through different things; but I was trying to look at these cultural complexes as though individual people are passing through a structure, a set of forces that exists independent of those people. So, the large cloud of fear is very obvious, it's associated with all of that infection stuff. What about death, what about sin, what about this terrible thing? What about the pictures I've seen in the newspapers of people covered with blotches, and what about being associated with all of those "bad" people—the fags, and the people doing drugs, and the foreigners, clearly the sources of rottenness in our culture? That is how a lot of people constructed it, of course.

So that was the fear; and that would often shift to anger; and then, by the mid-eighties, the growth of ACT-UP, and the powerful world of activism; the entire world of political statements, people would identify strongly with that. And they would essentially turn fear into anger and do their best to take all of their feelings, all of their projections, all of their experiences, to put them into a political focus. This was a very strong thing, enormous histories of that, enormous excitement over that, enormous pride over that, and of course it did change the way that AIDS was treated, it even changed the way it's spoken of. But that's always been something that has its own problems: It is, in some ways, a distraction. It is the ego distracting itself from the terrors that are beyond the ego, it's the ego saying: I'm in charge of this illness, I'm in charge of all this, and I'm going to make it into political anger.

And even in 1993, I think I was first talking about this—I gave a talk that was titled, "At three in the morning," talking about playing the piano at three in the morning—a piece of music by Tori Amos, "Not the Red Baron," which is her song about AIDS[5]—it's very oblique, it's very subtle, it's very

[5] Tori Amos, "Not the Red Baron," in *Boys for Pele* (Atlantic 892862-2), 1996.
Paul Attinello, "Closeness and Distance: Songs about AIDS," in *Queering the Popular Pitch* (edited by Sheila Whiteley and Jennifer Rycenga), Routledge, 2006, pp. 221-31.

personal. But I was also thinking about three in the morning in a hospital room, because hospital nights are very long—I don't know if you know this, I don't know if you've gone through this. Inevitably the bed isn't quite comfortable, and usually you aren't feeling very well, or something might be wrong anyway—the nights just seem to go on forever sometimes, it's hard to get to sleep, the slightly plastic-y sheets... So, at three in the morning: that is when all the activism and all of the political strength and the assertion that we can change this vanishes; and all you are left with is your body, which is sick. So, my question is always, at the level of activism: What is activism going to do, when you are in that condition? It's going to do nothing. You're facing your own body, your mortality, your death. You're facing all of your feelings and all of your sensations, and there's nothing you can do to turn that into politics. So, to really grapple with that, and to really stand in that, was really big, there.

SC: Is this what you meant when you were "Open to psychosis"?

PA: That is something a bit different. Remember, I've spent some years looking at artworks about AIDS, especially music, because that is my profession, but I would end up talking about artworks in a lot of areas. And it's interesting: all of this fear, and even terror—that terror reference that you mentioned—I was thinking of a raw and the cooked thing, that I want to go into further as I expand this material. When something is really raw—as opposed to, the cooked form will be: We will have a march, and I will make a sign, and we will try to get the government to improve our medications. But the raw thing is terror: I'm dying, I'm rotting, this is horrible, this is the end. So, there is a lot of madness in there; and some of the artists, especially Diamanda Galás—I don't know if you know her, an amazing Greek-American singer, very scary; her brother died of

AIDS[6] in 1986, and he taught her performance art. So, while she was learning this extraordinarily complex singing technique, and a certain amount of stage presentation—she is mostly a concert singer, but very experimental, very complex—she started to make all of this—rage, terror, you know, she was doing the Greek thing. (I can say that, I'm half Greek!) Greek culture does have that core of crazy anger, crazy terror, crazy rage, and she has always really invested in that and presented it on stage. And a few other people, there are different artists who would do this. But trying to look for the real terror/madness/craziness/rage that is embedded in the fear of death—we try to pretend it's not, we try to put it in hospitals, but—we think we're civilized, and this stuff comes up and it all is stripped away.

SC: Before we go into that I wanted to look at "Paranoia." What do you mean with paranoia?

PA: It's interesting, this goes in different directions... There are three or four different versions of paranoia here, of course. One of the more obvious and simpler would be: Oh look, it's foreigners who bring HIV into my country—it's always about "them," it's always the exotic ones, of course.

SC: But if they come with a big check, they're welcome...

PA: Well, it depends! I did get deported from Australia, even though I was expecting to have a job there... But paranoia: One of my favorite examples is the oldest piece of music that I have about AIDS. December 1983, I think, so—my god, the same month Reid died. So, Frank Zappa, he was the first, believe it or not. He wrote this ridiculously grotesque pornographic musical called *Thing-Fish*,[7] and the opening prologue is about AIDS. It doesn't show up again for the rest

[6] Diamanda Galás, *The Shit of God*. New York: High Risk, 1996.
[7] Frank Zappa, *Thing-Fish*. London: Rykodisc, 1984/1995.

of the show; it will basically be this crazed, incoherent voice making all sorts of strange mistakes and imitating a sort of Amos 'n' Andy style, it is very, very bizarre; and it will be a story of a kind that was hanging around a lot in the eighties. You can still find this kind of story in a lot of books, the kind that say, AIDS was *created*. It is about the American government designing a virus and trying it out on black guys in prison and—I'm trying to remember the phrase he uses—"sissy-boys." So it will be about the government wanting to get rid of people that it doesn't like.

SC: *Stranger Things* style?

PA: Of course, of course. And it's completely understandable.

SC: From those that would think, I'm a good guy, this shouldn't happen to me.

PA: Of course. So, you can see all of the heavy good/bad, God/Satan—it is drenched all over this illness. So bizarre; and still today.

SC: Purity and impurity?

PA: Absolutely. You know, the people who really get uncomfortable about this, even in the patient groups in northern England where I'm a member—usually white gay men don't find it terribly hard to talk about it, and some of the women from Africa are willing to talk about it. Straight men, generally no. But a lot of the white women in England, and what one might call regular, everyday women in many cultures, do not want to talk about it. They will feel completely—it marks them as them as the Sinner. This is all the sinner thing—the tainted one, the horribly ruined one... There's a wonderful song—I keep talking about songs today, as I say this is some of my background—there's a wonderful song from a group in Melbourne, Australia, where a songwriter wrote this lovely thing about, "I've got a secret."[8] The lyrics are all about a woman who is just standing in a grocery store buying food, and thinking, I have a secret; and she says hi to friends, and she says hi to the person at the cash register... she's terrified that someone will find out her secret, that she doesn't blend in properly.

SC: From "Paranoia" to "Death as black hole, or event horizon."

PA: I think I used to think... is this a bizarre sentence? I used to think I knew what I thought about death.

SC: Do you?

PA: Well, actually... One of the other things that happened to me in 1987—in the late 1980s I actually had three support systems: one was my Jungian analysis, another was a small writing group with Terry Wolverton in Los Angeles, where I was doing some of the first poetry and short story writing that I had done in my life, a wonderful experience, I was really glad to do that. And the third was—I'm not a particularly religious person, but my 'buddy' John Shinavier at AIDS Project Los Angeles—this is when I was living in Los Angeles, rather than San Francisco—was a member of an ashram in Florida run by Ma Jaya Sati Bhagavati, who was a spiritual teacher. She had come from New York—her background was a sort of wild Italian-Jewish mix, a wonderful woman, very much of the—when you think about spiritual teachers, the ones that are sort of the "mad" ones. There is a tradition of this in Buddhism—the ones that don't behave very well, that are rather noisy—she tended to explode with food and energy and generosity and these

[8] Jane Bayly, "Secret Life," in *Positive Steps*, Melbourne: Positive Women (Victoria), 2001.

sorts of things, and a very noisy woman, so she didn't look like a spiritual teacher. But she was wonderful for me because she was just full of life, at a point when I was really dampened down. And she gave names, Hindu names. After I'd known her for two or three years, she would regularly visit California, a big sort of festival thing and everybody would hang around and eat all day for the entire weekend. She had given a lot of people names; she was calling me Poet, because I had sent her some of my poems, but she hadn't given me a "real" name. And at one point I asked her; and she actually looked embarrassed, which was not a very typical look for her, she was very hard to embarrass [laughter]. And she said, "Well I did give you a name, but I didn't think you'd like it, so I haven't told you." So, I asked, "What is it?" She said, "Well, I decided to call you Nachiketas." Who's Nachiketas?

Shall I tell this story?... I have to tell this story.

The Katha Upanishad, which is from about 600 B.C., around the time when Buddhism and Taoism start to appear, in the middle of the Upanishads, in the middle of these hundreds of years, practically thousands of years, when they're building up this tradition of the Upanishad tradition of Hinduism, where they're making this more spiritual, more subtle, they're explaining things... The Katha Upanishad actually starts with a short fairy tale, and the fairy tale has a boy, Nachiketas, who is a Brahmin, a young member of the priest caste; and he's watching his father, who is sacrificing cattle and food to Yama, the god of death. Except the cattle are kind of old, and the food is from yesterday, and everything is a bit third-class and cheap and ... not the way you're supposed to do it. So, the boy says, "Father, why are you doing this, this is not the sacrifice you're supposed to be making." And his father is very embarrassed and very offended, and says, "Well, go down to hell yourself." The boy is very literal-minded—this is a very good name for me—so he goes down to Death, to stand outside Yama's house. But Yama is out doing his work in the world, collecting the dead, taking care of the dead; and his servants don't know what to do with a living boy, who is not supposed to be there. So, they shut the door and they do nothing. The boy waits for three days, and after three days, Yama comes back; and Yama is extraordinarily embarrassed because this is against all sorts of rules of politeness, anything due to a Brahmin child, this is an incredibly rude thing to do. And he says, "I'm so sorry, for the three days you've waited I will give you three boons." So, the first one is, let me go back to my father and make him not angry at me, so I can go home, that's easy; the second one is, teach me to make the sacred fire, and they do that. And the third one, the boy says: "Tell me the secret of death." And Yama says: "I can't tell you that. Even the gods don't know that, I'm not allowed to tell you that, how about if I give you something else—would you like houses, do you want dancing girls, do you want cattle, what do you want, I'll give you anything." And the boy says: "Tell me the secret of death." This is perfect for me, really—stubborn and irritating and a little clueless, it's just wonderful. And so, finally, Yama breaks down and says: "The secret of death is life." And that leads to the entire Katha Upanishad, which is the great text on rebirth—the idea that death actually leads to life. So that was the name that she gave me: the obnoxious little boy who really wants to know what's going on, and is staring straight at the worst stuff. Which, I suppose ... the thesis is another version of that, isn't it?

SC: It's a continuation. I like your story because it's the story of someone who went through something difficult, with so many people dying, people you loved—but you are here to honor them, to tell their stories, while you tell your story; but also saying this out loud and proud here, which doesn't happen very often. And of course you have your own style to make it easier, but I think it's really interesting. And... "Nothingness."

PA: What do we do with nothingness? That is one of the hardest things that can... That is probably *the* hardest thing; because it never changes. Whatever we do with it, it doesn't change, it never speaks back to us. All of our cultural projections and our personal anxieties about death—they never get answered. Which is why we speak about it so much: why so many religions and philosophies spend so much time there.

SC: At the end of your work, you talk about "The Passionate Body." What do you mean?

PA: Well this was actually wonderful, this happened here, in Küsnacht. There was a seminar here at the Jung-Institut with Marion Dunlea, a wonderful body therapist, body analyst. They've had a number of people who specialize in body psychology working here—many of them are absolutely brilliant, not many are terribly articulate; some of them don't explain what they're doing very well, but they do it brilliantly. It's much better when they actually work with people, which I've seen them do. This woman, Marion Dunlea, could actually talk about what she does. She's just come out with a book, and it's been successful.[9] She gave a wonderful seminar just down the hall, four or five hours, with the room full of students; and worked with a lot of us individually. And it was very, very charged—I was one of the people she did pick a couple of times, which was amazing—stuff that I'm sure for anyone else would be trivial, but for me was absolutely startling. At one point she said, come up here and let's look at this—we were looking at a corner of the room; and I stood up and, because my legs

[9] Marion Dunlea, *BodyDreaming in the Treatment of Developmental Trauma*. Oxon: Routledge, 2019.

had been crossed and I'd had my iPad on my lap taking notes, my leg was asleep. So, I did what I would do, which was: grinned, looked embarrassed and sarcastic, shook my leg, and tried to walk forward. And she said, stop! Your leg's asleep, just wait until it recovers! Now this sounds incredibly obvious and incredibly simple, but you know, as we do in so many things here, as you make these discoveries yourself or with your patients, there will be some very basic structure. And of course, what is completely normal for me is: the ego is in charge, and the brain is in charge, and if the body objects, it has its marching orders, right? I'm not interested in listening to the body, I'm going to tell it what to do. So, she was quite amazing.

But one of the things that happened: towards the end of her seminar, I was starting to write—I suddenly thought, I know what the outline of this thesis is, and I started to write down a lot of these chapter headings, ending with: "The Passionate Body." Thinking, suddenly: even though we're so accustomed to thinking of AIDS as all about death and collapse and destruction, really this is eros, this is sexuality. Even drugs—we always go, oh, drugs are bad—but drugs are *exciting*, right? There is this desire to be, to do, something bigger; it may be flawed—drugs often are—but there's this passion there to exist, and one of the reasons there's so much rage and anger and intensity is that the body really wants to be alive. So, this is all about passion, and existence. I want to be alive, I want to have sex, I want to be here, I want to feel—and that is actually the core here, that's not just a gloss-over, this would be the positive aspect—no-no-no. It's not always a light thing, or a cheerful thing, but this passionate body is really at the core of it, which is why it started to drive the thesis.

And it's interesting—that evening we did have a seminar on thesis topics, which is one reason it was so exciting to suddenly go, "Oh, I know what I'm doing!" I presented last of the five people in the room, and Philip Kime, who held the seminar, looked at me and said: "'The Passionate Body' is the last chapter—what if that's the title?" And I remember actually shaking, starting to shake at this, and getting into a very intense discussion late at night here at the Institute, which is very strange. And at one point, Philip said: "You know, sometimes in analysis people discover that the interpretation of their lives can completely shift—retroactively." Suddenly, the last thirty years mean something *different*.

SC: It seems so clear...

PA: Yes, and you can see the body—my body gets a little charged even as I talk about this.

SC: Looking at the news—you know I live in Berlin, and very often, in the newspaper, and even in advertisements from the government or the region, there is news about—AIDS is back. Berlin is very open, very libertine, a little bit the way you describe San Francisco ... you wrote about the aging patients. As an aging patient, why do you think AIDS is "coming back," if it is coming back?

PA: I don't think it's coming back among the aging patients, I think we're sort of a different group—I think it's coming back among the uninfected. But the interesting thing about the aging patients is: We can be a little ridiculous. I'm 62, and I'm probably—let's see, 1981 or 2 to 2019, so call that 37 to 38 years. And diagnosis is 32 years ago... It is true, scientifically: the presence of the virus does damage the body. So, it is said that we are all a bit physically older than we would be. Interestingly, my new doctor is really excellent—I've been really lucky over the decades, on four continents, to have really fantastic doctors; but my new doctor is fairly energetic, very Scottish, very focused, and he did say: "Yeah, that's not proven. I'm not interested—I want you to be in better shape." So, all right, I'll do what I can; but there is a tendency for us to be a bit more damaged. But what is even more interesting, and kind of chaotic, is—older people with AIDS, long-term or not long-term—many of us overinterpret everything. You look at the Facebook groups for long-term survivors, or even not particularly long-term survivors—everyone is anxious about everything that happens in the body, thinking somehow: this is AIDS, this is death! But no, that is just what is going to happen to people your age, or maybe a little older. So, it's an interesting panic. And it tells you how little we're prepared for the regular weaknesses of the body. Which, again, is probably that awkward tendency towards isolation.

SC: I want to get your opinion on the government need to be out and loud with an informative campaign; so, inform the generation of young men and young women aged 20 to 25, maybe younger, about something that happened twenty years ago, thirty years ago—it's not long ago—as if we lost what we'd learned: how to take care of each other... I was shocked when I saw that this was coming around again.

PA: Of course. Well, think of the huge, long-term problem of the urban West, of people being too separate. If we were in more of a village context, or if we were just more connected, it wouldn't be so shocking when people got a bit older and more fragile. And also, we wouldn't be so worried, because younger people would be taking care of other things and we'd be taking care of them, and all that kind of thing.

SC: But there is also something else that links to your thesis: new angers, new paranoias.

PA: Of course: it's coming from outside, it's disastrous, it's death, no one to help me... And of course, all the way back to: at three in the morning, in the hospital, or not in the hospital, when it's just you and your bed and your body, which may not be doing so well. Or are you just worried about it too much? This is a pretty universal experience—some people handle it better. You know, here we are in Switzerland, and so many of the people here are so tough and so athletic and that's so powerful, it's impressive (I should do more of that). And they will create a particular attitude—I can take control of this, I can handle this—that I think is wise, I think they tend to be pretty clear about it. But everyone else does tend to let themselves go in modern culture, don't they? It's a tough thing.

SC: To conclude I would like to ask you—why among various Jungian approaches and views, you chose the cultural complex? How does it fit?

PA: A lot of people have written about single cases, and there are a lot of wonderful—you know the longest and biggest is Robert Bosnak's *Dreaming with an AIDS Patient*[10], that was very famous, really wonderful, from the mid-eighties; and a lot of other Jungians—and a lot of non-Jungians—have written about individual patients. For me the problem with that was, in each case—actually the Bosnak is a good example.

Bosnak's patient is a young man from Texas who's gay but doesn't want to be gay, who's considering becoming a priest, it's 1985; and for the first couple of months with Bosnak he's trying to figure out who he is and what he wants to do in the analysis, and Bosnak has particular opinions of his own about what he should do or shouldn't do. Then he gets sick—suddenly very sick. Recovers a bit, they realize he's HIV-positive—they realize he has AIDS, it's 1985, they

[10] Robert Bosnak, *Dreaming with an AIDS Patient*. Boston: Shambhala, 1989. [Reprinted and expanded as:] *Christopher's Dreams: Dreaming and Living with AIDS*. New York: Dell/Delta, 1997.

don't make those distinctions—he has AIDS, and expectations are ... low. He'll live for three years, during which Bosnak will have a very intense analytic relationship with a lot of dreams, a lot of really close connection. Of course, the guy doesn't really want to think about AIDS much—he wants to think about being a priest, and not being gay, or being gay, and—because he's from the South and he's living in Boston, at one point he's trying to deal with the fact that a very supportive black church is willing to support him becoming a minister, and he has to decide how he feels about that [laughter]. So, he's dealing with all sorts of complexes and fragments and elements of his own, and behind it will be all of this stuff about AIDS that I'm constructing as a cultural complex. From my point of view, all of that exists simultaneously with all of the personal material. But it takes a long time for them to get to that. And interestingly, from my point of view, I think that by the end of Bosnak's book, I think Bosnak really understands, and has—can I say, transformed his experience of what AIDS is, and death and sex and... Bosnak himself is straight, but he is willing to imagine an erotic connection between them, and he's really—he really loves this patient by the time he dies. The patient, who is called Christopher in the book ... he gets part way there, or a bit more than part way. It's interesting, it's almost as though—and I'm sure this happens a lot in severe illnesses—it feels as though the analysand is piggybacking his awareness, his individuation, on the analyst's. He doesn't get quite as far, but he gets far enough that he can die, relatively, in peace. And I was thinking—that's just the biggest example. I've seen this in other clinical cases that I've read—it felt as though if people understood, knew, how big this is, this particular cluster of elements, then the analyst would much better be able to see where do we go, where do we need to go, rather than waiting for the darkest, heaviest stuff to come up in the course of everyday work. Obviously, you need to let the patient move at their own pace, but there are so many cases where it feels as though a little more.... Well, you know, one of the things you'll see throughout the psychological literature around AIDS is analysts and therapists and psychologists saying, Gosh, this is big and scary, with a surprised tone: "Oh my gosh, this is much scarier than I thought it was" [laughter]. And I think if we had a better idea of what that was before we are sitting watching a patient work through it, I just think that would be so much more powerful.

SC: Thanks, Paul. I look forward to reading your book.

PA: I look forward to finishing writing it [laughter].

C.G. Jung, Anima/Animus, Homosexuality, and Integrity

John Beebe

SC: Dear John, thank you so much for joining Breakfast at Küsnacht. We are in Wroclaw, Poland, at an interesting conference on Jung and society. I would like to start this interview looking at your intellectual biography. Therefore, could you share the central steps in your intellectual biography/journey?

JB: My relation to psychological work began when I was a 17-year-old college student. I saw a notice at Harvard that was seeking volunteers to work in a public mental hospital for children in Waltham, Massachusetts. The sign said, "Help a child who is mentally ill," and I realized that I had always assumed that only adults would be mentally ill. I started with a series of one-to-one weekly walks with a cool, oppositional 14-year-old boy, and eventually took a part-time job working on an inpatient unit with autistic children. I was an English major at the time, but I took an elective course taught by Clyde Kluckhohn and Henry Murray about personality and culture which included some material on Jung. I began to take pre-med courses, and eventually applied to medical school at the University of Chicago, where I took an elective course Eugene Gendlin taught in the Psychology Department. He impressed me with the value of focusing on here-and-now bodily felt experiencing. When I got to San Francisco to do my medical internship, I went into therapy with a Jungian analyst who used a Rogerian technique when listening to patients. Eventually, with encouragement from Tom Kirsch, who was my supervisor during my residency at Stanford, I decided to go into Jungian analytic training.

SC: Who are the authors and the research areas you consider essential for your own development and work?

JB: My work with Gendlin included some field testing of the focusing manual he had just developed, and my name was on the first paper about that research. I got very interested in Carl Rogers, and then later in the work of Hellmuth Kaiser, which I brought into my psychiatric residency as a way to talk with patients that included both reflection on the feeling in each communication and also the need to take responsibility for what was communicated. My analysis inspired me to bring the same rapt scrutiny to my dreams. Von Franz's work on fairy tales influenced my work on film. I combined her work on the inferior function with Isabel Briggs Myers' understanding of "good type development" and eventually added to both to conceive an eight-function dynamic model of types. After completing analytic training, I found Kohut's Self Psychology a good way to continue to work on the therapeutic interaction as a place where both empathy and integrity are essential. This led to my book, *Integrity in Depth*.

SC: Which other areas do you consider fundamental in your own intellectual biography (also beyond psychoanalysis)?

JB: I found the Richard Wilhelm translation of the I Ching with Jung's Foreword invaluable for learning to recognize archetypal situations in an objective way and intuiting how to bring them into Tao. This led me to appreciate moral psychology in a Chinese way and paved the way to a long engagement with the training of Chinese psychotherapists, which is ongoing.

SC: When did you realize (and decide) you wanted to become a Jungian analyst?

JB: At age 31 in 1970, after five years of my own Jungian analysis.

SC: John, who was Carl Gustav Jung? Or rather, who is *your own* Carl Gustav Jung?

JB: Sometimes when I think about Jung, Poe's "Imp of the Perverse" takes over, and I recall Maurice Chevalier coming back for the second time as a movie star in America, after a long and dubious period of disgrace because he had collaborated just a little too much with the Vichy government. For a while he was *persona non grata*, and then he was a great and wonderful entertainer. He appeared in *Gigi*, a film by Vincente Minnelli that won the Academy Award, and sang the song, "I'm Glad I'm Not Young Anymore." Sometimes I think to myself, if Jung came back, he would say "I'm glad I'm not *Jung* anymore." That's my Jung, the Jung who was glad not only that he was not a Jungian but even that he's not Jung anymore, because he goes on evolving, and we go on carrying his project forward. The Jung I first heard about, between 1956 and 1957, so over 60 years ago, is not the Jung I think about on a daily basis now. There has been some evolution in the image of Jung in my mind over that period of time. So, I'm sure he is not Jung anymore and he is probably glad about that!

SC: What do you think is Jung's relevance today, at the beginning of the 21st century?

JB: It remains his openness to what presents itself from the unconscious. It is not his attempts to close those questions, but his openness to hearing from the unconscious. In a sense, it is his granting space for what he originally called a "compensation" to the conscious attitude, and gradually began to call an "objective psyche," because there is some kind of capacity for objectivity beyond our normally conditioned minds that is constantly sifting, commenting, and mirroring our ideas in such a way that we actually have the chance to examine and reconsider them in the light of another perspective. I think that remains his gift to us, and that becomes a lifelong process for those of us who believe in this capacity of the mind to correct itself at that level through some kind of synthetic, imaginative process that starts by seeming just another form of our subjectivity, but then turns out to be far more objective. That, I think, remains his great gift to us.

SC: To look into the irrational?

JB: I wouldn't say that. Because here is where my work on typology has made me emphasize the book *Psychological Types* and its enormous difference from the book *Symbols of Transformation* as we now know it, in which Jung starts with the idea that the conscious mind is rational and the unconscious mind is irrational. He does say that in the correspondence that he made with Hans Schmid-Guisan about psychological types sometime between 1915 and 1916, which is still several years before the type theory completely consolidated, and he wrote the draft of *Psychological Types* and completed it in 1919. Those were such germinal years that you really have to ask, what was Jung thinking at the beginning of 1912, what was he thinking at the end? What was he thinking at the beginning of 1913, what at the end? I've done that over the years, and it's very interesting how fast his mind changes. And if you move with him from what he thought in 1912 to what he puts into *Psychological Types* in 1919, you find that he no longer says the unconscious is irrational and the conscious is rational. He says there are actually eight types of consciousness (or as we now would call them eight function-attitudes of consciousness), and fully four are irrational. That, to me, is among his greatest contributions; yet people still aren't taking it in. Far more interesting than the theory of archetypes is that there really is such a thing as irrational consciousness, and that it is organized. For all we know, what's sitting in the unconscious is unrealized reason, not the irrational. In other words, the equation of irrational and unconscious just can't be sustained after a close reading of *Psychological Types.* But, see, everybody loves the idea of the irrational hiding in the unconscious. What I would prefer to say is consciousness emerges out of the unconscious. But so many people have criticized the idea of *the* unconscious that who knows if we have the right to say even that. We could go back to Freud, and say that what emerges comes out of the *id*—the it, and perhaps a nicer thing than "it" to call "id" would be "that." Then we could admit that what emerges out of *that* is sometimes *insight.* Maybe we should talk about *that* when trying to name the unconscious, and insight when we talk about consciousness. It's *that* which is speaking in us to help us arrive at insight, and *that* which we're trying to relate to as analysts when we struggle to accept those insights. If we put it that way, then we would realize that what *that* gives us in the way of insight could be reason itself, or it could be something unreasonable that nevertheless makes sense. It could be play, it could be parody, it could be satire; it could be so many different things, but it is consciousness we can learn from. So I feel like we want to free the unconscious, *that,* from being chained to the notion of it being without useful consciousness, and if we also de-link conscious from rational, which my study of psychological types has helped me to do, we can get a depth psychology that better appreciates the complexity of consciousness.

SC: Can we dig deeper into an important part of your own work, the personality types? First, I will ask you which are the eight types Jung is talking about, and which are the four that are the irrational. Then from that, can we go to your own work?

JB: Sure. Well it's only in Chapter Ten of *Psychological Types* that you get to his eight types of consciousness. They come after some all-but-unreadable material that comes before. It's very difficult to read, and who can stand to read it all? And if you do read it, you're not necessarily always satisfied. *Psychological Types*, like many masterpieces, is a very strange book, filled with so many odd things. But it is Jung's book, every bit as much as *The Red Book* is, and this time he disgorges his conscious mind, and at the end he creates a lovely organization that unpacks all the ideas that have come before, ideas his mind has been kicking around since he first engages the type problem around 1904. It was then that he started noticing different ways of relating to the word association test on the part of the subjects themselves. He started with a two-type model focused only on the functions of feeling and thinking, though at first he doesn't even use the word "feeling" for what he opposes to thinking—his own feeling wasn't well enough developed to name it as such in other people, so he called the person who leads with feeling the "value-predicative type." The person who leads with thinking he called the "objective type." And these became before long his extraverted and introverted types. The "value-predicative type" was usually in his mind an extraverted feeling woman and the "objective type" was usually an introverted thinking man. For the longest time, he mixed up types of consciousness with masculine and feminine and with objective and subjective and located these opposites unfortunately in women and men. So, he thought, the woman who comes in and is value-predicative says, "Oh, Dr. Jung, it must be so hard for you to sit in this hot room doing this association test. Oh, the beautiful salmon color on which the print is made," and gave him all these assessments of value, trying to turn the testing situation into an exploration of the relational field between them to see what value it might possibly contain as the helplessly extraverted person, hopelessly stuck on feeling. And her opposite is the man, who was so stiff, sitting straight at attention trying to give nothing but objective associations to satisfy Jung, equally stiff and looking at his watch to time the associations, as one-sidedly introverted in a typically disciplined masculine way. We can only imagine that Jung in his white coat was trying to be as objective as possible and his masculine subjects would with strict introverted drill give their associations one after the other saying absolutely nothing about the testing situation, unlike the women who insisted, for subjective reasons, on making it social and extraverted. So, the two types that emerged for Jung from the Word Association testing situation became feeling, which Jung decided to call extraversion, because it turned toward an object, and thinking, which was the same as introversion because it sought the right answer within. And, unfortunately, that two-type model lingered a long time in Jung's writings, so that as late as his 1925 English seminar we find him saying that, because he himself is an introvert and can think, he must be an introverted thinking type; and thus the soul-figure that he met in his active imaginations between 1913 and 1916, his anima, Salome, because she is extraverted, has to be an extraverted feeling type. I think that's absolutely ridiculous. Salome, the belly dancer who asked for the head of John the Baptist and lifted it off the platter to kiss it, to pay him back for not, as a holy man, having given her a kiss before, is hardly an extraverted feeling type. I also think that much as Jung would have loved to have been an introverted thinking type, he was not one.

SC: What was he? What do you think he was?

JB: I think Jung was an introverted intuitive type. It was Maria Moltzer who in 1916 came up with the idea of an intuitive type. We must credit her with recognizing the function of intuition as a type of consciousness. And he puts this category, citing her, in *Psychological Types*. Now of course, he doesn't confine himself in that book to only a

dominant function as defining someone's type, because by then he has taken up Otto Gross's idea of an auxiliary function. So, to say that I think Jung was primarily intuitive rather than thinking, I am still agreeing with him that was an intellectual intuitive. I just have to disagree with those numbers of times that he sounds like he believes he is primarily a thinking type, which reflects the long period before in which he equated introversion, which he had always recognized as dominant in himself, with thinking. I think when he suggests that he is an introverted thinking type he is conflating the introverted attitude type of his dominant function, which I believe to be intuition, with the *function type* of his auxiliary, which I believe is extraverted thinking. I am aware how much Jung aspired to do introverted thinking, and how often, in solitude, with the help of Philemon he got there. But that is Jung writing in colloquy with his genius, in an altered or heightened state of consciousness. Everyday Jung excelled at extraverted thinking. He was marvelous at explaining depth psychology to people! It came naturally to him. People who know only his worked-over published writings often talk about how they find Jung difficult to read, or how obscure he is, but if you read the reports of his lectures you find he's one of the great explainers of depth psychology. He was a great teacher, which you can see particularly when you read the Tavistock Lectures. It's just dazzling, in these lectures that he gave in 1935 in English at the Tavistock Clinic in London, how clearly he gets across his basic ideas. Jung was a great explainer of psychological ideas. What he couldn't do as easily in the midst of his busy working life was to think as profoundly as he wanted to. He really wanted to be an intellectual, maybe even a philosopher, like Kant, of psychology. But his thinking was more extraverted than Kant's. He was a *Kulturphilosoph*, a culture philosopher . . .
SC:—A *kulturkritik*, as the Germans say . . .

JB: Exactly. That was absolutely who he was and what he most loved to do with his thinking, and the object of its attention is not his own mind, but the mind of the world. That's extraverted thinking. But that doesn't account for Jung's aspiration also to do introverted thinking. He didn't want to be confined to explaining other people's ideas. I always felt the real reason he broke with Freud was because in being the Crown Prince of the psychoanalytic movement he was confined to being Freud's, so to speak, general. Freud's whole theory was an extraverted thinking theory created, as Jung would say, by an introverted feeling man in the second half of life. And Freud's theory is absolutely his anima. He had his immediate followers wear a ring to declare fealty to never turn on the sexual theory, as if they were medieval knights swearing their fealty to a lady.

SC: His eros.

JB: That was his eros, his theory. An extraverted thinking theory. And so, Jung could become Freud's general, because Jung could use his own strong auxiliary extraverted thinking to explain psychoanalytic theory to psychiatrists, especially in extraverted thinking America. He sold American psychiatry on Freud. And when he broke with Freud, he couldn't get American psychiatry back. That ability on his part was too confining for him. Not only was Freud trying to make him toe the line and not go too far, but the very fact of having to be somebody's general, following that extraverted Freudian line of thinking, was keeping Jung from developing his own thinking. The only way he could learn to think more deeply was to return to himself and to see how his own soul and spirit figures wanted him to develop his mind.

In *The Red Book*, Salome delivers him from a narrow focus on rational thinking to a greater acceptance of the role his native introverted intuition can play in the development of his consciousness. She offers him his own gift for prophecy and magic. And then, by finding Philemon, a retired magician, he actually found an introverted thinking type in his unconscious who could help him think as profoundly as he needed to develop his own psychological theory. When he could be alone enough with Philemon, as when he went away to Bollingen, which he called the "Shrine of Philemon—the Repentance of Faust," then Philemon could come up, then Jung could do introverted thinking, and do psychology at the depth that he really wanted, because introverted thinking has a remarkable capacity to name and define and understand at very deep levels; and that Jung could get to. But unlike Salome, Philemon brought to Jung a mental gift that was not altogether natural to Jung already. Rather it was a true expansion of Jung's ability to think that added an introverted dimension. Philemon thought like a Gnostic Alexandrian philosopher, and when Jung learned that he could add to his own extraverted psychological thinking how, with introverted thinking, Philemon could define the *pleroma* and the *creatura*, a new depth surfaced in Jung's writing. Jung becomes successfully original at creating his own depth psychology with the help of an introverted thinking type wise old man, Philemon, who can offer Jung in midlife what he could no longer find in Freud.

But if you think of Jung as a man, apart from what he gets to theoretically by creatively plumbing his own depths, most of the time you see an extraordinary ability to *know* things with phenomenal introverted intuition and a very good capacity to explain that in reasonably coherent terms to the modern world's extraverted thinking mind. There I think you get the core typology of Jung. You don't get the whole of the man, because he did so much else. His trickster extraverted feeling is fantastic, for instance. And sometimes his introverted sensation becomes a daimon. In fact, he couldn't have gotten to the typology if he hadn't channeled the introverted sensation. Yet his inferior function is extraverted sensation—that is his anima. You can feel that all the functions of his consciousness had a tendency to live in him, and that he was willing to move around in his own typology. The type theory he presents in the book *Psychological Types* organizes consciousness as a kind of polyphony. I think that makes his complex, eight-function attitude model of type really lovely. It matches other notions of complexity that we've been educated to appreciate in the last 25 years. I believe that complexity theory makes it easier to see what Jung was doing with his theory of types. That theory represents his first recognition of the full complexity of consciousness. It allows consciousness to be both rational and irrational, both introverted and extraverted, thinking and feeling, and sensation and intuition, and for all of these functions to express themselves through our complexes. Jung's theory of types is a phenomenally interesting model for the unfolding of consciousness, and it makes clear to analysts trying to make the unconscious conscious that when consciousness comes, it comes out on an already self-organized complexity before it can inform the choices of an ego.

SC: Listening to you, two words come to my mind: intuition and masculinity. In 1985 you contributed to a book edited by Andrew Samuels, called *The Father*. When I was a student at Cambridge University, I went to a book seller and I found your own book, the book you edited, titled *Aspects of the Masculine*. Thinking of Jung and Freud's relationship, it is interesting again to think of the father, the mature father, versus the mature man. Since you wrote that contribution, since your work on the *Aspects of the Masculine* in this complex society, what is the masculine, what is the father, what is the *new* father? And how does this link with intuition?

JB: It's interesting that you bring up *Aspects of the Masculine* and the father, because after I published that a colleague of mine in San Francisco, Arthur Colman, who had written one or two books about the father, said he admired my introduction to *Aspects of the Masculine*; but he wondered why I didn't take up more of what the father meant to Jung. Or, he wondered why I didn't take up the fact that Jung doesn't really get into that subject very much, except in that very early essay about the significance of the father in the destiny of the individual, or something close to that (and it turns out to be not much more than an analysis of number symbolism in dreams, it's very limited). In my own meeting with Jung's son, Franz Jung, he said, "My father was someone to get to know on holiday or weekends, but actually he was in his study all the time. Emma Jung raised us, and when we needed advice, my father couldn't give it to me."

He told me that when he was going to school, he thought he would be a doctor because his father was a doctor. You'd have to know that Franz Jung's type was almost surely introverted sensation, which happens to be an orientation that is typically valued in Swiss culture. Usually, when people have introverted sensation, their first idea of what they should do with their lives is wrong, because they don't have the right intuition; whereas someone like Jung had that sense that what he was going to be was a scientist. In his own way he had the "dream of a science," as Sonu Shamdasani puts it, very early, and went to medical school and had a coherent line. It wasn't that way for Franz Jung. So, when he was in school, whenever he got a lower grade on a science test, Switzerland being Switzerland, his teacher would say "if your father only knew." And it was just too humiliating, so he realized he wasn't going to be able to do that. He talked to his father and said, "Father, I don't know what I want to do." And Jung said, "Well my son, I really can't tell you what to do, but I will give you a sum of money and you can travel all over Europe and you can try this and that and see what appeals to you." By then Franz must have been, by American standards, out of college; I'm not sure exactly where he was on the educational track, but he was old enough to take a trip on his own like that. Of course, Jung had borrowed this suggested plan from what the philosopher Schopenhauer's father had done for Schopenhauer. It shows how little Jung knew about his own theory of typology as applied to his children, because if you tell a young introverted sensation type to go somewhere looking for what they're going to do next they usually haven't the intuition to follow through.... Of course, Franz Jung was too smart to take the offer; he knew it wouldn't work for him. Instead, Franz went to see Emma's mother, because she was the extraverted intuitive that gave everybody in the family good advice. She was in many ways the good father in that family. She said, "Well let's think about this, what do you want to do? Well ... I seem to remember you working when you were fifteen with your father on Bollingen. And I seem to remember you got really into that. Is that true?" And he said, "Yes, I just loved that," and so forth, so she said, "Don't you think you could be an architect?" and of course that was exactly what he was going to be. He became an architect, and a very good one. But we heard just today at this conference that Franz's father never referred a client to him. So, in one sense, I have to say that Jung was a dud as a father.

SC: A dry father, as Andrew Samuels would call it, perhaps?

JB: Well the English word I chose is "dud," which means someone who just doesn't quite perform as expected. I think there was in Jung not only his actual father who died young, but also an internal, archetypally "dead father" (to borrow for Jungian use an object-relational term from the followers of French psychoanalyst André Green). The fatherly advice Jung is recorded as giving to people was often more wooden. For example, he told Tom Kirsch's mother Hilde that she shouldn't leave Nazi Germany and go to Palestine. He told her to stay, because Germany was her home. She would have been killed if she had stayed there. I mean, Jung wasn't able to look ahead with objective sympathy in a protective way...

SC: At the reality in the society? At the real happening? Too deep, perhaps?

JB: I just think that Jung was not a father for individual people. For me, a father is a parent first of all, more than that he is a man. For me, the essence of a man is not whether he's a father, although, God knows I have probably developed my own masculinity along those lines, and so contradict my own theory! A "father" is someone who fosters, parents, protects. A man with a real fatherly instinct does not cheat on his wife. You don't do that if you really are a father of a family. Jung was far more heroic than fatherly. But Jung wanted to believe his own midlife myth, that he had sacrificed the hero in himself when he had the dream of killing Siegfried. I think what that dream told him he had sacrificed was the false hero, the role of Siegfried as the son of Sigmund that he had tried to live with Freud. When he gave up on being Freud's Crown Prince, he didn't sacrifice his superior hero function, he simply stopped using his auxiliary father function of extraverted thinking, explaining someone else's ideas as if it were his major masculine role in life. What he found in the active imaginations he records in *The Red Book* was the heroism of his own superior function. You can see that emerge in the miraculous way Izdubar is finally constellated. This ancient Sumerian hero, a Gilgamesh-like figure with an intuitive worldview, had been threatened with cultural extinction upon hearing from Jung about modern science, but he is somehow kept alive by Jung as a fantasy with a purpose. The moment when this ancient hero's introverted perspective is released to assume its rightful place in the sky of Jung's active imagining psyche is for me the moment at which Jung's own introverted intuitive function becomes constellated as the dominant within his typology. Jung himself became the culture hero who in accepting his own intuitive standpoint became a role model for the value of irrational consciousness in the age of logical positivism. Jung's heroic feat in the face of the accusation of mysticism he had to endure was to make us trust intuition again, more than modern science was willing to allow, and what a wonderful role model he became! In that sense, he was a magnificent example of self-affirmation for those of us who are also predominantly intuitive, an archetypal father serving to show that intuition, though irrational is more than superstition and can actually function as a consciousness in a useful way. So, though I would probably have hated to have Jung as my personal father, I have been delighted to accept him as my lodestar. He was not the same kind of intuitive as I am, an *extraverted* intuitive, but he fathered me by example. And that is good. And I should point out that his son Franz did find himself. And finally, Jung was as good a grandfather as he was terrible as a father, in my opinion. He was a very good grandfather. His living grandchildren attest to that.

SC: When the responsibility to father his kids was less strong, then he could give the grandchildren everything he was not able to give to his kids.

JB: Also, those were the years after his heart attack, when he was entirely with Emma, finally, and Toni was no longer in the way of contained functioning as a couple. Those were the years when Emma could put her foot down, say he didn't need to work, and he'd stay downstairs with her so that they could pass the evenings together. He'd ask her to tell him about the grandchildren. And she would tell him all about the grandchildren. So, when he met the grandchildren—

SC: So, he could really connect.

JB: —they found he knew more about them than their own parents did, because parents are too busy to find out everything children are doing. But Jung, with the education of introverted sensation Emma, had all the facts at his disposal. That was all part of a late bloom of a really marvelous *humanitas* that comes out of Jung toward the end, particularly the last ten or fifteen years. It is very beautiful and very different from Jung playing the genius and posturing and also making the colossal mistakes he made in those years of exploration. He became quite a better human being.

SC: And to me it sounds like that the more he reached an age—maybe getting closer to death—the more he became at ease with himself, while Freud didn't. Freud died suffering, physically, and maybe even psychologically.

JB: Freud was a remarkable man, nonetheless.

SC: Absolutely.

JB: I like the way Peter Gay describes Freud. I am told that there is a lot to complain about in Peter Gay's biography. But I love his description of how Freud, who as a young doctor had been addicted to cocaine, at the end of his life, suffering from cancer of the jaw, refused to take any kind of opiate. As Gay puts it, "The old stoic had kept control of his life to the end." The stoicism that Freud lived—he really exhibited, far more than Jung actually did, a pagan consciousness in the sense that he refused both Judaism and Christianity in favor of a classical kind of stoic humanism. I sense in him at the end, a true wish to keep his consciousness clear, so that he could stay present to his suffering.

This was Freud's integrity, which I think you can feel in other key moments of his life. There is a dream that Freud had, that I regard as a Jungian dream. I've focused on it in some of my writings. It is the dream of his self-dissection. We don't know exactly when Freud had this dream, but it looks like it was about 1897. There is a moment in the dream at which he is operating on his pelvic region, and overlaying it is some paper made of *stanium*, a form of tin foil that has a distinctly silvery quality. It's strangely present, this overlay. He doesn't know what to make of it, so he carefully lifts it up and puts it aside. That is Freud's discovery of the anima. That was his encounter with *luna*, the feminine principle, and he didn't know what to do with it. It is a cultural thing that covered, in an unexpected way, the most private area that he was so interested in—sexuality. The night before he had this dream, he had been talking to a woman about H. Rider Haggard's *She*, the very text Jung always used to talk about the anima. Well, the dream goes on that after the operation he is feeling very unsteady on his legs, and at that point a tall man, who was an alpine guide, picks him up and carries him, because he can't do it just himself. They start moving across a bridge and then the two of them can't go any farther, and Freud realizes that they're not going to be able to make the crossing over into this place they're trying get to. But the children will be able to make the crossing. I hope you can see why I call this a Jungian dream now, because I think that alpine guide was none other than Jung. And it is a precognitive dream. There is the self-analysis out of which emerges the problem of the anima that Freud doesn't know how to deal with but has the integrity to set aside for later study, and we see him then realizing he needs to accept the help of the Alpine guide whom I associate with Jung, who carries Freud farther, but even they only get so far and find that neither of them is going to be able to get all the way to where they need to go. It was left to the rest of us, the children, the next generations of analysts, to take up what these men left unfinished. What I love about that dream is that I can feel Freud's integrity all through it, recognizing the limitations of his ability to complete his own ambitious project by himself. In it he is keeping track of what still needs working on and may be better accessed after his own death. In this, he is trying to be as scientific as he knows how. I think we have to respect that. I see Freud, as Jung and von Franz did, as an introverted feeling type, and I think in his lifetime he was still trying to put together a rational feeling view of what analysis could add in terms of value to the modern psyche. In other words, there is the idea of the unconscious as irrational and conscious as rational, "where id was there shall ego be." Freud did find a way to make us recognize that there is a rationale for the analytic process, which is its potential to make the unconscious conscious. Jung picked up on that big time. So, Freud got the psychoanalytic project started, but Jung saw the importance for our culture's development of what Freud set aside. I find it thrilling that Freud's dream seems to have anticipated that this progression would be necessary, and that it would not be completed in a single generation.

SC: You touch upon dreams, integrity, and anima, all at once. Let's try to differentiate them. What is integrity? You wrote about it.

JB: First of all, it is a complex notion; it has at least three or four meanings. The three meanings are found in the standard definitions of *integrity*. The word probably was coined by Cicero, who had a tendency to make nouns from adjectives that had represented certain ideas or values. *Integer* was an enormous value for the ancient Romans. There is an ode by Horace, Integer Vitae, that begins with the word *integer,* that is about the Roman who could live what they would have called an upright life, and we would today call a life lived with integrity. But the way we have the right to speak of a life "of integrity" is because of Cicero, who turned *integer*, an adjective that means incorruptible, into a noun that pointed to the quality required for that to be the case. *Integer is* "lack of corruption." It's the basis of virtue sustained over time in the face of moral tests, remaining whole or entire. Entire is a better word than whole to convey how integrity actually operates; the *entirety* it points to is our willingness to summon everything in our ethical nature and experience that is relevant to the particular situation that is challenging us. Integrity doesn't mean *everything in the psyche* can be included, it means everything *relevant* will show up. All that is relevant would be closer to Husserl's phenomenological idea of wholeness than the notion of the Self in totality that we sometimes get from Jung, and I prefer it. Integrity is entire in the sense of being untouched, complete and of a piece morally, all of which under test, means standing for something, living by values that endure for others to follow. As you can see, it's a very complex notion, three or four ideas connected with each other that have to be teased out. What it amounts to in practical, everyday, psychological terms is embracing a form of moral desire. That is a willing sensitivity to the needs of the whole, and a real wish to serve those needs, rather than to cherry-pick the part we want to take care of. Like all the people who have cheated in business to be able to feed their family: "I've got to take care of my family. What happens to those people I do business with—I can't take care of them if they're bad businessmen." That is a very common attitude. But integrity cares as much about the businessmen and their families as you care about your own family, because it's all connected. It's all relevant, and you try to find a way to do what's right because you have a willing sensitivity to the needs of the whole rather than the needs of particular parts of yourself you wish to advance. There is something about that, which becomes a practice. And though it is standing for something, it's more standing for that process than just for a particular value. It's seeing what the total effect of one's actions and choices is going to be on everyone one can possibly think of at the moment one makes them and being willing to learn about the people that one didn't think about. Because that comes up later in dreams and in their wounded comebacks to you because you left them out. And being willing to take that on, which means you have to embrace continually a certain amount of shame and not being able to see all of the impact. But loving the process of learning it—that to me is integrity.

SC: De facto. What are dreams?

JB: Well, "news of a difference" is an idea that I like from Gregory Bateson, which he said in *Steps to an Ecology of Mind,* one of my favorite books. I had a chance to hear him lecture from parts of it when I was a resident at Stanford in 1970. There was much interest then in the implications of the emerging field of neuroscience. Bateson assumed that as doctors we already knew that neuroscience in the modern sense had begun with Hodgkin and Huxley's experiments on the squid axon, which had demonstrated how the action potential of the nerve impulse travels along it. This work had become seminal from the 1950s on. The giant squid was a marvelous choice for these studies because such creatures are, well, eight-functional and also exquisitely sensitive creatures, picking up vibrations all the time. But Bateson pointed out that if you conceive what travels along the squid nerve axon to be an electrical impulse, then you will never get to what that sensitivity is communicating. You are just measuring its intensities. Rather, Bateson said, we should realize that what is travelling along the nerve axon is news of a difference. If you accept that, then you will be prepared to understand the interaction that he called in his last book, *Mind and Nature.* Mind is that thing which is constantly noticing the changes in the nature of things around us. That, I think, is what our dreaming process is. Dreaming is our squid axon revealing that it is constantly picking up news of a difference.

When I'm working with a dream, I'm trying to see what that difference is. I start by assuming that the dream is not wasting its time. As Jung says, this is the reality of the psyche, and so I better attend to it. I gave a paper as you know this weekend, called "Why is This Real?" If the psyche is real, I have to say, "Wait a minute, why is this dream real? What news is coming my way via this dream? What is the difference that the dream is picking up?" The dream is picking up on the fact that everything is changing and only you are not changing with it. The dream shows me what the difference would be if I would pay attention to it, or shows me the degree to which I'm not attending to the difference. I'm looking for where is the difference, what is the attitude toward the difference? The dream is my most objective window on that difference, if I know how to read it.

SC: Dreams are very important. In dreams you can find your shadow, your persona, your anima, your animus.

JB: All of the above. And for the record, men have an animus and women an anima.

SC: What is the anima, and what is the animus?

JB: Well, Hillman says, and I agree, that the anima serves the instinct for reflection. The anima helps a man reflect on all the things he does with his privileged agency. This inner capacity for reflection becomes, like a trusted wife, an access point to integrity. Whereas, when I see the animus in women, I see something that focuses upon how much integrity is there, and takes enormous satisfaction when things are being conducted, particularly by men, with integrity, and takes enormous exception to men when their actions are not conducted with integrity. The anima is thus a healthy insecurity in a man, and the animus is a necessarily severe monitor in a woman. But, as I say, men and women have both anima and animus. You could say that the anima offers an opening, in something like a safe and protected way, to the possibility of reflecting and becoming closer to one's integrity, and that the animus is not so willing to wait until that happens. The animus, like a *spiritus rector*, is there to tell us when it isn't happening. The animus, in the original formulation of Jung, based on gender roles familiar to people within the families of his time, was there to help a woman make sure that things are going as they must in the family, and the anima was there to help the man use his privileged agency with a certain empathy for its impact. But now that we are in a much less gender-polarized world, I think we have to say that—

SC: —That concept to which you refer was very controversial, or gave a basis to those against Jung to attack him.

JB: Yes, his original formulation was sexist and rigid. Now that I can speak outside it, retaining the possibility of both archetypes appearing in both genders, and stay just with what I myself experience, I see that my animus stirs non-stop at the lack of integrity in political leaders, for instance, or in other analysts, or whatever. It drives me crazy. It's not patient with a process of getting to integrity, so much as it is absolutely clear that this is unacceptable, and at a very deep level. I also have found a need to make a distinction within my work on the archetypes that carry the types of consciousness, between the animus and the anima, on the one hand, and what I call "the opposing personality." I am someone who likes to follow in a tradition, so because Jung is my ancestor and I don't want to dispose of what he gave me, I still use the terms anima and animus. But I try to clarify them. The common English language meaning of the word "animus" is very similar to what I'm calling the opposing personality, a state of mind in which one, sometimes in a snarky way, speaks back at something one dislikes subjectively, mainly as a way of defending one's own interest, however one-sidedly. That is not what I do when my animus speaks out. Then I have a deep awareness that a lack of integrity is occurring, and any outrage I express is not just me defending myself.

I have seen both opposing personality and anima or animus appear alongside the ego in movies where the main characters are a man and two women, or a woman and two men. If you get the typology right, you will see that one of the characters of the opposite gender from the hero or heroine represents the inferior function for that dominant function character, while the other character that is opposite in gender from the hero will use the same function as the hero but with the opposite attitude and be his or her opposing personality. I love to learn psychology from movies. One of my favorites, an American movie that was considered to have one of the finest screenplays of all time, *Broadcast News,* stars Holly Hunter as an extraverted thinking woman. She is the heroine of the film. William Hurt plays an introverted feeling man, who is an animus figure for her. He is very handsome and somewhat dubious as far as his integrity, and she is very righteous and severe about it. The whole movie is about whether the two of them can come together as to what integrity is and thus establish an integrity in depth. Holly Hunter's character, Jane's best friend is an *introverted* thinking man, Aaron, played by Albert Brooks, who is constantly making snarky remarks, very attacking and snide. So we see the woman, who has a strongly dominating *extraverted* thinking ego, with two male figures to compensate her: one represents the part of her that almost, like a tic, has to push back and prove to everybody that she is smarter than they are: this is her introverted thinking opposing personality. And then she has this other figure, who is much more complicated for her, who represents her real animus, who is not nearly as straightforward, not always acting with integrity. No one in the whole film quite comes together in a stable partnership. That represents exactly where America was in the time the film was released in 1987, seeking but not attaining a culture of integrity.

That is the year that for many of us it became clear that America had seriously begun to lose its way; and as I see it has not succeeded in regaining its integrity since, even though the sincerest of our recent presidents, Obama, certainly tried. In 1988 we had a terrible election, in which the first George Bush ran on the "Pledge of Allegiance" to the American flag, because his opponent, Michael Dukakis, who was a member of the American Civil Liberties Union, had opposed the idea of children being required to say in schools, "We pledge allegiance to the flag of the United States of America and to the Republic for which it stands, one nation *under God....*" Dukakis felt that the words "under God" should not appear in the pledge recited by school children, because it implied that everyone had to have a belief in God, leaving no room for atheism. Bush used that as his campaign issue. And Bush had gone to fine schools, he had a father who knew everything about foreign affairs. The cynicism of making that his top campaign issue—and the fact that Dukakis was not a good campaigner, he didn't know how to deal with it—gave me, for the first time, a political depression. I mean that I actually was clinically depressed for about three months. I didn't take medicine; I had an analyst at that time, so we talked about it. But I absolutely could not believe what was happening to America, and I knew it boded very ill. I have never been prouder of a depression than I was of that one, because my psyche picked that what was happening in the culture *was* depressing. That depression was an expression of my animus. And that led to my writing the book, *Integrity in Depth*.

SC: The integrity of your animus. The integrity brought by your animus.

JB: The insistence of my American spirit, that demanded more integrity from my surroundings. That prepared me for what has come ever since. And of course, the election of Bill Clinton didn't solve it because of his affair with Monica Lewinsky.

SC: Not even Obama's.

JB: No, and Obama certainly, at a personal level, had far more integrity than almost any president in my lifetime, including Franklin Roosevelt, who was a greater president. The situation we have now is exactly what follows from earlier failures of integrity. My generation was so complacent after the resignation of Richard Nixon. We imagined that we had solved something, that our time had come. And before we knew it, Ronald Reagan was our president. By 1988 it was really very clear that we were in a very serious decline, which we are still in. I hope that now that we have a gargoyle as our president, and are starting to stand up to him, we have a chance to put the spire back on Notre Dame. I would like to see us begin to show some integrity in how we hold the problems of the world that are ours to fix.

SC: I didn't know about the use of "God" by Bush in 1988, but a few weeks ago you might have heard, our own Italian disgrace, Salvini, our interior minister, used the Virgin Mary the day before the election. He asked Mary to look down and to actually let him win the elections. It is interesting how sometimes these people use God in the very wrong way. But then thinking of Bush Senior, also, the speech he gave on September 11th, 1989, when he talked openly about the "new order," an order that is going beyond the bipolarity of the East and the West. Well then, actually, the Iraq war came, and many, many other things came. That's why in my presentation I talk about the uroboric, the cyclic turn in life that is not going towards something only positive...

But anyway, I would like to ask you a more specific question about the anima and the animus. If we read the books, it was stated as gender binary: anima for the man, animus for the woman. As you alluded to, post-Jungians like Kast, Giegerich, gave a new opinion about it, that it is not gender related, not gender specific. What do you think?

JB: Well for me, empirically, I long ago came to this. There was a time when I was looking at dreams all the time, and so systematically that I could dare to say: it's three to one. The anima, or animus, is the linking point between conscious and unconscious and that vital bridge, that figure that shows up in dreams of men, three times out of four will be a female figure. Even in a homosexual man, there will more often be a female figure. Whereas, it was the other way in women—the bridging, enlightening figure in dreams was three to one male to female.

I was once at a Jungian congress long ago, talking about the dream in which I clearly found my anima after years of wondering what it would look like. It took the form of a Chinese woman who was an introverted sensation type. Introverted sensation is the inferior function in a person whose dominant function is extraverted intuition.

She was sitting alone in a room and she didn't have anything, because her husband was out drinking and gambling and not bringing money home. I thought that was a representation of my tendency to chase intuitive possibilities, and it was leaving her with too little. The woman in the dream was a woman I actually took my laundry to at that day. She had a launderette and she was definitely an introverted sensation type. She folded the clothes very neatly and was very precise. So, in the dream she had nothing, and I really took that seriously, that I was going to have to take better care of her. I began to make room for myself, and it actually changed the way I worked with patients, because I would attend to introverted sensation—to the inside of my body—and I noticed what I was doing in the therapy was very like what my dream was saying, but in a way I would never have thought. Those are the years when I was, like yourself, a candidate in analytic training, and I was reading the complete works of von Franz and the complete works of Jung, chasing after every dream and after every archetypal association I could think of. There were many! In those days I used to have severe migraine headaches. And what I realized, as I began to think about the introverted sensation anima that doesn't have anything, I was listening with bated breath to everything. I was so intensely interested and not wanting to miss any part of the dream or its symbol, that I wasn't even breathing as I listened to my patients. I had this enormous carbon dioxide retention. No wonder I had a headache at the end of every day! What I realized was, wait a minute, I'm going to have to take the time for me as I listen to the patient. For a long time, my patients had to listen to my breathing and actually I changed the entire way I worked, because I learned to attend to what my body was telling me and not just what my intuitive mind was telling me. And (like anyone else who would do this) what I found was that by paying close attention to the tensions in the smooth muscles of my body, inside my gut and elsewhere, I got hold of all kinds of material that my patient wasn't talking about, and wasn't dreaming about, and where their affects were, and where their transference towards me and their frustration with me, and where other people's frustration with me—which is certainly understandable—was. Very soon after I started doing this, I dreamed of the same figure. She was feeling much better now, her husband was taking her out for ice cream. That was just the beginning; I mean, there was a lot more than ice cream that she needed. It became a real work, to tend to my body while I was listening to patients. But I made the decision that since in each therapy session I'm here too, I have to notice what's happening to me. I have to speak from that awareness of the inside of my body when necessary. In the long run doing that unlocked many therapies and made my life as a therapist so much richer.

So, I'm saying that the true anima or animus is the thing that carries the inferior function, which is the transcendent function, only in the sense that it's the bridge. It is not the answer. And that's the mistake in some readings of psychological types. Yes, the inferior function is, as von Franz says, essential; but it positions you so that then you can pick up on other things, which are the shadow things. Nowadays I would be more interested in the man who was out drinking and gambling not as a symbol of my dominant extraverted intuition, but as something much more primitive and much more ego-distant, you could say, or distant from my usual self-conception, which is my extraverted sensation. I didn't drink and gamble, but there is some part of me that is a bit of a beast. It takes the form of gluttony among other things; thank heaven I don't have serious addictions (except perhaps to work!). But I really think that I had to come to terms with that part, and that's a whole other thing.

In terms of how this applies to women and to the post-modern: A colleague of mine who was at the same conference as me when I was talking about my dream about the Chinese laundress approached me quietly after. As a postmodern Jungian, she was doctrinally committed to the opinion that the animus is something that belongs to the sexist past of Jungian analysis and we need to get rid of it, because it's getting in the way of how we see women. But she said to me, "Please don't tell anyone, but I have a Chinese man in my dreams!" So, I would say, as long as we don't make it absolute, Jung is sort of right, and there is something about otherness in relation to your biological gender that will want to symbolize itself as contrasexual. But let's look for that in a three-to-one ratio.

SC: Three-to-one is a very good approach!

I would like to ask you a final question, which is about individuation. I remember in Prague in December 2017, you—I would say courageously—stood up and said that during your training you were told by someone that a homosexual man, or a gay person, cannot individuate. I want to add to this something that happened to a colleague of mine who is training. When he was looking for a training analyst, he was told by a male analyst, "Well, I would strongly suggest that you not start the training. The first thing you have to do is work on your homosexuality." He got shocked. He didn't start working with this person and he is training now, and he is going to be a fantastic psychoanalyst from my point of view. What is your take on this? Before you answer, this is a problem I often face when I see new patients in Berlin. They come in and say, "But you are a Jungian—he was Nazi, he was a sexist, he was against homosexuality if you look at the anima and animus." This is an issue we have to talk about.

JB: Oh, it's a big issue, yes, and I've certainly been a pioneer in a variety of senses. I am told (of course you never can believe everything you are told in training, but I am told) that I was the first openly homosexual person to be open at the time of their admission. I felt if you are going to be admitted to an analytic institute you don't want to hide something as fundamental as that. I was by no means the first person who was homosexual who was admitted, and I noticed when I would travel around the world how many homosexual men were married or in the closet all over the Jungian world, and that the homophobia in Jung was still alive there. Jung, however, was very important to me, not as the homophobe to be overcome, but as the man who did make room for me. For instance, he says, "In view of the recognized frequency of this phenomenon [homosexuality], its interpretation as a pathological perversion is very dubious." (CW vol 9.1, para. 146). That's a remarkable statement.

SC: Absolutely.

JB: I published a case that I found, as a lecture to an Analytical Psychology club, of Joseph Wheelwright when he was in training to be a Jungian analyst before there were institutes. Jung was his supervisor for his control work, and it was a gay case. The man was dreaming of gay marriage. It was a wonderful case, and there was essentially no homophobia in Joseph Wheelwright's 1939 case report. It was very clear that Jung had given him plenty of freedom to explore the experiential world of this particular patient. And there was no wish on the part of Jung or Wheelwright to change this man's sexual orientation.

I remember the way things looked in the 1960s. I graduated from Harvard in 1961 and I graduated from Medical School in 1965. The big gay movement breakthrough was the Stonewall riots in New York right after Judy Garland died. Some drag queens were celebrating the memory of this iconic figure for gay men (including myself), and somebody tried to arrest some drag queens at the Stonewall bar and they fought back. I was so moved in San Francisco, not by that, but by the fact that Judy Garland had died, that I took a picture in a window in San Francisco of a rainbow in colors, and this was long before there was a rainbow flag, it was just because Judy Garland had sung "Somewhere Over the Rainbow" in *The Wizard of Oz*. There was a colored rainbow in the shop window—this was two days after she died. I don't know how it was made, it seemed to be made of embroidery or something, but it was quite a beautiful thing. I took the picture through the window, and in the photograph my reflection appears in the window, and the rainbow is over my head. It was like I marked the moment at which something changed.

When I applied to the Jung Institute of San Francisco in 1970, Tom Kirsch was my supervisor. I was a second-year resident at Stanford in psychiatry, and he was encouraging me to apply to the Institute. Tom was someone who needed to know who you were when he supervised you, so he wanted to know who I was, and I told him that I was homosexual. That was something that people didn't talk about that openly in training at that time. It was still illegal in California to be homosexual at that time, so it could have been a basis for being dropped from the psychiatric residency. He was very helpful with that and wanted to know if I would be interested in Jungian training, and I said I don't know whether they are going to accept me, because I know what happens in the Freudian psychoanalytic institutes. I'd had a friend who applied and there the personal psychoanalyst talked to the training committee, and my friend was told that he would have to change his sexual orientation, or he couldn't continue with the training.

SC: To *change his sexual orientation*?

JB: Oh yes, that's how homosexuality was handled in the standard psychoanalytic world in America before 1970, you know. And since he obviously wasn't going to make the required shift, they dropped him. He then applied to another analytic institute and this time, rather cynically, he decided to time it. So, he got in and he waited, and then at a certain point he told his personal analyst that he was homosexual. He timed it, and 48 hours later came the letter to leave the analytic institute. With that knowledge and background, and it was only four years before that I'd heard this, I was naturally concerned. I talked to Tom Kirsch about it, and he said well, I will check. He went and talked, and he came back and said there is no rule. It's how it fits into your life. So I have to say that the three people who admitted me—one was the first graduate of the C.G. Jung Institute in Zürich, William Alex; one was Joseph Henderson; and one was Elizabeth Osterman—all felt very good about how open I was, that I was willing to talk about this, and they were very, very welcoming of me. Joe Henderson wanted to know if the relationship I was in at the time was a stable relationship; Bill Alex wondered why the Freudians didn't accept homosexuals and wanted to know what I thought about that; Elizabeth Osterman wanted to know something about my relation to my mother, and just in general what my relation to women as well as men was like. I said I feel a little anxious, and she said, "Please don't. When we talk, we say we believe in the individual, and we mean it." So, they all were very affirmative and that took a lot of courage. It wasn't until 1975 that our fantastic assemblyman, Willie Brown, who became Speaker of the California State Assembly, got consenting adults legislation passed in California, which was a breakthrough. It wasn't long after that, that the American Psychiatric Association dropped its classification of homosexuality as a mental illness.

In 1977, when I was on the verge of becoming an analyst, I had a dream in which I am going into a store that I had actually seen at Harvard. It was a store called "Design Research," which was a place that had all of the most recent in trendy designs from Scandinavia, and so forth. I went into the furthest reaches of the store, like into the "Holy of Holies," you could say, where Athena would be in the Parthenon, of this store. I wanted to see the latest things and I looked at the salesperson—I think it was a woman—and I said to her, "I'm gay," and she said, "You're right on." That dream exemplifies what I meant about the objective psyche.

What I hardly knew, rather than being a liability, it turned out to be an advantage!

So, I was a bit naïve, and this is where the story you heard comes. I wrote up my control case in 1978, and the theme I chose for my control case, was a woman who I felt was going to have an erotic transference to me and I felt that as a homosexual man maybe I wouldn't know how to handle that. Because it seemed to me that somehow if you're working with a woman and she develops an erotic transference to her analyst, and you're homosexual, it's sort of like cheating! You're supposed to be a heterosexual man and I didn't know what to do about that. I got an older male analytic consultant to help me, and it turned out that really wonderful things happened in dealing with that case, where I could really feel the woman's sexuality coming toward me and genuinely find a way to deal with it. But one of the big issues was whether to talk about my homosexuality with her, which I eventually did choose to do. How we worked on that in analysis together, and how that opened up a point of connection created a meaningful analysis. I wrote that up in great detail, and I was certified. Now, because that certification took place not in San Francisco where I had trained, but in Los Angeles where I had to go (because in those days we had a deal where we would go to each other's cities often to be certified and some of the analysts would be from Los Angeles and some from San Francisco, and so there was a little bit of sharing of training by the two California institutes), one of my examiners was to have been Tom's mother, Hilde Kirsch, a very well-known Jungian analyst and someone that I had gotten to know just a little bit. She had read and really liked my paper, but she had some kind of illness that required hospitalization, so she couldn't be present for the exam. I wanted to go and see Hilde and her husband, James (who was Tom's father). They both were very closely identified with Jung—Hilde had been a patient of Jung's and James maintained a long correspondence with Jung. So, I went and I talked to them, in a kind-of "feeling my oats" way. And you know, Hilde really liked me and liked my paper, and James was jealous of the fact that Hilde was that interested in my paper. I said, "Well you know, there was a time when Jungian people would say that a homosexual person couldn't individuate." And James, who was the most dogmatic and at times the most unrelated of men when he got into his thinking (he must have been an introverted feeling type, because when he got into his thinking, he became so dogmatic), said, "Well, a homosexual can't individuate!"

SC: From a dogmatic point of view!

JB: He knew perfectly well ... but couldn't avoid saying that. Now, to be fair to James, he had to do something about my inflation, so I understand. But it was very clear that there was that dogmatic idea that the anima is heterosexual, and if you're not heterosexual you haven't realized the anima. You just have a mother complex. Of course, I knew perfectly well from my own analysis that I had an anima, and that she was female, and that deepened my homosexual relationships just as the anima deepens heterosexual relationships (or complicates them!). But in any case, he was voicing the old opinion. And I realized I had a job to do, that I was going to have to talk about that, and I have, in different writings, and said what I think about that. It's terrible to use the anima and animus as a theory of love. It's just a mistake! I mean, the anima and the animus connect you to the Self and then the Self does the loving of whoever the Self loves; and it's always a mystery. And it is through the eyes of love you see the other person in a way that you have to live up to or not, depending on how much integrity you have. The fact that the anima and the animus can be sexualized doesn't say much, because any archetype can be sexualized. The daemonic, the trickster, the opposing personality, particularly. A lot of the sexual acting out that takes place between the analyst and the patients come when the analyst and the patient have the same function with the opposite attitude. Though I am not sure whether it was her primary or her auxiliary function, I'm convinced that Toni Wolff, in her relationship with Jung, opposed her extraverted intuition to Jung's introverted intuition, something no one else he knew would have been able to do. She was not his anima, therefore, but a kind of real-life opposing personality. That's the role that she often took with him in life, according to Joseph Henderson. Emma, more ladylike than Toni, would always try to be polite when Jung was in one of his horrible moods, but at such times Toni had the temerity to look at him and say (as Joe told it, she would do so in Swiss German), "You bastard, shut up, stop stinking up the air with your shitty mood." This was something Emma couldn't do. So Jung was getting from Toni a needed pushback. I don't doubt that this cost her a great deal, but the opposing, and not the anima role people unthinkingly assign to her, was the role he often needed her to play. In other words, we don't always know what archetype a partner in a sexual relationship will end up personifying, and it is naïve to imagine that will always be anima or animus. That is not even the most important role in development those archetypes play. The anima and the animus can certainly be sexualized when projected; but, when kept inside, the connection they serve is the one to yourself, which is invaluable. In that regard, I have noticed that the presence of a well-functioning anima or animus can be just as important to a homosexual person as it is to a heterosexual person.

SC: Thank you John. I hope this video, with what you just said, your personal story, will help to clarify a myth, or wrong myth, about Jung. But also in your book, *Aspects of the Masculine,* you quote Jung working with a patient, the patient is saying, "I came here to cure my homosexuality," but actually Jung worked with him to cure him of his immaturity as a man, as a masculine person, so to help him become a mature masculine, whatever this is.

JB: I think you are absolutely right. And you know, declaring one's heterosexuality or homosexuality, whether you do it proudly or as a problem, is just a starting point. I mean we are hardly mature when we are young. We have to grow up. And that, I think, is what Jungian analysis is made for, the maturation of the personality; and I think Jung was, in many ways, very good about that.

SC: Thank you John. It was a great pleasure.

JB: Thank you.

C.G. Jung and the I Ching

Ursula Brasch

SC: Dear Ursula, thank you so much for inviting me to your praxis here in Germany, a very beautiful praxis, close to the Black Forest. For me, it's very interesting to be here, because you're an expert on the I Ching. But before we get to the I Ching, could you share the central steps in your intellectual biography/journey?

UB: At the beginning of my Chinese studies I studied classical Chinese. At that time, I got to know the ancient Chinese philosophers, the Chinese classics, and in particular the I Ching. At the same time, I studied European history and politics. The analysis of Chinese and European cultural history influences and characterizes my thinking still today.

SC: What are the authors and the research areas you consider essential for your own development and work? Which other areas do you consider fundamental in your own intellectual biography (also beyond psychoanalysis)?

UB: Marie Louise von Franz's scientific work on Jungian psychology accompanied me from the beginning. Likewise, Erich Neumann and Edward F. Edinger. With Gerd Rudolf's scientific work on structural psychodynamics I developed my understanding of the treatment of structural disorders. The most important authors for me are Richard Wilhelm, who translated the I Ching, and his son Helmut Wilhelm, who became a significant sinologist. Among the contemporary philosophers, I especially appreciate Francois Julien, who is also a sinologist and philosopher.

SC: When did you realize (and decide) you wanted to become a Jungian analyst?

UB: Towards the end of my sinology studies, I dealt intensively with the I Ching. Through Richard Wilhelm, I came to know C.G. Jung and his writing, beginning with Jung's foreword to the translation of the I Ching into English. That was the trigger for my desire to become a Jungian analyst.

SC: Ursula, who was Carl Gustav Jung? Or, better: Who was, or is, your *own* Carl Gustav Jung?

UB: Well, my own Carl Gustav Jung is the one who discovered the collective unconscious, and who had this close friendship with Richard Wilhelm, and who was the one who opened the psychological door for the work with the I Ching. So, this is what he is personally for me, and of course he is the one who developed his own approach to describing the psyche, which is very much connected with how I understand the psyche myself.

SC: What could be Carl Gustav Jung's relevance today, at the beginning of the 21st century?

UB: Well you see, lots of these modern psychotherapy approaches, like schema therapy, are somehow connected with Jungian ideas. Because the schema therapy is very much orientated to what Jung discovered, or developed, about the complexes. So, lots of his ideas can be renewed and reworked in our times; and it is very interesting, and a still helpful and very supportive therapy approach. This is what we can use today, and what we can make out of it until today.

SC: Jungian psychoanalysts are very fond of dreams. What are dreams?

UB: I would say dreams are your personal and very individual mirror. It is a mirror with many dimensions. So, you can look on the surface and then you see all your relationship problems. The dream is compensating what you actively have in your life now. But then you can go deeper, and you can see the deeper levels of your psyche, images that belong really personally to your psyche, and what you individually are. This is the best source of meeting oneself, in the dream. And you can take it, or you can leave it. It is not something that is overwhelming you—okay sometimes they are nightmares, but usually the dream is just coming, and you can try to understand it or not, but anyhow it's helpful.

SC: How can we understand it? Can we understand it by ourselves? Or do we always need somebody else?

UB: Well, it's easier to have somebody else, and it's easier to have somebody supporting you to read these images of the psyche, but not influencing you. This is why we as Jungians do all this symbolic work, to understand the different symbolic meaning of the dreams and connect it to your individual experience. So, this is why it is very helpful to have somebody you trust to talk with. And during the process of analysis sometimes you get an idea, you get a clue about your own inner pictures, and this helps you to step-by-step understand your own dreams. So of course, I would say it's helpful to have somebody, and of course it's helpful to become your own expert.

SC: Jung said he had nobody to tell his dreams to; not even Freud, since they parted. But in May 1929, Richard Wilhelm sent Jung *The Golden Flower*. And Sonu Shamdasani underlines in his edited version of *The Red Book, A Reader's*

Edition, that suddenly Jung stopped writing and painting *The Red Book*, the *Liber Novus*, and started to dig deeper and deeper into *The Golden Flower* and alchemy. He met alchemy through Wilhelm, we could say, or this is what Shamdasani says. Can you tell us more, something about Jung and Wilhelm, their relationship?

UB: Yes, you know of course we know little about that. But what I think, was that it such an amazing meeting, and it was such a wonderful coincidence that they met. Richard Wilhelm at that time was one of the most profound sinologists in the old Chinese classic works, and he gained a deep wisdom during his studies, because he stayed for 25 years in China. He went very deeply in this classical Chinese material. But of course, he was not a psychologist, he was a Protestant priest; but he was very open-minded, and he was not a person who tried to put things he got information about into his own system. He was open-minded enough to look at it as a phenomenon. And that's something you can see when you read his translations. He did not do it in a very narrow-minded sinologist's approach; he tried to understand the text in its meaning. Sometimes he put it a little bit into this Christian terminology; however, he tried to really get an idea of the meaning of the text. So, this was his great effort. And I think this was something Jung realized and could appreciate very much, because in one sense this was pure material he got, pure material he needed to include in his own work about the archetypes and about alchemy. And of course, it was a confirmation about his collective unconscious concept he discovered at that time. So, this was really an amazing synchronicity.

SC: You mentioned meaning, the concept of meaning. Shamdasani underlines that in psychotherapy, "Jung sought to enable his patients to recover a sense of meaning in life through facilitating and supervising their own self-experimentation and symbol creation." This is interesting to me because after years of working on his inner side, writing, dreaming, painting, meeting *The Secret of the Golden Flower* (or writing the comment to it), he was able to leave the inner work. To find the strength to go into the outer world. To present his ideas. And here is where he also met his followers. He was not alone anymore.

UB: No, he was not alone anymore. And of course, this was why the I Ching was so valuable for him, because in these 64 hexagrams, the I Ching describes complex situations. These were generations of Chinese experts who worked on the I Ching. It was, *it is*, a very old book, and it was continuously commented on until, let's say, in modern days. And it was not him who had to do this, it was already done. It was only the thing to see, to discover it, and to understand it in this way; for example, to understand the hexagrams in their psychological meaning, psychological background. So, this was really a good opportunity to demonstrate how psyche expresses itself in this, let's say, philosophical and also very archaic source of wisdom, which is shown in the I Ching.

SC: Jung, thanks to Theodore Flournoy, got closer and closer to alchemical texts since 1910. But he also got closer and closer, although superficially we could say, to the Asian culture.

UB: Yes.

SC: Yoga, meditation, the mandalas and their center, the Tao, and then the I Ching. Why do you think that is? What was he looking for there, that we in Europe couldn't find?

UB: Well, you know, in *The Red Book*—you mentioned *The Red Book*—there he had a fantasy about the opposites. And he was not calling it *yin* and *yang*, it was just that the one begets the other one; that the one creates the other side, which was the beginning also of his shadow concept. He found this when he got an idea of Lao Tzu's *Tao Te Ching*, and there, in the very first words, is a very precise description of the *Self* concept which was also Jung's concept. In these few words everything is explained: the two opposites, the shadow concept, the transcendent function; and the inner subjective opposites and the outer object opposites, like the shadow and ego, or like the unconscious and the conscious. This whole system is based on a concept of the unifying symbol. And the unifying symbol, like we have it in the Zen Circle, is something you find in Asian tradition. The Christian tradition is more orientated to the Trinity, and so the beginning, the very first beginning in the unifying symbol, which is significant in the circle—this was something he found in the Asian culture.

SC: Jung wrote to Wilhelm on May 25th, 1929: "Fate appears to have given us the role of two bridge pillars which carried the bridge between East and West." Jung also wrote, "My acquaintance with alchemy in 1930 took me away from it, from the *Liber Novus*. The beginning of the end came in 1928 when Richard sent me the text of *The Golden Flower*, an alchemical treatise. There the contents of this book found their way into actuality and I could no longer continue working on it" [on the *Liber Novus*]. And then he continued, "The text [*The Golden Flower*] gave me an undreamed of confirmation of my ideas about the mandala and the circumambulation of the center. This was the first event which broke through my isolation. I became aware of an affinity. I could establish ties with someone and something." Ursula, what is the content of *The Secret of the Golden Flower*?

UB: It is the combination of the idea of entity, duality, and quaternity, which means it is a very impressive work on the symbolism of the numbers. Which is, of course, connected to the mandala, because you again have the cycle there and then you have the quarter within the cycle. The whole thing is based on how a human being can become aware and, let's say, conscious, within the darkness of all these influences that create the world and the personal being. It is again, let's say, an idea of how to find a position in your personal life according to your fate, which is also mentioned in *The Golden Flower*. And, of course, it is a very interesting description of the individuation process, because *yin* and *yang* can be seen as *anima* and *animus*, the concept Jung developed also. But the thing is that *yin* and *yang* are not valuing. *Anima* and *animus* are very complicated concepts because they are very much valuing. This was also a problem Jung had with this concept. In *The Golden Flower* you have the philosophy of *yin* and *yang* as qualities of the psyche, and how these two qualities create each other in a sense of gaining more consciousness about yourself. This is, in short, what *The Golden Flower* is about.

SC: What about the I Ching—what is the I Ching?

UB: Well, this is a bigger question. The I Ching says about itself, that it can describe everything. It could describe everything that happens in the world, so it is a unifying description of everything that happens in the world. And the I Ching says that all of these things that happen in the world are not chaotic. All this is happening according to a certain order, and the I Ching helps to discover this certain order. Even in terms of conflict, or despair, something like this, it can help to give you an idea, or to find your way back to what your inner *Tao*, your inner path, or inner truth, is. It helps you to find a new position in what seems to be chaotic, in the sense of just trying to understand the meaning of a certain situation; because you get an idea of what you don't see, what you don't understand, and what you don't *want to* see, of course. So, it helps you to find your own place within things overwhelming you.

SC: Let's try to help those reading this understand how it works. Imagine a patient comes to you, and this patient has a problem: I have a job offer on the other side of the world. I don't know what to do. Shall we ask the oracle, the I Ching?

UB: Now, interesting enough you mentioned two things. The one thing is, the I Ching helps you to find decisions, to make decisions. And you mentioned that the I Ching is an oracle—and of course you can see the I Ching as an oracle. But this is not the expression we like to use in modern times, because it's too obscure. Insofar as the I Ching says that it has a structure, it can bring structure, a sense of order into, let's say, chaotic things. The I Ching says it doesn't matter when you ask something, or how you ask something; but, if you ask something, you can get a certain answer. And it's up to you to give this answer relevance. So, you can ask your best friend this question and he will give you some advice. And the I Ching says about himself, I'm like a well, and you can take fresh water out of this well, or you can just pass by. When you take away the word "oracle," we can say, the whole thing—we are in a psychological field, everything around us—is psyche. So, the question is, which position you find to get an answer to such a question. And if you cannot find an answer within yourself you can use a mirror: you can use a friend, or you can use the I Ching—in other words, something in this psychological field—to get advice, or to get a new, helpful, or supporting idea. But with the I Ching it is amazing, because it is containing this great wisdom. So, it's a very wise friend you can ask. And here again, we are at the unifying symbol. Jung is coming from the *unus mundus*, and from alchemy; here again, you find it. The I Ching says everything is contained in everything; everything is in this psychological field, and the question is which position you take to get an answer, and to get an idea about it.

SC: I have an intriguing question. Does it work with everybody? I am sure you have encountered, maybe not a patient, but people who came to you and asked you, "What is the I Ching, I heard you are an expert about it?" Maybe because they have a rational mind, a conscious-oriented mind, they would say, "Come on, how does this work?" Have you ever encountered somebody that was at first sight against it, or not able to understand it, and then proved that the I Ching (or the oracle) could really support you in your life?

UB: Well you know, when somebody is coming and is really skeptical about it, then there is a little curious light within them who wants to know it. Those who are really not interested, and who are really not thinking about these things and are not interested in these questions and in this idea (that I can ask a book a very personal question), they won't come and ask me to do the I Ching with them. So of course, these are always people who say okay, I can go along with it, that I might get an answer while throwing coins or throwing the sticks. And this is already, let's say, the idea that there is something greater, a greater wisdom beyond what I see; and I am interested enough in getting an answer from this side. This is why when people are coming and asking to do the I Ching with me, these people are really interested. They are really interested in taking the risk. And again, the I Ching is answering in a symbolical way, with this universal symbol, so that everybody, with some help like with dream interpretation, can understand the answer when there is a person helping them. This is what I do; I try not only to translate, but to discover the meaning of the symbol for the proper situation the client is coming and asking.

SC: Modern technology enables us to have the I Ching on your iPhone, your smart phone. Does it work?

UB: Yes, of course it works. It doesn't matter; it's not important whether you do this ritual and very magical things with coins, or the sticks, or even shake your iPhone. You also can look at an image and immediately it is meaningful to you. So, it's not so important how you ask the book—you also can open it, and then you get a hexagram. The only thing is with throwing the coins or the sticks or also shaking the iPhone is that you get the lines and the comment on the lines. So, it is a practical question of which method you use. But to say it symbolically, it doesn't matter. When you want to swim, it doesn't matter if you jump into the lake or if you just approach the lake slowly; when you want to swim you swim. So, when you want to ask the book, just ask.

SC: Can you ask the same question multiple times?

UB: Yes, you can, of course you can; but I know what you mean. So, there's one hexagram which is very amazing and always astonishing to people, because when they ask the same question several times the I Ching answers that they should not bother him any longer. This is Hexagram No 4: Youthful Folly. There the text says: "The young fool seeks me. At the first oracle I inform him. If he asks two or three times, it is importunity. If he importunes, I give him no information. And this is something very amazing, and this is maybe also something very obscure. It seems to really have a certain intelligence. There are some people who are working with the I Ching and who say this is like something superficially talking to you; however, what it is, it is as if the I Ching makes contact with you in this very personal situation you are in. And this is so amazing, and so helpful. So, you can ask several times, then sometimes you get too many answers which are confusing, or you can ask several times and then you get this hexagram which tells you that you should not bother the I Ching, because it doesn't give you a second advice. But there is also a hexagram which says, please ask me a second time. This is Hexagram 8: Holding Together: "Inquire the oracle once again. Whether you possess sublimity, constancy, and perseverance. Then there is no blame." Then maybe the question was not the real question you had.

SC: Can we look into technique, how to formulate the question? A few minutes ago, I asked you: A possible patient, neighbor, friend comes to you with, "I have a job offer on the other side of the world. What can I do?" What is the first thing that you do when looking at this question?

UB: Yes, you know, when looking at this question, when you say, "What can I do?" well, then it is, what can you do? You can do many things. What makes sense is to find a very precise question about what is really affecting you. Is this job interesting for you because you want to escape from a situation here? In that case, then maybe the question would be, why do I want to leave my surroundings here? Or is the question actually, "What am I expecting about the new job on the other side of the world?" Or, "What will be the consequences if I take this job and leave my life here?" So, you see, when starting with the question, there are lots of different questions behind it. This is why the question finding process is so important, because then you really find out what your real question is, and what the real motivation is behind the question. This is an important step in your personal conscious work you have to do when asking the I Ching, when asking the oracle, you know. When you know your motivation, and when you know your proper question, then the I Ching is able to answer very precisely, very much referring to what is really affecting you. And this is the same like the dream. You can understand the dream in two ways: in a final way, in the sense of what is the development in the dream? What helps me to understand my situation now and gives an idea of what will develop out of this situation? Or it's answering the "why" question. I don't like the "why" question very much, because it does not make so much sense to explain the past. It very often makes sense—and this is again much more connected with the I Ching—to ask what is the situation now, what can develop out of this situation, and what is important for me now to understand, to survey, to accept, in the sense in order to be in accord with my individual development, which takes part now in this situation. This is why we can talk about I Ching to be an oracle. Because the I Ching says, "I see the seed in a situation and I can tell you something about how it will turn out, how it will develop." This is the great relevance of the I Ching. And this is also the differentiation to all the other things, because it is really referring to the proper situation. Then you can get a very individual answer.

SC: Step one is to find the correct question. Step two is to throw the coins or sticks, open the book, shake the iPhone. With the coins (which, as far as I understand is the method you use the most), how do you use it? How does it work?

UB: Usually you choose three coins, personal coins, your coins; it can be coins from your currency, or it can be Chinese coins, it doesn't matter. They have to be three similar coins, of course, in terms of size, and in terms of weight. And then you begin with making a definition, because the coin has two sides: usually a side where a number is mentioned and the other side with a weapon. And you have to give a definition to these two sides, meaning one side is representing the number three, and the other side is representing the number two. I usually give the advice that the side of the coin that shows the number represents the number 3, because 3 is the first irregular number, which is much more dedicated to what is meant with heaven. The weapon side is representing the earth, the archetype of the earth, and this is much more represented through the number 2. So, this is why I give this advice. When you have found your personal definition for the two sides, you go along with this during your whole life, or when you are asking the I Ching. So, when you throw three coins, you add the numbers you get, so you can for example get 3x3, then you have the number 9. The number 9 is a long line, non-interrupted line. Or you can throw the coins and you can get 3x2. This is 6, and this is a *yin* line. So, the results you get are connected to *yin* or *yang*. Numbers 6 and 8 are connected to *yin*, and numbers 9 and 7 are connected to *yang*. 9 and 6 are changing lines, and 7 and 8 are staying lines. And of course, the I Ching is the book of changes, so you can see with these changing lines, represented by the changing numbers, the I Ching shows at which point of the situation the situation is going to change into a beginning, new, transforming situation. So, you throw the coin six times. Six times throwing you get a hexagram, because you get six lines. (Every time you throw the coins you get one line.) When you have thrown it six times you have got the hexagram, and with the changing lines then you look at the book and identify which hexagram you got, and then you read the comments.

SC: You said that there are 64 hexagrams, and now I see that you have not one, but two I Ching books.

UB: Yes, I have the German one and an English version.

SC: Can you give me an example of how you work with it, how you support a patient with decrypting the answers, reading a hexagram.

UB: Yes, of course I can. I remember a woman coming, she was in her mid-40s, and she had serious problems with her partner. And like it always is, it is a typically complex situation. There were lots of emotions, which were struggling with each other. So, she was afraid about maybe this is going to separation. She was angry with her partner. She felt alone, she felt helpless, she was mourning, and of course you see all these different emotions are connected with different experiences in her life. For example, her mourning was because she remembered another situation where she lost an important person in her life; and her anger was because she felt that there is something between them which was like a blockade, and that she could not come closer to her partner and she did not know what it was. Her anxiety was, of course, that it will come to a separation. So, she was mixed up with all these different emotions, and, well of course, she wanted to ask the oracle where the relationship will go or develop. Then I told her, okay, if you ask a question like this, maybe you think that something, or this decision (this is not a decision), that the whole situation is influenced by a sort of fate outside of you. And then she said yes, well I feel like that—it's not me anymore acting in this relationship, it's as if these things are happening around me. And then I said, well then maybe you are too strongly connected to your fate or to circumstances you cannot influence, and I think this is the reason why you feel so overwhelmed. The question is, what is really connected with you, what can you do in this situation, so that you feel more capable? With this instruction she realized, "Yes, I am also part of the situation, and I cannot delegate the solution of the situation to my fate or to my fortune or to this book." I have to find my own way to get along with this problem I have. Then I asked her to tell me more about the problem she had. Then she talked a little bit more about the blockade. She said that they have this relationship, and she loves this man, but she always thinks that there is something standing in between. And her husband was divorced from his first wife, this was his second marriage, and she said, "I think he never arrived in our relationship." When I asked her what she meant with "arrived" she said, "It is as if he is always a little bit absent." Okay. So, and then (to shorten this a little bit) I asked her what she wants to ask the I Ching, and she said, "My spontaneous question is, how will this relationship turn out in the near future?" Then I said well, this is what I said before. You are delegating the question to your fate. You can do this, of course; you are allowed to ask everything. But it's more helpful, more practical and more useful for yourself when you ask a very personal question. So, then I said, "I hear that you are a bit doubtful about this relationship," and then she said, "Yes, of course, to be honest. This is not the relationship I want to have." And I said, "Well, can you try to get an idea of what question you really have?" Then she replied, "Maybe the real question is, how do I feel in this relationship right now, and how about my personal emotional energy to go along with this partner?" because she was also thinking about separation. So, she became aware that she had been projecting her idea of separation first onto her partner. And then she realized, "Well I also thought about separation, and my question is, how am I personally and emotionally involved in this partnership, and how do I personally want to go along with it?" So, we threw the coins, and she got hexagram number 12. And hexagram number 12 is, in the English translation, "The Standstill/ Stagnation." So, the first reaction was, okay it is now again fate; the I Ching says that they will separate. So, when you project it on the objective level, when you project it outside of yourself, then you can say, "Okay, the meaning of fate is separation." Then I always go back to the personal, the inner motivation and the inner complex situation. So, then we talked a lot about her not being connected with herself and with the situation, and not being connected with the partner. Because hexagram "Stagnation," number 12, describes two powers, heaven and earth, which are not coming together, because the two energies are separating away from each other. So, the question was: What is really her inner problem about not really saying yes to who she is, who she is in the relationship, and also saying yes to her aggression and her anger she has towards her partner? Because of her aggression and anger she was unable to share her feelings with her partner and always excluded herself. Then we talked a lot about the fact that aggression and anger sometimes can help to come into contact; as long as she is in the stagnation and repressing her anger, she cannot feel herself and her partner. So, there is no feeling in the relationship. And the missing feelings lead to stagnation. And when she is not connected with all her feelings, she is not connected with herself, so this is also an inner stagnation. We talked a lot about how this hexagram "Stagnation," this complex situation, is referring to her inner psychological situation, to her objective relationship level, and also to the objective world she is in. Then she came to the point where she realized that this mourning aspect of the whole situation (because she was afraid that her partner will leave her, or that a separation is coming)—this mourning aspect is one of the first separations in her life, because there she could not show and express her feelings (because she had lost a beloved person). She could not express her feelings, and she covered these feelings inside herself. Outside, she always played the nice person and she was very successful with it. But of course, this inner part was always separated. The transforming line was the line number 6 at the beginning. And the 6 at the beginning says, in short, "When ribbon grass is pulled up, the sod comes with it." This was exactly what was happening. She tried to pull out the grass, but what was coming with it was the mourner. And she saw that she had to re-process this, because, she said, "I have to re-find my lost feelings, because I realize now without these feelings I cannot arrive in a true relationship with my partner." And so, she realized the blockade she had projected into this situation because, she said, "Maybe the idea that he was still connected with his former wife was a projection." It was not what was happening with him. This was something that was happening with her; that she was unconsciously connected with something that had happened in her life before, and which was her problem. So, then this was a very long process that we worked on—this inner stagnation she had, where she had lost herself in this situation when she was a girl. Then she could find the courage to express her proper feelings, let's say "negative" feelings (there are no negative feelings, but meaning these not very much accepted feelings); that she could express this in her relationship with her partner and in all the other relationships she was involved. This was a process over several weeks, and suddenly she felt more alive, because she had more feelings. She was not so depressed anymore. She had not been obviously depressed; this was really a depression which was very much hidden. And so, she felt alive, and said, "I feel much more alive." And what happened was, of course, that she went out, and she met two other men who seemed to be very interesting. Her partner became jealous, and they got into a great discussion about their relationship, and the whole thing led to good progress in their relationship. So, you see, what at the beginning could be understood as separation in the sense that they are going to separate as a couple because he is the problem, went into a completely other direction. She could solve a subjective, inner problem, and then see that this and stagnation is something meant within her. Taking the responsibility for that, she could solve the relationship problem. And there was no separation at all. She got the courage to talk with her partner about his first marriage and all the questions she had. Of course, she also had to manage this mourning process, which was her own story, and the whole thing led to a better understanding of the situation.

SC: Usually it is said that psychoanalysis is the development of the personality, of your *own* personality, your true personality. But this story, this case you just mentioned, sounds to me like a revolution. Do you believe psychoanalysis is meant for revolution, and which kind of revolution?

UB: Well, you know, "revolution" is a political word. I think we Jungians would prefer to talk about *transformation*, changing, and, well, when we go back to what I described with this woman. Of course, it was revolutionary for her to take her projection back; to see where her proper problem was, because people avoid this. Everybody knows we all prefer to project and we prefer to see the problem in the other. So, this is a sort of revolution when you are able to do that. Because you always have to engage, really, your whole courage to do it. This is what Jung says, nobody likes to do it, to meet his own shadow, because his shadow is ugly, and the shadow is always challenging us. This is the part, when you talk about revolution—it is the challenging aspect of the whole thing. "Challenging" also means that you really have to go through the suffering and also go through the joy. Lots of people are afraid of being happy and of being joyous, as sometimes they prefer to suffer. This is also a sort of revolution, to accept that if I come to this point where I realize who I am, as in this woman's situation, then I really feel happy and I can enjoy this progress. Sometimes this is revolutionary, because then you really get an inner connection with yourself, like a new inner stability. And you must be honest to say, "Well I solved something, and I've got an idea of something about myself and I am proud about it." So, I think this is revolutionary; but I would not use this word. I would say when you take a chance to do this transforming process, even if it's harmful and even if it's shaming, and even if it's sometimes very sad, there are also other feelings around it, and this makes you feel more like who you really are, with all the variety of feelings you have. And of course, it also helps you to find your position in the proper situation now; not fleeing into the past, and not seeking for whatever may be in the future, but really having arrived in this proper situation in your life. This is for me something that is really connected to a feeling of vitality, and of being connected now.

SC: Thank you Ursula. It has been a pleasure to listen to you.

UB: Thank you very much, thank you for this interview and these interesting questions.

Otto Gross: "The Personal is the Political"

Gottfried M. Heuer

SC: Dear Gottfried, thank you very much for accepting my invitation to talk about Otto Gross. As you know, this is a series called "Breakfast at Küsnacht." Perhaps, for today, we can call it "Breakfast Beyond Küsnacht"; although Otto Gross is also linked to Küsnacht—to Carl Gustav Jung. But the aim of this interview is not to compare Jung and Gross as twin brothers, as you did in your book. I really want to look at Gross and his work. Before doing so, could you share the central steps in your intellectual biography/journey?

GMH: I was born in northern Germany some five months before the end of the Nazi regime into a family dedicated to art. My father was a secondary school teacher and had been standing up for what in those times were called "degenerate" artists, i.e., the German expressionists. So, for as long as I can remember, I've been doing drawings, painting—and continue today with stone-balances and photography. After secondary school, I studied commercial graphic arts in Berlin, followed by a teacher training at Hamburg art school and university. That was in the mid-1960s, and I became interested in and engaged with the politics of the students' movement, initially triggered by early aspects of feminism, leading to an interest in psychology, family dynamics, et cetera, including ecology. My then girlfriend and I contributed to the Berlin anarchist journal *Schwarze Protokolle*, and collaborated on a book of my drawings, published by the anarchist publisher Karin

Kramer, Berlin.[11] With increasingly conservative politics, there was fear of a return to the horrors of the Nazi times: it became law that students engaged in radical politics would not be allowed to become teachers, and to the west of where I lived—the direction from where the prevailing winds came—the greatest concentration of nuclear power plants was planned to be built in the mouth of the river Elbe. In the early 1970s, my then girlfriend and I emigrated to England. Having read most of Wilhelm Reich's works, we were interested in having Reichian body-psychotherapy, which, at the time, was unavailable in Germany.

SC: What are the authors and the research areas you consider essential for your own development and work? Which other areas do you consider fundamental in your own intellectual biography (also beyond psychoanalysis)?

GMH: In my mid-teens I read Jung's *Memories, Dreams, Reflections*. Later, as I mentioned, Reich's works were very important, also David Boadella's, *Wilhelm Reich: The Evolution of his Life and Work* (1974, London: Vision Press); A.S. Neill, *Summerhill*; Georg Groddeck's works; Emmanuel Hurwitz's *Otto Gross. Paradiessucher Zwischen Freud und Jung* [*Otto Gross. Seeker of Paradise Between Freud and Jung*] (1979); apart from—again, later—reading Jung's works, starting with *Psychology and Alchemy*, as I was fascinated by the imagery. I studied most of Winnicott's works, and then, in the 1990s, Andrew Samuels's books became a further turning point for me, helping me to realise what I had already found in Gross: that the personal—including individual therapy/analysis—is identical with the political.

[11] Due to the political situation, we published this under the surnames of our respective grandparents: Gottfried Hell & Julia Hartkopf (1974). *Täglicher Terror. 20 Tageszeichnungen* [Daily Terror 20 Daily Drawings]. Berlin: Kramer.

SC: When did you realize (and decide) you wanted to become a Jungian analyst?

GMH: Ha! I could almost say, "I didn't," because someone else did: Through contact with the London libertarian/anarchist group *Solidarity*, with which we had already been in touch before emigrating, I became friends with Peter Eedy, an Australian chef who was doing a therapeutic massage course with Gerda Boyesen, a Norwegian Neo-Reichian body-psychotherapist. I went to see her to ask whether I could have individual therapy with her. She kindly agreed, and then asked me—and, looking back, this is really *the* turning point in my life (apart from meeting my wife five years later!)— "Have you ever considered becoming a psychotherapist yourself?" Her question hit me totally out of the blue: I had never *ever* thought of that before, so I could only stutter, "I—I—haven't even studied any psychology at university," to which she responded, "Well, maybe that's not necessarily a disadvantage..." I joined her training, and became a body-psychotherapist. Having qualified, Peter Eedy invited me to lead therapy groups in Vienna—for the first time in some 50 years, we brought Reichian bodywork back to where it had originated!

SC: How did you become a psychoanalyst?

GMH: I worked for some 15 years exclusively as a body-psychotherapist, in a number of European countries (Germany, Austria, Switzerland, France, Finland, Yugoslavia) North, Central and South America, and Australia; yet increasingly realised that, although I was touching the body and working with it, the unconscious was largely ignored. This also meant that transference/countertransference was not considered. In the mid-1980s, a Canadian Jungian psychotherapist, Jim Healy, joined the Boyesen Centre, and inspired me to consider a training in Jungian Analysis, which I started in the late 1980s. In the mid-1990s, I began working on my Ph.D. on Otto Gross, with Andrew Samuels as my supervisor. In 1999, I co-founded the *International Otto Gross Society*, and co-organised 10 congresses in: Berlin; Graz, Austria; Munich; Vienna; Zurich (at the Burghölzli, where Jung had diagnosed Gross a schizophrenic!; and another one at the Café Voltaire, where Dada was born); Dresden; Malente, northern Germany; and Moscow. We published congress proceedings in excess of a total of 5,000 pages. After the ruin of the Society following a change of leadership, I initiated the *International Association of Otto Gross Studies.*

SC: This brings us to the question: Who was Otto Gross?

GMH: He was an early psychoanalyst who lived between 1877 and 1920—also a medical doctor and psychiatrist—who had a major influence on the theory and clinical practice of psychoanalysis. His qualifying medical dissertation was immediately published in book form, and he started a promising career as a psychiatrist, publishing texts in some of the most prestigious journals of the time. He travelled as a naval doctor to Patagonia before he was drawn to psychoanalysis. As a university lecturer, Gross was the first to bring Freud's psychoanalysis into academia in 1902 at Graz University. Initially, all the early psychoanalysts praised him: Freud himself wrote to Jung, "You are really the only one capable of making an original contribution; except perhaps Otto Gross." Ferenczi wrote to Freud, "There is no doubt that, among those who have followed you up to now, he is the most significant." And Ernest Jones remembered that Gross "was my first instructor in the technique of psycho-analysis," and added, "he was the nearest approach to the romantic ideal of a genius I have ever met."

However, when Gross linked psychoanalysis with revolutionary politics—we might say he was not just a psycho-analyst, but also a psycho-anarchist—he was considered to have gone way too far with the radical political changes he suggested, and also with his very Bohemian way of a promiscuous lifestyle, taking drugs, et cetera. For this he got what in today's language we would call "blacklisted": he was excluded from the psychoanalytic community that struggled then—as it still does—for scientific respectability, because he took Freud by his word, who had written in 1907 that our neuroses have their origin in the society we live in. I believe it's true to say Gross had arrived at that conclusion already earlier, influenced by anarchist ideas. They helped him to realize the close interconnection between his individual rebellion against his authoritarian father and the patriarchal structure of the nuclear family and the surrounding society as a whole: He recognized the identity of the personal and the political. Gross saw how previous revolutions had foundered because, as he put it, the revolutionaries of tomorrow were still carrying the old character structures inside. He fervently hoped that this could now be prevented with the help of psychoanalysis. This came to a head between him and Freud at the 1908 1st Psychoanalytic Congress in Salzburg, when Freud bluntly told Gross in regard to his radical political activism that as psychoanalysts, "We are doctors, and doctors we shall remain." Yet Gross stated later—and we might consider this as almost as his response to Freud: "I have only mixed with anarchists and declare myself to be an anarchist. I am a psychoanalyst and from my experience I have gained the insight that the existing order is a bad one. And since I want everything changed, I am an anarchist." In Roman antiquity, the term *damnatio memoriae* was used, the erasure of a person's name from documents and monuments, et cetera. This happened to Gross. For example: in the first edition of "The significance of the father in the destiny of the individual" (1909), Jung acknowledged that this paper was based on his having worked together with Gross—in the course of their at times mutual analysis. In later editions Jung falsified history by omitting any reference to Gross.

A further example worth mentioning is the origin of the term schizophrenia: as a psychiatrist, Gross had initially coined and used the term *dementia sejunctiva*, literally, "split-off madness" (in published writings since 1904). Eugen Bleuler is generally credited with inventing the term "schizophrenia" in 1908. Synchronistically, this was the year of Gross's analysis with Jung at the Burghölzli, of which Bleuler was the then director. And "schizophrenia" is nothing else but the Greek translation of the Latin term *"dementia sejunctiva"*! In a cruel twist if fate, that exactly was Jung's diagnosis of Gross—wrong, as it turns out, according to careful analysis of the known facts, including Jung's case-notes! When Gross broke off his analysis, Jung almost reacted like a spurned lover and diagnosed him incurably mentally ill with schizophrenia, predicting that he would probably have to spend the rest of his life in closed institutions. This was done in arrangement with Gross's father who used this diagnosis to start legal proceedings against his son in order to be legally made his guardian—in which he partly succeeded.

Shortly after his death, a close friend, the Austrian satirist Anton Kuh, spoke of him as "the most stolen-from psychoanalyst," writing of him as "a man known only to very few by name—apart from a handful of psychiatrists and secret policemen—and among those few only to those who plucked his feathers to adorn their own posteriors."

SC: What are the key areas, or aspects, of his investigation? What was he concerned with?

GMH: He did not use the term, but the first thing that comes to my mind is trauma—the trauma of the child in the traditional, patriarchal family. That was one of his main concerns, and the other connected to what I've mentioned before: to see the family structures (the intra-familiar politics, so to speak) in the patriarchal family linked to the authoritarian patriarchal structure of the rest of society. Gross movingly writes how the child is born with a longing to be loved—unconditionally—and how, in the traditional family, the parents' response to this comes with a condition, a "yes—but only if you become like we are." And the child is forced to succumb, since s/he cannot survive without love. Again, without using the term, what he does is describe the origin of the superego. For Gross, this is *the* basic conflict, which, he says, rents asunder all of humanity: the conflict between self and other, or, as he put it, the conflict between *dem Eigenen und dem Fremden* (that which is one's very own and that which is the other's). With Gross's work, Jung's concept of the archetype of the *wounded healer* comes to mind (although, again, the term, of course, didn't exist then). Gross developed his concepts from the basis of his own traumatic experience as a small child in the stifling atmosphere of the late Habsburg patriarchal society in a provincial town in southeastern Austria.

SC: Could we say that it is precisely this traumatic experience of growing up in a patriarchal environment (with an authoritarian father and a sick mother) that led to his proposal of a matriarchal society, as a compensation for the patriarchal one?

GMH: Yes.

SC: Yet his lifestyle was in contradiction to the matriarchal view that he espoused, and actually only served to reinforce the patriarchal attitude that he despised. Could we say that he was infected by what Jungians term a parental (negative father and mother) complex?

GMH: Well, yes—although I often feel that this term can easily be used with a somewhat hostile undertone, as if it's the person's own fault. I'm thinking of lines from a poem by Rumi, which I believe Gross would have agreed with,

> We started off pure gold.
> Then people began
> polluting us
> when we were too young
> to fight back.

SC: I agree that a complex should never be seen as a person's own fault, but it seems to me he was not conscious enough to deal with it and the consequences. Therefore, on the one side he proposed a matriarchal society; yet, on the other he involved himself in multiple relationships at the same time. How do you reconcile the theorist and the man?

GMH: Well—especially from today's perspective, with so much greater knowledge about the effects of trauma compared with what was known over a hundred years ago—we may say that when an early deprivational trauma is too deep, healing can be very difficult. As with many of us, his ideas, which he wrote about, did not—sadly, painfully, tragically—correspond to the life that he was able to live. Didn't someone say, "History happens between what we aspire to and what we actually do"? In spite of the moving way he was able to write about the plight of the child in the family—with a degree of compassion unmatched by any of his psychoanalytic contemporaries—Gross was unable to care for his own children. He had a son, Peter, together with his wife Frieda, and another son in the same year of 1907 with a close friend of his wife, Else Jaffé, who named her son also Peter. The latter Peter died seven years later, and Peter Gross became a medical doctor like his father, and died in the early 1940s before he could complete his training to become a psychoanalyst. In 1908, Gross had a daughter, Camilla, with the Swiss writer Regina Ullmann. I met and interviewed her before she died in 2000. Gross's youngest daughter Sophie, with the nurse Marianne "Mitzi" Kuh, was born in 1916 and is alive in Berlin.

Gross hated his father and was locked, really, into a lifelong battle with him: in 1913 he said, "I want to die young, preferably by killing an investigating judge, so that we both die at the same time" (his father having written a world famous *Handbook for Investigating Judges).* Gross also mused, "Blowing up all of Vienna—that would be *wonderful!*" At the same time, he was capable of the insight that one of the tragic long-term after-effects of trauma can be, in his words, "the will to rape and be raped," the sado-masochistic trap of handing down onto others abuse suffered in early childhood.

For the whole of his life Gross was financially dependent on his father; and when his father, Hans Gross, died in 1915, Otto Gross continued to be financially dependent on his mother. I think he was attracted to a romantic version of matriarchy, stemming from his longing for motherly love (which apparently, he hadn't received much of). Clearly, although he never mentions him in his writings, he was influenced by Bachofen's ideas—which were very popular at the time.

In 1905, Gross went to Ascona in Switzerland—in today's words, we could call it the counter-cultural capital of the whole of Europe—where he met two German anarchists, Erich Mühsam and Johannes Nohl, who, I think, helped him to channel his rebellious feelings towards his parents and patriarchal society into the direction of anarchist politics, imbued with a strong sense of spirituality. Gross wanted to revive the cult of Astarte, one of the mother-goddesses of the Middle East, and is rumored to have initiated religious orgies in the woods around Ascona. It must have been there, in Ascona, that he was also introduced to the works of the Russian anarchist, Peter Kropotkin, who had published a very important book in England in 1902, which was written as a kind of anti-Darwin book (if we simplistically reduce Darwin's ideas to the survival of the fittest and the fight of everyone against everybody else). Kropotkin wrote a book entitled *Mutual Aid: A Factor of Evolution* in which, rather than fighting against each other, he observed cooperation in the animal world. Actually, in the years that Gross frequently was in Ascona, Kropotkin wintered in nearby Locarno. It is hard to imagine that they never met in person, but there is no documentary evidence for that. Kropotkin's ideas of mutual aid have recently been confirmed by latest research—I am thinking of Antonio Damasio's latest work on the important factor of cooperation. Of course, Frans de Waal's discoveries come to mind, too.

SC: In your book, on page 10, you write: "Gross's concept of dialectic intersubjectivity is based on the anarchist principle of mutual exchange between equals in the psychoanalytic relationship." Could we consider Gross to have been a pioneer of relational psychoanalysis and intersubjectivity? It is a very interesting link.

GMH: Absolutely, yes, intersubjectivity: analytic writers speak of "the relational turn in analysis"—meaning the change from the traditional doctor-patient relationship with the all-knowing doctor and the patient desperate for the doctor's help, which is hierarchical with the doctor up here and the patient somewhere down there. We could call this a one-person psychology, because the focus of the therapist—the analyst—is exclusively on the sick or ill, neurotic patient. The relational turn marks the change towards a two-person psychology where the psychology (meaning the feelings and emotions, transferences) of the analysts/therapists, are also taken into account.

This concept of "mutual aid" had a profound influence on Otto Gross: he basically transferred this political way of relating—both individually as well as collectively—into the analytic practice. Much later, Jung ingeniously refined this concept in the form of his transference diagram of the mutual relationship between equals, where all four corners of the created rectangle, standing for the analyst's and the patient's respective consciousness and unconscious are seen as being in constant two-way-communication/interaction:

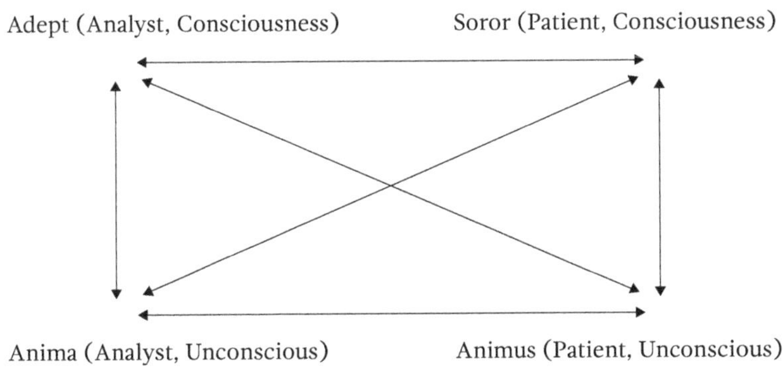

Gross analyzed his friends and patients—without making all that much of a difference between these, just as Freud and Jung did, then—and let them analyze him, in turn: in today's language, we could speak of a kind of co-counseling, *avant la lettre*.

When, after the 1908 Salzburg congress, Freud referred Gross to Jung for analysis to treat Gross's drug addiction, Gross brought this practice of mutuality in equality into the analysis. Jung wrote to Freud, "I have let everything drop and have spent all my available time, day and night, on Gross, to best further his analysis . . . Whenever I got stuck, he analyzed me. In this way my own health has benefited." This is the first testimony of a mutual analysis in which—at least periodically—both partners worked with each other as equals! Jung felt so close to Gross that he experienced him as his "twin brother." I do believe this experience in the mutual analysis with Gross later helped Jung to understand the alchemical images of the *Rosarium* in the way he did.

SC: What you just said is important to underline that Jung and Gross were the first to engage in a mutual analysis, long before Ferenczi.

GMH: Oh, yes. People who write about the origins of relational analysis usually speak about Ferenczi and do not mention Gross. Ferenczi was influenced in this way by Gross. They were friends, they were close together, they even had the same political ideas until 1908, when Gross was rejected for his political ideas. We could say Ferenczi towed the party line; he held back with his political ideas, which were at the time quite similar to Gross's. Melinda Friedrich, a Hungarian Gross-scholar, told me that Ferenczi continued to express radical political ideas in his writings after the Salzburg congress—but only in Hungarian, a language Freud did not understand... So, Ferenczi lasted another 22 years before he, too, became another "black sheep" of the psychoanalytic community.

SC: Perhaps it could be that Ferenczi was less of a self-destructive *puer* type than Gross. For Ferenczi, Freud was a positive generative figure, whereas Freud stirred up Gross's negative father complex. Could it be that his theories came too early for the nascent psychoanalytical Viennese circle, and that his approach lacked the appropriate filters required by such a milieu?

GMH: In his theories, Gross was, I feel like saying, a peaceful man. I am saying this because another one of his most important legacies is—and it is linked to the mutual communication as equals—he wrote (and that continues to be of immense value, from my perspective, in any kind of relating, be that in our personal relationships, in our professional relationships, also intra-psychically as well as interpersonally, and also politically in any context), "the highest goal of every revolution is to replace the will to power with the will to relating." That feels to me a much more profound formulation of what was later turned into a slogan (not with reference to Otto Gross), "make love not war." For me, this is one of most important legacies that Gross left to us as a potential for healing—ourselves, each other, and the world.

SC: This relates to my second question, which would be: What is his relevance in the 21st century? I sense that what you just said *is*, really, his relevance.

GMH: Yes, that is the greatest relevance that I can see. I mean, as I was kind-of sketching out earlier, he was instrumental in many of the most important changes of psychoanalysis, when psychoanalysis was really in its very early years. And I feel that it is important to notice and to take note of that, and not to overlook it and say, "Oh he was just a crazy drug addict and we don't need to bother with him." What is important for us today is this: the idea of replacing the will to power in any relationship with the will to relating. Gross understood this in the context of the personal being the political, and he linked this—and in this also he was decades earlier than Jung—with a spiritual, religious aspect. He saw relating on a deep level as always having a spiritual, religious component. He speaks of "relationship as the third, as religion."

SC: ...Which can only be if there is a relationship, a profound relationship, between two human beings that is brought by equality, equivalence, and mutuality.

GH: Yes.

SC: What is psychoanalysis from Otto Gross's perspective? What is the aim of it? Perhaps revolution? In your book you cited Coline Covington (2001): "Analysis is essentially a tool for revolution." But I wonder, which kind of revolution? There have been many revolutions in the past 100 years. And we can also refer, as you do, to Andrew Samuels's use of the term *tikkun*, healing the world, healing the soul. Healing your soul could be your own revolution: individuation, to become yourself, to become the person you have never been. What is (was) psychoanalysis for Otto Gross?

GMH: He literally saw psychoanalysis as a "preparatory work for the revolution"—his words. As I mentioned earlier, Gross realized that all the revolutions of the past have failed because the revolutionaries were concerned with outer change, and were not able to realize that within themselves they carried the old structures, the old hierarchical *power* structures, so that their efforts ultimately only produced a copy of what was before.

SC: A compensation of the previous status. Look at '68, a "failed" revolution due to a return to *will to power* rather than a search for long-lasting mutuality.

GMH: Absolutely—although I do not see '68 as a failure. Gross saw the chance, the opportunity, via psychoanalysis, to change these inner structures so that they would not be able to turn the outer revolution into basically more of the same, into what existed before. That was his fervent hope and belief. That was the chance, and that's where he felt abandoned by Freud, bemoaning "the repression of the final revolutionary conclusions . . . by the ingenious discoverer of the exploratory method" (emphasis Otto Gross). You asked what kind of revolution, and in that context, you mentioned healing. *That* is the revolution that Gross envisaged: a healing, both individually—healing from our individual wounds with the help of psychoanalysis—and simultaneously, a healing via a change of the outer, hierarchical structures of patriarchal society that caused these individual wounds. Again, in the sense of the identity between the personal and the political.

SC: I also wonder whether—call me a romantic—revolution can only happen through and thanks to love. Again, the difference, between *will to power* (where there is no love) and the relationality of the revolution that Gross talks about, is key.

GMH: I absolutely agree with you on the love, yes.

SC: Let me read to you another quote from your book: "Our pain doesn't come from the love we weren't given in the past but from the love we ourselves aren't giving in the present"—this is by Williamson. You talked about Gross's longing for love: the fact that he hated his father (who he perceived as authoritarian and castrating), and the absence of his mother due to her illness. This, to me, is about love and hate, where hate is compensating love and love compensates hate. Is this where he was trapped—unable to love himself, and constantly seeking it in others?

GMH: Yes.

SC: And this is also what Jessica Benjamin, Susie Orbach, and their feminist psychoanalysis is all about.

GMH: I very much agree. Yes.

SC: We could also add Bowlby, Winnicott, et cetera: the key is love.

GMH: Yes. This is another thing that actually Freud, very early on, wrote to Jung: "Essentially, the cure is effected by love!" And it is interesting to realize that this is not something that Otto Gross said—although he could have said it, he would have absolutely agreed with that.

SC: There is another sentence—this time your own—which touched me deeply, and perhaps this is the big difference between you and Otto Gross. You wrote, "In the process of learning to love, I am also learning to feel loved, to accept love for myself." He didn't give himself the chance to be loved and to stay there. He always had, perhaps, to move on, as he couldn't believe that the love was given by this bad man. Jung was a medical doctor. Taking care of patients—or his wife, or a lover—could be a place to stay. I say it is because the relationship between him and Jung was very strong. Jung was contained, somehow by Emma. Maybe by Emma's wealth. Without Emma (and his mother, sister, cousin, Sabina, Toni, Marie-Louise, et cetera, as the numerous facets of his anima), perhaps there would be no Jung as we know him today, who knows. Jung grew up in a society, because of his father, that could not accept polyamory. But when he met Otto Gross, he changed his mind. While Otto Gross, somehow, was coming from a different point of view. Society is not embedding me; society is something that I have to get rid of. It is interesting that Jung could continue to work, could come back from his night journey, because he had a safety around him, psychological and not—there his anima stepped in. Gross never had this. This is my fantasy.

GMH: I felt touched by what you were just saying about Gross being probably unable to believe that he could be loved. I hadn't really looked at him in this way before, and I am moved by that and I believe it is absolutely true. I see that as possibly the root of his, we could say, sexual restlessness. To have one woman after the other, which, in the way I see it, was—well, in the way the women he was with wrote about their relationship with him, they did not feel loved. His wife felt close to suicide even whilst she was pregnant with his son—that was not a healing love relationship.

SC: This brings to my mind a patient who is very, very successful professionally. We could say he has a parental complex not unlike Otto Gross: with a mother and father who were unable to provide a secure-enough base. When he comes in, he is very sad, very depressed and unable to relate. Like Otto Gross, has a series of lovers with whom he doesn't engage. It is interesting for me, considering these parallels between Otto Gross' story and my patient. Professionally successful in the public sphere, in both cases, however, there is a lack of ability for mutuality and relational ability that creates the impossibility of love in the private sphere.

GMH: The impossibility to live his ideas, which we initially were referring to. At the same time, it seems right to me to call him a sexual revolutionary. The writer Werfel claimed that Gross had invented the term "sexual revolution." On the one hand, we can see from today's perspective that his was a sexual revolution very much from a male perspective: men should have the right for multiple sexual partners, but when one of Gross's lovers—Else Jaffé—engaged with another man, he got very cross! On the other hand, Frieda Weekley, who later became D.H. Lawrence's wife, wrote in her memoirs that Gross had awakened her soul that had lain coiled up and asleep in her. Gross also wrote that for a man to be able to truly love a woman, he needs to be in touch with his own homosexual side. I think implicitly this relates also to what we were saying before about a capacity to validate one's own lovability. In this context it is also important to mention that he was the first psychoanalyst who did not pathologize same-sex desire. It took the analytic community almost another century to reach that conclusion—if we can truly say so, and if biases really do not continue to linger...

SC: Like Marcuse, who said that the philosopher can live a particular life but, you know, his philosophy is something else.

GMH: Which it shouldn't ideally be; but of course, as I say, I guess it is for most of us, if not for all of us, that way.

SC: Let's go back to Andrew [Samuels] and plurality.

GMH: Yes.

SC: Linking to this: in the book titled *Love and Sacrifice: The Life of Emma Jung* by Imelda Gaudissart (2014), there is a sentence in a letter from Jung to Freud (McGuire, 1979, Letter 175), where Jung says, "The prerequisite for a good marriage, it seems to me, is the license to be unfaithful." How much of Otto Gross is in this sentence? How much of Jung is in this sentence? Or even Freud, if we also look at the relationship between Freud, his wife, and his sister-in-law?

GMH: It takes me back to what you movingly said a moment ago about the inability, or the incapacity, to believe that one is lovable, which I think applies to Gross as much as to Freud, as well as to Jung. All three of them, we can say from today's perspective, have been sexually traumatized. And a terrible ongoing continuing legacy of this can be—just as the man, the client that you referred to a moment ago—the "I am not really lovable, so...." There is a line from a Goethe poem, "*Und bist du nicht willig, dann brauch' ich Gewalt*" ("If you do not accede to my wishes, then I will use force"). And tragically, though I do not mean to excuse what all of these three men did to the women they were involved with, *that* is the source. In my feelings, as in the line from the Goethe poem, it goes more in the direction of power, of conquering women, than in the direction of love and healing. It is that fatal legacy, again, that I mentioned earlier, "the desire to rape and to be raped"—and we may understand "rape" here in the widest sense of emotional as well as physical, including, of course, sexual abuse.

SC: Which sounds very difficult in these past few years of the 21st century. We had hoped a few years ago that things were progressing in a different way, but now it really looks like a worldwide regression to old threats.

GMH: Well, yes. However, I am also thinking of the American philosopher and psychoanalyst Jonathan Lear, whom I quote in my book on Gross. In his *Radical Hope* (2008), he speaks of a hope which can be found after all negativities have been faced, and trusting that there is sufficient goodness in the world for things to turn out alright¾even if there is nothing rationally knowable on which to base such faith. I'm with him in this!

SC: And there is a psychosocial, or political, need to look into this, I would say, psychoanalytically. Like Andrew [Samuels] says, in the book *Politics on the Couch*, there is a possibility for psychoanalysis to serve as an additional tool to history, sociology, et cetera; to look into what is happening from a deep, deep psychological point of view.

GMH: Yes.

SC: When you and I first met in Prague in December 2017, at the "Analysis and Activism" conference, you told me the story about how you spent a considerable amount of time looking for Otto Gross's grave in Berlin Pankow. Would you share more about this, perhaps?

GMH: It has been part of my research to find out where he is buried, and there is only a line in Emanuel Horwitz's book, the first really groundbreaking account of Otto Gross's life and work published in 1979 (sadly only in German language) where he says that Gross was accidentally buried in a Jewish cemetery in Berlin; "accidentally," because he was not Jewish. There were originally six Jewish cemeteries in Berlin, but of course they did not survive the Nazi times unscathed. So, based on what is left of them and what is left of records that had been kept, I did research and contacted the various administrations, but there was no trace of Gross. Raimund Dehmlow, one of the two men with whom I co-founded the International Otto Gross Society—the other one was Gross's grandson Anthony Templer—has some theories that possibly a rich industrialist who helped Gross financially may have given Gross a grave in his family plot, but, so far, that is an unsubstantiated rumor. The place of Gross's burial remains unknown.

SC: Finally, my last question for you today would be: How is the society going to honor—I was about to say celebrate, and perhaps it is a reason for celebration—the 100th anniversary of his death in Berlin, which happened on the 13th of February of 1920?

GMH: As I mentioned earlier, the original *International Otto Gross Society* foundered around power issues—another irony of history!—and it does not exist anymore. I subsequently initiated the International Association for Otto Gross Studies, and we had the tenth International Congress in October 2017 in Moscow, which was absolutely wonderful, especially as it coincided with the hundredth anniversary of the Russian October Revolution. I imagine that Otto Gross would have been very pleased about that. Also last year, the first Portuguese translation of his most important later works, where he links psychoanalysis with radical politics, have been translated and edited in Sao Paulo in Brazil by Marcelo Checchia, and he and I are considering the possibility of having the next International Otto Gross Congress coinciding with the hundredth anniversary of his death, in Sao Paulo in Brazil, in 2020, which would be absolutely wonderful. It's in the southern hemisphere, and all the previous congresses in various European cities have all been in the northern hemisphere, so it would be really great if we managed to do that. So that's the plan at the moment.[12]

SC: Thank you Gottfried. Thank you very much for your time today.

GMH: Thank you very much for giving me this opportunity.

---

[12] Reviewing our conversation in June 2019, I would like to add that sadly, the plan of an International Otto Gross Congress for early 2020 in Sao Paulo had to be abandoned due to the political changes in Brazil in the autumn of 2018, which immediately affected any potential university-sponsored activities. Unfortunately, further efforts to hold a congress on the centenary of Gross's death in Berlin, also came to nothing due to unforeseeable organizational difficulties. At present, it seems likely that *Association of Jungian Analysts,* London, is going to host an event of an as yet indeterminate size to mark the occasion.

C.G. Jung, Depth, and Transformation

George Hogenson

SC: George, thank you very much for having accepted my invitation to take part in "Breakfast at Küsnacht." Could you share the central steps in your intellectual biography/ journey?

GH: My intellectual work began in philosophy. As an undergraduate I focused on the basics of Western philosophy, and specialized more deeply on East Asian, particularly modern Japanese, philosophy, working in Kyoto, Japan, under the direction of Professor Masao Abe. Upon graduation in 1970 I entered graduate school at Yale University in the Department of East Asian Studies, focused on the history of Buddhism. This work was interrupted by four years active duty in the United States Air Force, after which I returned to Yale in the Department of Philosophy. Shortly before leaving Yale I bought a copy of Paul Ricoeur's *Freud and Philosophy*, which did as much as anything to shift my focus to the philosophical issues inherent in psychoanalysis. In the course of writing a paper on the problematic of time in Leibniz I happened on Jung's essay on synchronicity, and Marie-Louise von Franz's book, *Number and Time*, which I incorporated into my seminar paper. I had by this time determined that I wanted to do my dissertation under the direction of Professor Rulon Wells, who had taught the Leibniz seminar, and in the course of conversation with him he suggested that I work on Jung. Family complications resulting from the death of my father disrupted this plan, and it was in fact a return visit to Japan and a conversation with another mentor, the Jesuit priest and mystic, William Johnston, that finally convinced me to work on Jung. I completed my dissertation on Jung and Freud in 1979, and, after substantial revision and editing, published it in 1983 as *Jung's Struggle with Freud.*

From 1979 to 1986 I was on the faculty of the Yale School of Organization and Management where, based on my experience in the Air Force and additional experience during my four years in graduate school, I taught courses on political behavior in organizations and chaired the faculty research seminar on international security and arms control. In 1986, I moved to Chicago to become the deputy director of the MacArthur Foundation's program on international security and arms control. It was at the Foundation that I also became involved with the newly formed Santa Fe Institute and the study of complex adaptive systems.

In 1989 my friend, William Borden, professor of clinical social work at the University of Chicago and an expert on the work of W. D. Winnicott persuaded me to take a clinical course in adult psychopathology—essentially to give clinical work "a try." I was, at that point, looking for some new area of intellectual and personal engagement, and found the clinical course fascinating. I therefore enrolled in the clinical social work program at the University of Chicago, completed my degree in 1991 and began to practice as a therapist. In 1994 I was admitted to the analyst training program at the C.G. Jung Institute of Chicago and received the diploma in Analytical Psychology in 1998. My thesis, on evolutionary theory in Jung, drew heavily on my interest in complex systems theory and formed the basis for much of my subsequent work on Jung's theory of archetypes.

In the 20 years since I completed my analytic training, I have been involved in teaching at the Jung Institute in Chicago and served from 2011 to 2013 on the Executive Committee of the International Association for Analytical Psychology and as Vice President from 2013 to 2019. In addition to my private practice, which forms the center of my work, I have been exploring the theory of archetypes, largely from the point of view of complex systems theory and more recently the structure of systems of symbols, applying research methods associated with emergence theory and fractal geometry. Having stepped down from the administration of the IAAP I look forward to more opportunities to teach and continue my writing on these and other subjects.

SC: Who are the authors and the research areas you consider essential for your own development and work? Which other areas do you consider fundamental in your own intellectual biography (also beyond psychoanalysis)?

GH: In addition to the works of Jung, I have been influenced by a wide variety of sources. Paul Ricoeur's *Freud and Philosophy* was certainly decisive for first stimulating my interest in psychoanalysis broadly construed. My background in philosophy has been particularly shaped by Leibniz, Kant, Nietzsche, Kierkegaard, and Heidegger. My interest in Buddhism began as early as adolescence when I first read Suzuki's books on Zen Buddhism and continues to this day. Having attended St. Olaf College as an undergraduate I also have a deep familiarity with Christian, and particularly Lutheran, theology.

In the sciences, I have focused my attention on developments in complex systems theory, where I have been deeply influenced by the work of Stuart Kauffman and the theoretical roboticist, Horst Hendricks-Jansen. Other major influences have some from the developmental psychologist Esther Thelen and the theoretical biologist Susan Oyama. Over the last few years the work of the physicist, Harald Atmanspacher, has become a major area of study for me, along with a variety of materials in quantum mechanics and other areas of physics.

Clinically, I am probably closer to the classical tradition in Analytical Psychology, although I have paid considerable attention to the developmental school and make regular use of the writings of that group. I have been fortunate to be able to work closely with a number of analysts from several traditions in Analytical Psychology, most notably Jean Knox, Joe Cambray, John Merchant and Murray Stein, who was my first analyst. More recently I have been examining the work of Wolfgang Giegerich.

My research interests over the last 20 years have focused largely on the intersection of Analytical Psychology, particularly the theory of archetypes, and complex systems theory. I have also been examining the nature of symbol systems drawing on the theories of George Kingsley Zipf and the development of fractal geometry.

SC: When did you realize (and decide) you wanted to become a Jungian analyst?

GH: I was persuaded to explore the clinical side of Analytical Psychology around 1989 and found clinical practice to be the most rewarding activity I had encountered. Thirty years later I continue to place clinical practice at the center of my interest in Jung.

SC: George, who was Carl Gustav Jung?

GH: It is an extraordinarily interesting question. You and I were talking yesterday, which prompted me to give a little thought to that, and what came to mind when I was reflecting on that question was a peculiar thing Jung comments on in *Memories, Dreams, Reflections*. In the later part of the book he comments that after his wife's death, which was quite late, around 1950, I can't remember the exact date now, that he realized he could finally build out a part of the Bollingen tower that had previously been unused and that it would be, unlike the other parts, entirely his. He felt finally that he could separate himself at this rather late age; he must have been in his late 70s or even around 80 years old at that point. And when that thought came to mind, it occurred to me that trying to define who Carl Jung was raises the question of whether Carl Jung himself could define who Carl Jung was. I think it's arguable that Jung's entire life project in one degree (as I suspect it is for most—actually for anyone who probes deeper into their own psyche) for Jung himself was to find out who he was. And to the extent that that's the case, it's a little bit presumptuous for anybody, including people who have worked on Jung and studied him—I studied Jung for over 40 years—it's a little presumptuous to say, "well this is who Carl Jung was." We can obviously go on in great detail about what he did, what he wrote. I'm not trying to evade your question. To me it's an extremely interesting question, and one that provoked in me, when we were talking about it, and I reflected on it quite at length overnight, thinking about what that question really implies about Jung, more than might appear on its face.

SC: So, let me help you make it more difficult! What do you think is the relevance of Carl Gustav Jung or Jung's thinking in the 21st century?

GH: In the 21st century, what's the relevance of his thinking in the 21st century? Well, this is rising up as a subject of quite a bit of discussion in some circles recently. What's the relevance of *The Red Book* for the 21st century, what's the relevance of Jung? Andrew Samuels, an analyst in England, wrote an article in one of the British newspapers a few years ago now, stating that the 21st century would be the "Carl Jung Century."

SC: He wrote it for *The Guardian*.

GH: Yes, it was *The Guardian*. I got a copy of it from Andrew; he is an old friend of mine. I've known Andrew for a long time. But what's its relevance for the 21st century? Well, you know, I'm going to connect to that a little elliptically, because first, a lot of my own work on Jung goes back to the early relationship that Jung had with Sigmund Freud, and one of the interesting little tidbits about Freud, of course, was about the *Interpretation of Dreams*, for which he is most famous. *The Interpretation of Dreams* was actually written and was ready for publication in 1899, but Freud allegedly persuaded his publisher to put the publication date in as 1900, because Freud felt (obviously in retrospect for good reason) that *The Interpretation of Dreams* would be a defining text for the 20th century. So, he wanted it dated to 1900 instead of 1899, which, I suppose, would have implied that it was the last text of the 19th century. So you have an interesting question that a lot of people are talking about, which is, since *The Red Book,* which was kept hidden, largely to a much lesser degree than most people realize—there was a lot of material from *The Red Book* available in pictures and accounts, in Jung's seminars he talked extensively about the material that actually shows up there. So, it wasn't really an entire mystery, but the fact that it was actually published or made available in 2009, I think, raises this question, not *what's* the meaning for it, but *does it have* some meaning for the 21st century? And one can say that the degree to which it captivated the public imagination at the time of its publication tells you something about the desire, of at least a significant part of the population, for something like *The Red Book* to appear at that time. I have clients in my own practice who have *The Red Book*, for whom having *The Red Book* was an important thing. Now, do they read *The Red Book?* I don't think so. Do they look at *The Red Book*? Yes. Reading through the translation is not undertaken lightly, although there are a lot of discussion groups that show up around the country in the United States, I suspect there are in Europe as well, where they are reading *The Red Book* as a project.

I think the thing about *The Red Book,* or one of the things that fascinates me about *The Red Book* (and fascinates me about Jung in general)—and some of this goes again all the way back to my very earliest work on Jung and Freud—is Jung's very strong emphasis on the importance of the image for psychological well-being; imagery, for example such as imagery associated with religion, and imagery associated with many other phenomena. And one of the things that we have clearly done over the last several centuries—you can call it the Enlightenment or whatever—is wash out of culture a lot of the deep imagery that Jung was interested in, and we have replaced it with an absolute wild proliferation of imagery through the media and so on, movies and such. We seem to be surrounded by images, but I think people in many respects feel that those images lack substance. They lack depth to them; not in all instances, but there's a certain lack. And Jung comes along with *The Red Book*, and even though there some of the imagery is rather peculiar (no question about that, some of it is mystifying), I think there is a felt depth to that text that speaks somehow to some degree of desire, need, in the culture.

Whether it can stand up over 100 years the way that Freud's did ... now just keep in mind that Freud himself pretty much dropped *The Interpretation of Dreams* as a guiding text for his own work. He moved away from dream interpretation fairly early on and into free association as his principle analytic method, so it's not as if *The Interpretation of Dreams* as a psychoanalytic text defined psychoanalysis for the entire 20th century. It didn't under any circumstance. It's not clear that *The Red Book* needs to define Analytical Psychology for the next 100 years. But I think Jung had probably a deeper sense than any of the other psychologists or psychoanalysts that modernity, in general, has lost the dimension of depth to human experience. We have moved it to a more superficial level in some ways, and that is the real origin of a lot of the distress that we experience in the world at this point. Finding ways to engage that loss or engage that sense of emptiness at some level, and finding what was in fact needed to remediate that kind of loss and rebuild those senses, was really very much at the center of what he was working on in *The Red Book*. A lot of the other material sort of fits into that way of thinking about psychological distress, if you will. I hesitate to call it psychopathology, because I think Jung was trying to get away from the idea that when a person comes in, say, to see an analyst, there is something fundamentally wrong with them; or that there is some kind of disease, in some broadly construed sense, that needs to be cured, in some broadly construed sense. He is very clear, all the way through, that the way he sees the person who comes into the consulting room is that they are confronted with a situation where the means by which they engage the world are no longer working adequately. It's not that there is something wrong with them. It is simply that the strategies they have used up to that point to cope with the world, or as he puts it adapt to the world, are no longer working. Therefore, they need to seek new and constructive ways of engaging the world around them, engaging other people, engaging their relationships, and most importantly engaging their own experience of themselves. That requires this exploration into parts of their psyche that they have, up to that point, neglected to look at.

SC: Yesterday[13] you mentioned that *psychoanalysis* could only be that period between 1907 and 1913 when Freud and Jung were associates working together, which is a very strong statement. I like to think of psychoanalysis as a

[13] During a seminar at the C.G. Jung Institute Zurich (fall/winter semester 2017/2018).

science of the depth (or science of the soul) that started—obviously—from Freud's *Die Traumdeutung* (1900), and that developed with Adler´s and Jung´s research and work. A science that has three great masters and many, many, other contributors that developed this science over more than 120 years. This is why, I always claim—*ad absurdum* and provocatively—that every Jungian is also a Freudian (although with distinctions).

I do not like the etymological distinction between psychoanalysis (deemed to be exclusively Freudian and post-Freudian) and Analytical Psychology (deemed to be Jungian and post-Jungian). Instead, I propose that our work started from (and it is still very much about) the insights gained from the unconscious and from dreams´ interpretation—as well as other sources—and that this is called psychoanalysis. Also, I propose that our methods diverged since Jung and Freud´s split[14]—while the core of our work is, although with great distinctions, the same: the cure of neurosis. And in this context, dreams are fundamental. What are dreams for you?

GH: Well first let me clarify that comment about the period of psychoanalysis. That was not my formulation, that's the formulation of my friend David Henderson, who was a psychologist and scholar in England. I think it's worth clarifying that what I believe David was talking about when he made that remark, and I think it is important for analytical psychologists but I also think it's important for psychoanalysts to realize that (I'm putting words into David Henderson's mouth but I believe that it's something along these lines) there is a degree to which when the two of them were working together, when they were collaborating with one another, we had a more complete system. We had a

[14] although there is still someone who proposes that Jung was kicked out from IPA (Andreoli, 2019)

more complete conception of what was happening in the psyche. We had Jung working with materials in ways that Freud wasn't and vice versa, and then if you put the two of them together, if they could have successfully collaborated and continued to work together, we would have a very different animal than we have. So, with the psychoanalysts over here and the analytical psychologists over here and "never the twain shall meet," I think one could make the case that we have split the psyche between the two groups. And both of them, to the degree that they stay locked into the model developed by their master Freud or Jung, have a hard time getting a complete picture of the psyche, and that's what I think he was talking about. Now what I think you can say about the Jungian community, the Analytical Psychology community (and I'll come around to your question about what dreams are; I tend to sort of go like this to get someplace), I will say quite straightforwardly, that they tend to know a lot more about Freud and the post-Freudian psychoanalytic theoreticians than the other way around. The Freudians, for 100 years, have worked very diligently not to read Jung, even though there's an awful lot of Jung that you will find in those post-Freudian psychoanalytic theoreticians. I was in China about a year ago, and gave one of the keynote addresses to the Chinese psychoanalytic congress, and there were quite a number of Western psychoanalysts there. I talked on the same material I talked about yesterday, on the Schreber case and *The Red Book* because it does have this bridging quality that both Jung and Freud were looking at. And I will say that after my talk there, which was a somewhat different version than the one you heard, quite a number of the Western psychoanalysts came up to me and were very, very appreciative of hearing, many for the first time, about some of that very early history, of in fact the collaboration between Jung and Freud and what the circumstances of their disagreements were that didn't fit into the sort of mythology about why they split from one another. So that's clarifying, I wanted to be clear about that comment I do think there's an argument that can be made that when Freud and Jung split there was an unfortunate breach in the way in which that thinking about depth psychology took place. From my standpoint the Jungians have done a pretty good job of trying to bridge through that but certainly not a perfect one.

Dreams. Yes, we are fascinated by dreams. One of the things to keep in mind about Jung, thinking about dreams: Years ago when I was working on Jung and Freud, people used to ask me to say in 25 words or less, what is the difference between Freud and Jung, what is the simplest possible encapsulation of the difference you can come up with. My answer in those days was that for Freud, in some fundamental way the unconscious is a place of disorder, or disease, or disturbance. It disturbs you. All the material that is in the unconscious, because it's there by the way repression, is always knocking on the door to upset the conscious ego. So, it is a place of disorder. For Jung, on the other hand, the unconscious fundamentally is a place of health. *Fundamentally* a place of health doesn't mean there are not a lot of things that can be very disturbing when you operate, but the basic objective (if you will, to the extent that the unconscious can be said to have an objective in its own right), is to enlarge and complete the personality; not to overwhelm it, to disturb it, knock on the door with bad news about how you feel about some frustrated desire in childhood.

There is another very, very important distinction, I think, between Freud and Jung on the nature of the psyche (and this will come around to dreams), which is that again for Freud, with the majority of what goes on in the unconscious (and there are some fine points in defining the unconscious for Freud) what is disturbing is material that originates in the past for the individual that is put there by repression and retained. It has energy and it wants to discharge that energy. But the reaction to the unconscious, from the analyst's point of view or the personal point of view of the unconscious, is always retrospective; it's always looking backwards in one's life. Whereas for Jung's notion of the unconscious, he doesn't deny this, and on the contrary he readily admits that there are things in the unconscious that have that historical personal basis, but the unconscious is fundamentally forward-looking. It's what he calls the teleological model. Material that comes from the unconscious always has some dimension to it that is trying to move the psyche, move the individual forward in time rather than simply deal with material that has existed in the past. So, when you get to dreams, the dream book, *The Interpretation of Dreams* for Freud has this very retrospective dimension to it. He takes a dream, and he will say well that's because once upon a time I wanted to do this, I was envious of somebody, or I had these desires, and of course most of it ultimately goes back to Oedipal and sexual desires. Jung will come along and ask the question, where does the dream want to take you? So, to me as an analyst, you can sit down and talk to somebody, somebody comes in with a dream and you can talk about a lot of the associations and the current state of affairs and so on, which was very important to Jung.

Another thing he says about dreams is that they tend to have a lot to do with the person's immediate circumstance. The immediate is not what happened in childhood or ten years ago or anything else, but what the problem is that you are currently dealing with. The dream then tells you something, it gives you another point of view. And I think an important thing about dreams, there are some jokes about people taking dreams so literally they go off and do things that maybe aren't the wisest things to do. I always say one should be aware of the fact that the dream is another point of view. Jung is clear about that too: don't always take the dream as the definitive answer to your problems. Ego consciousness has a perfectly legitimate role to play in all of that. So that is sort of one level of thinking about dreams. But there is another way you can think about them that goes a little bit deeper. That is sort of the technical analytic way of thinking about dreams, which I attend to, because I think sometimes Jungians have a bit of a tendency to get caught up in the mystery of dreams in ways that they can lose sight of just what these sort of basic elements that we're dealing with are. But dreams have a certain relationship to what Jung works within his technique of active imagination as well. There is a whole world that can reveal itself if you allow it to visit, to come forward. That world is a complex world. It is to some degree the world that he taps into in *The Red Book*. *The Red Book* is a complicated text. It's a complicated thing to understand what all is going on in *The Red Book*.

SC: If we follow your train of thoughts, dreams are another point of view: depth. *The Red Book* was a difficult moment for Jung as a man: depth. Both examples of finding a solution in depth. Why does current society, especially Western society, have such a great difficulty to go down deep, to look at the depth world to find answers, or a different solution?

GH: There are a number of things that can be said about that. I am personally very deeply involved in reading and keeping up with modern, very cutting-edge scientific literature. I read a great deal in the sciences and I read the technical material in science, not just popular books. So, I keep up on the natural sciences to a pretty substantial degree and try to bring a lot of that to bear on the work that I do from a theoretical standpoint. As far as I'm concerned, I believe that engagement with contemporary science is fully in keeping with the way that Jung himself was doing a lot of work all the way up to his collaboration with Wolfgang Pauli. But even in that instance, they were trying to mix the science with the psychology. And I'm not the only one doing that, several people are working that way. However, that said, it's perfectly, I think entirely, self-evident in the modern world from a scientific standpoint, that materialism (what the philosophers of science would call ontological materialism—in other words, that the world simply grounds itself at a material level, and in fact that psychology is, in some meaningful way, reducible to simple brain states, for example)—is extremely widespread.

One of the other things that has happened is, in my opinion, once you begin to get into those very deep levels of the psyche (Jung was pretty clear about this and I think it is exactly this), as you get down into the collective unconscious, or whatever kind of technical terminology you want to use, the material that begins to present itself has a very mythological quality to it. That began to be noticed not only by a Jung, it was really first brought up in relation to psychotic states by Eugen Bleuler, who was Jung's mentor at the Burghölzli hospital. He actually preceded Jung in taking note of the fact that with psychotic patients the discourse, the way that psychotic patients presented themselves or talked about themselves, had a very mythological quality to it. He took it very seriously and Jung did, too. Well, once you get into that space, myth very broadly construed, you are entering a space that traditionally has been interpreted and frankly regulated by the religious traditions. I think a case can be made that the religious traditions as we have them now, to a very substantial degree (along with the rise of the natural sciences), have relinquished a lot of their role in organizing and understanding that mythological dimension, and replaced it with a variety of other interests, some of which are other components of religious traditions, such as ethics, for example. But for others, which are much less concerned with understanding the mythological dimensions (and keeping in mind that for Jung and for Jungians, myth is not a pejorative term) it is the real essence of things. For example, we attend the

Lutheran Church—I have been a Lutheran all my life, although with that I have spent a great deal of time personally in the study of Buddhism and other religious traditions. But the Lutheran Church is still what one could call liturgically a high church; in other words, the liturgy is still very, very similar to the Catholic Mass. But you can go to a lot of Lutheran churches (and you can go to a lot of Catholic churches) and you'll see very well-meaning pastors basically just waving their hands during the Eucharist, during communion, during the Mass. It is fairly unusual, in my experience, to see someone—there is one of the pastors at the church we attend—really clearly take the symbolism of the Mass, which Jung spends a lot of time talking about, very profoundly, seriously deep in the way in of which he executes the Mass. It is a distinctly different experience from an awful lot of other perfectly well-meaning clergy, who simply seem not to understand what exactly is going on in that process in terms of its depth of meaning. Jung makes this remark in his paper on the symbolism of the Mass, which I think captures the essence of this problem. He says when you have that moment of consecration, the moment of consecration is, in fact, breaking through time and space, and it opens up the universe to this. So, the time and space open up, and you have the true presence. You can find the same thing in other religious traditions, it's not unique to Christianity by any means. If you are really involved in the deep structures of Buddhism, for example, you will see similar things, so this is a fairly universally available experience. But you know, this religiously began in the Reformation, and of course Jung grew up in Zwingli's Swiss Reformed Church, and for Zwingli, the Eucharist was just a sort of ceremony you did because it was something for remembrance. Jung has this very telling description of his first communion in *Memories, Dreams, Reflections* where he thought, well you know, the bread was stale bread from the bakery down the street and the wine was no good and it was the last time he ever went to communion, even though his father was the pastor. And he goes on in essays like *Transformation Symbolism in the Mass* and so on, to try to explore what the real depths of these religious processes, religious ideas and so on really are. And frankly I would not put out blanket characterizations of these things, but I think that that's a very serious problem in the West. And it ranges from your traditional churches—Catholic, Lutheran, Presbyterian, and so on, all the way across. It's a gradient, but basically I think there's such a loss of the deep sense, the profound significance, of those very basic elements in the religious tradition combined with the ascendancy of an intellectual tradition in the natural sciences that isn't interested in anything beyond, that takes its methodological commitments to the materialist worldview (in other words science can only really work on material states of affairs) and transfers that methodological commitment over to its metaphysical commitments, so that there is nothing other than the material side of the world. That combination is really lethal in some respects to the maintenance of a sense of depth in the individual. I'm sort of philosophizing, though, about culture. So, I think that something like *The Red Book* comes along, or when a person has a particularly profound dream, or some other experience takes place in life that breaks through that barrier that's been established in terms of accessing that area or that dimension of life, it is both shocking—frequently very, very disruptive to their life—and they don't know what to do with it. And we don't really have the institutions in place, in large measure, to help them deal with it. So that's sort of a cultural/theological/psychological way of thinking about some of these things, and how they fit together.

I have a very good friend—he's not officially an analyst, though he ought to be—named Roger Brooks, at Duquesne University. He works with a lot of veterans, a lot of military people who are suffering from post-traumatic stress disorder. He has some very interesting techniques for dealing with them, most of which, one could say, come from mythological traditions of dealing with warrior cultures where a particular kind of healing needs to take place. He will tell you, for example, of the number of men he has worked with who have come out of the wars that the United States is involved with right now, who, for example, still see in their dreams the men they have killed. They are still there. And he works with these soldiers to—and I may be putting words into his mouth but this is how I understand it—in effect, to reconcile themselves with those men that they have killed so that they can then recognize them as soldiers, too. And now we're working in a very, very deep level, these men, because the trauma that they have experienced takes them into the very depths. This is why so many of them are killing themselves afterwards; because they can't sustain that place that they have found themselves in after these experiences. But to oversimplify what Roger is doing, he takes these men frequently out into the wilderness, where they camp for periods of time and go through a lot of ritual cleansing practices and reconciliation with the men they have killed, and others. It is a profound way of working with them. But you have to be able to operate therapeutically in that very deep space along with them. Roger himself happens to have been a paratrooper, and so he has more connection to the military experience than a lot of people do. It's quite a profound way of working, but that's where it becomes mythological, at that point. When a person is in that space where the mythological is really the defining way of thinking about their experience, it requires somebody who is willing to be in the mythological space with them. I tell the trainees at our Institute—and I sometimes get a funny look initially, but I think they figure it out— that the analyst has to be able to inhabit the world that their patient really lives in. You have to be able to go into whatever their world is; and now if you don't feel like you're ready to do that as an analyst, then you had better be clear that you're not going to be able to do that, and know where those boundaries are. But you have to inhabit their world. Roger is very good as far as I can see, he can inhabit the world of these men, be there with them, and show them ways of coping with the sort of mythic dimensions of their experience in combat. And there are other ways that you can think about that. The same principle applies if you're dealing with people who have suffered other kinds of very severe trauma that open the wall that we build up between ourselves and that deeper world.

SC: Thank you George it's been a pleasure to hear what you have to say.

GH: Definitely. Thank you, Stefano.

C.G. Jung, Hegel, and Wolfgang Giegerich

Philip Kime

SC: Dr. Kime, thank you very much for your time and for joining Breakfast at Küsnacht. It's a pleasure to be here in your home. Could you share the central steps in your intellectual biography/journey?

PK: My background was originally psychology and philosophy; my first degree was in philosophy with an emphasis on metaphysics and philosophy of science. I then moved into artificial intelligence (master's degree) and then cognitive science (Ph.D.). While doing these latter two, I was teaching philosophy in Edinburgh for about a decade. I then did some postdoctoral research work in logic and psychology before starting on the process of analysis and training a few years after leaving academia completely.

SC: Who are the authors and the research areas you consider essential for your own development and work? Which other areas do you consider fundamental in your own intellectual biography (also beyond psychoanalysis)?

PK: For my own work, I am particularly influenced by central analytical metaphysics and philosophy of science (Wittgenstein, Quine) and I consider some of this area to have particularly wide applicability. I was very influenced by Kant and Schopenhauer in my academic days as there are strong Kantian metaphysical themes in some neuroscience work, for example. The best psychological education (what can really be called psychological, as opposed to academic psychology) came from Kierkegaard whom I read in my late 20s, early 30s. To pick just two, *The Sickness Unto Death* and

Fear and Trembling are still, to my mind, unsurpassed psychological masterpieces. Hegel was a later project for me, after I overcame the very negative opinions of Schopenhauer and Kierkegaard about him. I would consider Hegel's insights essential for psychology now, not any particular opinion, but the general geometry and emphasis on a broadly recursive approach. This is naturally why I also appreciate Giegerich.

Fiction is also often particularly good education. Henry James, particularly the late works, and Proust were major influences. Zola's "empirical novel" style of the Rougon-Macquart cycle was also of tremendous interest to me for some years parallel with beginning training. Arthur Miller's plays, when they are not being clumsily political, are a good source of applied psychology as often are the painfully accurate plays of Alan Bennet and Samuel Beckett.

I am very interested in academic work in mathematics as this really gives the necessary sense of just how complex topics can be and how subtle the concepts required to be adequate to them. Immersing oneself in this sort of think in some way is important to prevent being trapped in simplistic modes of thinking which pervade public and even professional discourse. It is not to do with the subject (interesting though that can be), it is about the education and sophistication of the mechanisms of thinking that are important in these areas which I find extremely important.
SC: When did you realize (and decide) you wanted to become a Jungian analyst?

PK: It was, I think, a Thursday night in the smoking room of the Prestonfield House Hotel in Edinburgh, 2000. I was working as an IT consultant to pay off the student debts and I had gathered information from several U.K. Jungian training programs, and I went there to smoke a cigar and to look through the literature I had received. I remember quite well realising, retrospectively at the end of the night, as is often the way with me, that in the course of the cigar, that I had decided. I didn't end up training in the U.K. but the decision was made somewhere in the middle of a Monte Cristo No. 2 that night.

SC: Let me ask you a very simple question: Who was Carl Gustav Jung?

PK: I'm not sure I could answer that, because I think the only way to answer that would be if you actually knew him, and I don't presume to know anything about the man himself other than what's been written about him; and I don't really think that is enough to presume personal knowledge. I think the best answer to that is that I don't know. I don't know who he was, and I'm not sure for people who are studying his work or claim to be following his work that it matters very much who he was. I think that it's far more important to spend one's time having an understanding of what he said, and what he thought. Mixing those two things up—who he was and who he was in his writings—I think, is the source of a lot of errors. I think people can get a bit carried away with assumptions about what he thought based on their assumptions about who he was. I'd like to keep those two things separate. As any analyst should know, anecdotes and legends are the worst foundation imaginable for a credible assessment of a person, and that is all we really have for someone of scant or no personal acquaintance. Autobiographies and biographies make, as Jung famously said, no appreciable difference to this. In terms of who he was as a thinker, or as a historical figure, however, that's a different question, and I think that is a bit easier to answer.

I would say my impression is that he is a relatively unique character in the history of Western thought. He was a very specific and important type of polyglot that we very rarely see. But, also, he was somebody who, while having or following a line of a particular theory he was developing, was extremely sensitive to the idea that theory is somewhat brutal, and that one shouldn't impose it when one's theory is supposed to inform a certain type of practice. So, I take him as a sort of pioneer of a type of psychology which advocates a theoretically informed psychological approach, rather than a theoretical psychological approach. I don't like to hypothesize about the kind of man he was, precisely because I think that leads to a certain type of mysticism and hero worship, which I think he would have been horrified by (he was, in fact, based on some of his quotes, such as the famous one, "Thank God I am Jung and not a Jungian"). I think that he is quite a character enough in his writings, so that we don't have to augment that with a certain type of excitement about his character in real life. I mean, let's face it, the practicing body of Jungians don't know anything about it. I think it's best we stick to the books rather than the fragmentary pieces of historical information about him. So, I don't know who he was and I don't think for practicing Jungians it matters very much.

SC: What do you think is his relevance, or the relevance of his work, now, in the 21st century?

PK: Now that's a terribly difficult question, because it depends on which part of his work. I don't think that just because one likes Jung, or has read Jung, or practices Jungian psychotherapy, or is enthusiastic about certain of his ideas, one should rush to an idea of Jung that is rather primitive in its granularity so that Jung is either just marvelous and relevant to everything or is not relevant to anything. His work is quite voluminous and has many different aspects, so it depends very much on which aspect of his work. For example, if you take some of his more traditionally empirical early works, around Volume 2 or Volume 3, and then also the synchronicity pieces where he sort of dabbles in what would now be considered empirical psychology, they have very little relevance now, I would say, because the methods he was using would not pass muster by today's standards. That isn't to say that the concepts are not particularly relevant, but the methods that he used were of the time, and so that aspect doesn't really carry very well into the 20th to 21st centuries. The relevance of the content of his ideas is a different matter. But it's a difficult one, because while there are some aspects which are in some respects a little bit romantic about his views, it is absolutely clear that there are certain timeless fundamentals that he was trying to get at, which couldn't possibly not be relevant to any time, because they're completely atemporal. In his best moments when he's talking about archetypes, he de-temporalizes them completely, partly due to his vaguely Kantian proclivities. That renders them relatively timeless in terms of their application, which opens up a whole area of study that is quite alive today. However, it is debatable—I think it's debatable, I know it's not particularly debatable in mainstream Jungianism, but I think it's debatable—how relevant a lot of the use to which he put mythology is today. Because there is a thread, I believe, of a fairly regressive longing for the past in there that you can credibly read into it, and I think there are good reasons why that doesn't have as much a place today than one might imagine. And I do see a lot of work in mainstream Jungianism, in my view, rather desperately trying to hold to and prove that these threads are still relevant today, when in fact I think there's good reason to think that they are not. But the way in which they are not is another question entirely. It's not that they are not relevant because it's just old-fashioned, that it's outdated—that is far too simplistic. It's the particular intentions that Jung had in bringing mythology to the fore as a solution to problems. I think that can be called into question today, but it requires quite a lot of philosophical analysis to understand the reasons why that's the case.

So, I would say that in general Jung's approach to psychology could never fail to be relevant at any time in history, because I think what drew me to Jung in the first place was one sentence. I forget which volume it was in, but I never forgot the sentence; it was the first sentence of Jung's I ever remembered. It was the one that still guides my particular admiration for him, the one in which he says that you learn a lot of theory, and you remember a lot of meticulous things that you studied, and then when the patient walks into the consulting room you forget all about it. That is so fundamentally correct an attitude towards the role of theory. It is not a dismissal of theory at all, it's a knowledge that theory has to be absorbed into the structure of one's approach, and then forgotten. But it's not entirely forgotten, it becomes the fabric of how you work. It's not something you apply, and that is a terribly deep insight which has to be learned over and over and over again every single time a patient does in fact walk into the room. So, the relevance of that and how that particular insight plays itself out in Jung's work over and over again couldn't be more relevant, because it is the fundamental structure of what it is to do therapeutic psychological work.

SC: This is interesting, because this is a question I posed to one of my clinical supervisors.[15] I asked, how do you put together theory and practice? And he said, "Well, they are two completely different and separate things. Theory is one thing; but when I'm in front of my patients there is much more. It is a rapport, the relationship, the intuition, the dreams they bring, how I feel and how they feel, therefore the transference and countertransferece." So, it's something that gets enlarged by the relationship with a human being.
PK: That's true, but the way in which it is enlarged is important. It has to be enlarged by a mind that has absorbed theory.

---

[15] Wolfgang Giegerich

SC: ...And structure even?

PK: Yes. Because one does need training in structure, so that one's approach is structured. It doesn't necessarily have to be structure on any particular lines. I'm not a particular adherent to the idea that it matters that for the purposes of practice, certain theories are correct and certain other theories are false. I don't think it matters that much. But one does need some structure. That's a very, very important question in psychology: how much structure is necessary in order to practice psychotherapy, for example, or psychoanalysis? And my answer to this is, a lot. You need a lot of structure. And it's a very subtle and very specific, and very special and unique type of structure. But it's not structure in the sense that it's a set of rules you apply when a patient walks into a room. Obviously, we all know there is a lot of that in mainstream psychology, where your patient says this, and then you say that. And there are certain approaches that have literal check sheets of things to ask and reply, and if somebody has this kind of affect then you have this kind of reply, and this sort of thing. This is utterly unpsychological. It is completely against what Jung advocated anyway. One does need structure, but it mustn't be structure as expressed in content. It must be real structure; its form must be structural. It mustn't be reified in content. The most egregious examples are when people will say, "Well, the patient says this to me and then I say to them, that's a good example of transference," or "that's a classic example of projection," or whatever. This is almost like a sort of psychological bingo, where you just say, "Aaah yes, there we are, that's that theoretical thing I've just seen, and this is the theoretical response." Or, you know, the awful idea, or aspect, of differential diagnosis, is that we've sophisticated our idea of the relationship between theory and practice simply by expanding the number of possible theoretical responses. So, the patient says this and I say, "Aah well that means this, or perhaps this, or perhaps this." Theoretically, that doesn't make any difference at all. That doesn't make it any more psychological just because you now have a logical disjunction of potential theoretical responses. That doesn't mean anything. You still have this hard and fast distinction between theory and practice; you still have this idea that there is theory that can be applied and you are just disguising it by saying that there are potentially multiple theories that can be applied. All you're saying is that there is theory, but there is also ignorance. Of course, there is; I mean, so what? So, the distinction between theory and practice is not entirely a legitimate distinction. I think this insight is one of his greatest strengths.

SC: When did you first encounter Jung's theory, and when—or how—did you decide to train to become a Jungian psychoanalyst?

PK: I'm afraid this is probably going to sound a little bit less fateful than a lot of people like to cast their initial encounters, because I don't really believe that those fateful encounters are generally very accurate. I think they're generally historical reconstructions. But this is what happened for me: I was on holiday in Canada with a friend of mine a long time ago. I was a young man, and I had done a degree in philosophy. I had read a lot of philosophy and bits and pieces of psychoanalysis. And we went camping in the middle of nowhere in Canada, as you can in Canada, when you are really in the middle of absolutely nowhere. And I had to climb a tree and hang the packs away from bears and I jumped out of the tree after hanging the packs up, and badly sprained my ankle. We were in the middle of nowhere, and my ankle went black and swelled up and it was very unpleasant. So, we had to row out of the middle of nowhere, and then drive to a hospital in Sault-Sainte-Marie, I think it was, in Canada. And they said, "Oh you've torn a ligament," or something. So, the whole trip was cancelled, and we had to drive back across hundreds of kilometers of

Canadian wilderness for two days to get back to where my friend was living. And, you know, I was in a bit of pain, and I needed to pass the time in the car, so we stopped at a sort of roadside mall, and there was a bookshop there. I went in and, it being a very long journey and I was in a bit of pain, I needed something to read. I looked on the bookshelf—I'd been meaning to look at Jung, the name was kicking around and I knew I was going to investigate him at some point—and I found Collected Works Volume 12, *Psychology and Alchemy* on the shelf. I thought, well that will do—it's by Jung, and it's a book.

SC: An easy one!

PK: Uh ... yes, I mean, it was just a book, you know! So unfortunately, because I was in Canada, it turned out to be the Princeton, not the Routledge editions which are available in the U.K. So, I ended up having to go through the Collected Works of the Princeton volumes, which I could not get in the U.K., because Routledge had the rights in the U.K., which was a huge pain. And so, I read *Psychology and Alchemy* while I was in the car, and I thought, well this is quite good, I think I'll read all of Jung. And it caught my attention partly because of his aforementioned approach to his notion of theory, which I had already been thinking for a while and was very keen on; and because it seemed to me to be a very good vocabulary. I had been thinking along psychological and philosophical lines and wondering what to do with this sort of reading and studies for quite a while, and I looked at this and thought: well, I understand this vocabulary and I can use this vocabulary, and it's important to have a vocabulary in order to speak about things that you're interested in. Before that I didn't really know how to frame the kind of thoughts that I'd been having. This frame just naturally fit and it was just good timing really, and so I thought, fine. I had formed a habit of doing philosophy. I got home and read a couple volumes and then started at the beginning and read all the way through. By the time I reached about the middle of The Collected Works, I realized that this was not only an excellent vocabulary, but it was a vocabulary in which you could say very deep and important things. Also, important for a young man at the time, it provoked a certain amount of admiration for what one's imagination of Jung as a man was. I mean, for a young, philosophically inclined man this is rather important. To be able to look up to the person who's the progenitor of certain ideas does matter, because it provides a certain kind of animal level connection with which you can motivate yourself to study and continue. And that worked for me, because I had read *Memories Dreams...* and he seemed like a decent, genuine man as well. That was nice, because by that point I had read Schopenhauer and things like this. Schopenhauer couldn't really be said to be a decent, genuine man, I mean he was a bit of a swine, and so were a lot of philosophers.

That's quite typical in philosophy, that you don't really want to know about their personal life, because it rather ruins the impression a lot of the time. But with Jung it largely didn't. And that mattered, because part of the content of what Jung was talking about is integration, and the fact that it's not that great having a disconnected intellectual theory, when your personality just doesn't reflect any of that at all; there is a problem there. He is absolutely correct about that; that this very, in the colloquial sense neurotic, Western idea of the genius (which actually is another thing that Jung mentions quite explicitly) is very disconnected. The Western genius is someone who's absolutely brilliant at one particular thing and almost has to be useless at everything else. He's an absolute swine in his personal life, or he's terrible at everything else that isn't his discipline. That is essential to the general definition of genius. His view was—and I think quite rightly—that no, that is not really impressive. It's not that difficult to neglect everything else apart from one thing and become good at it. That's not very impressive at all. By that time, I had been teaching in the philosophy department and I had seen this in real life. So this really resonated with me, the fact that I knew a lot of people who were relatively high up, some famous people in philosophy who had published a great deal and were quite well respected in the field; but I knew them as human beings and would go to parties with them, see them at dinner parties and in their everyday lives in their offices, and they were just dreadful people. I mean, not just dreadful, but infantile and in some cases really awful. That doesn't really inspire you with the sort of Socratic idea of philosophy, that it inspires and makes a good man. It obviously didn't, in my experience.

So, here was someone who was recognizing the fact that an integration of different sides of oneself was necessary in order for anything to count as development. That really mattered to me at the time, because I had become very disillusioned with philosophy as a result of the people who were in it. And I remember one of those clear moments that you remember in your life. I remember quite vividly. I must have been about 25, 26, something like this, maybe a little bit younger, standing outside the Usher Hall (a concert hall) in Edinburgh, where I was studying, and thinking, why do you want to be in philosophy? I was teaching philosophy at the time and doing my Ph.D., and (it was one of those awful moments when you are actually honest with yourself and you never really forget) I remember thinking to myself, well the reason I want to do it is because it sounds so good. If you go to a party and someone says, "What do you do?" to answer "philosophy" sounds so great. And I thought, my God, that's such a bad reason to do something! In that moment it broke. I was heading for an academic career in philosophy, and that moment broke my desire. I just thought, "No, I am not doing this."

SC: The same happened to me in sociology after my master's at Manchester and Cambridge. I felt disillusioned, because I had been working on Beck, Bauman, and Giddens for three, four years—especially on Ulrich Beck's concept of individualization. I had written two theses and was starting my Ph.D. on that, but I felt something was missing. What was missing, actually, was the psychological or psychoanalytical bit, which I found in Jung and his individuation theory. This is actually what my Ph.D. dissertation is currently about, but between one thing and the other I needed almost 12 years to let it grow, or materialize, on its own.

PK: Well, the problem is, in those sort of periods in one's life when identity is forming, it's a terrible thing to give up identity. One grows up, obviously, with and through an identity; and I certainly did at the time, as being a philosopher. And I count myself as just lucky to have had that moment, and those moments are extraordinarily interesting, because you remember everything about it. I mean, it was now 25 years ago or more, and I remember exactly what I was wearing, where I was standing, what I was looking at, what the weather was like in that moment. It is one of those rare moments of actual honesty, where you actually ask yourself, "Do I actually value this?" And you know you've answered that question "Oh, yes" many, many times; but you haven't really answered it, you've never really even considered it. You never really asked it. But then just by whatever accident, you're cursed to suddenly actually ask the question that you are forced to answer. And you find out to your horror at the time that the answer is "No"—and then you have no idea what to do.

After that, I was sort of casting around for several years wondering, given that that identity was not going to work because I could no longer justify it, I thought, "Well, what the hell am I going to do?" So, when I read *Psychology and*

Alchemy, I thought, "Ah, now here's a vocabulary which doesn't do violence to the thing that I had realized that I couldn't really give away at that moment, and it also has a lot of potential, and I feel a reasonable affinity with it." So, it wasn't the case that I read Jung and fell in love, it was more that I read it, and I thought, "I understand this vocabulary."

SC: It was quite synchronistic, what happened to you in Canada.

PK: Well, I have a very particular view on synchronicity, so I'll reserve judgment.

SC: This is a very good point to introduce the work of Wolfgang Giegerich. How did you move towards, or how did you get closer to, Giegerich from Jung? It is quite a jump.

PK: It would be a jump, except for the fact that my background is in philosophy. So, I was used to a certain amount of, I have to say, rigor, in the thinking of the kind of people I was reading. And Giegerich obviously has that. There is much more rigor in Giegerich than there is in most modern Analytical Psychology. So, it felt natural. But I came upon it somewhat against my will, because having a background in philosophy means that you have gone through the process, usually, of becoming very familiar with certain philosophers. As an undergraduate, I mean, you can't become familiar with all of anything, because there is just not enough time. I began most of what I consider my philosophical education after I finished my undergraduate degree in my own time, because that was more conducive to it. While I was doing my Ph.D. I read all of Schopenhauer and I was very, very keen on Schopenhauer. Later on—actually, while I was reading Jung, I was still just finishing off Kierkegaard, and they both, really didn't like Hegel. Schopenhauer more on a personal level, Kierkegaard more on a sort of principled level in terms of how Hegelisanism affected the church in Denmark. Not really having read Hegel (I mean, I had read a bit of Hegel by that point, but reading a bit of Hegel means that you haven't read Hegel—unless you've read everything, there is no point in having an opinion) I instinctively hated Hegel, because Schopenhauer was my hero when I was a younger man, Kierkegaard was my hero when I was a bit older, and they hated Hegel, so I thought obviously Hegel's an idiot. Therefore, I largely dismissed him, and I vaguely knew that Giegerich was a bit of a Hegelian so I thought there was no point reading Giegerich.

But I had learnt by that time that one's views on particular thinkers and particular positions are always essentially worthless, unless you put in the time to actually go through and read all of the basic works of the person that you think you don't like. I had done that enough times to know that an opinion that says, "I don't like this thinker or that thinker, or this idea or that idea," which is not based on doing the basic minimum reading of the primary works is essentially worthless. I've done it enough times and I am utterly convinced of this now. It's been horribly painful enough to have to do that, that nothing will ever dissuade me from this view. And so, it took a couple of years for me to realize that I couldn't hold out this dislike of Hegel anymore, because it was just utterly superficial and ridiculous given the fact that I hadn't read all of Hegel. And I didn't want to, because Hegel's famously unpleasant to read; but eventually I made myself do it. And, as always happens when one makes one's self do that, you realize you were wrong. I mean, not just a little bit wrong. Usually—it is really surprising to me—you expect normally in the world that if you have an erroneous view about something and then you actually study it, you will correct your view a little bit, and then it will be a little bit more accurate and nuanced. In my experience, that almost never happens. What happens is that you realize you were absolutely and utterly incorrect in your initial opinions; that you didn't understand anything. And most of the people whose comments you wanted to like because they were justifying your decision not to have to study it were also completely and utterly incorrect. I have had that experience so many times now it's a set belief of mine. It is a largely modern problem, inconceivable a century ago, that one can have a credible opinion based on a cursory brush with what remains the solid and primary mode of knowledge acquisition—reading. The bare minimum of reading required to have a credible opinion a couple of generations ago is today considered an impossible, monumental and even suspicious requirement. The consequences of this are obvious and increasingly apparent.

So, I did what was required with Hegel, I read all of Hegel and I realized that I was totally wrong. The last 100 pages of *Science of Logic* are sublime in the real Schopenhauerian sense of the word. It stills the will and makes you appreciate something, colloquially, "transcendental." As a preliminary to that, I had to go and read all of Kant first, because you can't really read Hegel unless you have read Kant and Schopenhauer and other bits and pieces. That was, you know, a lot of work, and a lot of it not very pleasant. And then I went back and looked at Giegerich, *The Soul's Logical Life*, and realized that I was completely wrong about him as well; and that actually, this was a terribly important analytical psychologist whose views were very sound, very deep, and one of the only credible voices I've really heard in Analytical Psychology in modern times. There is a lot of very, I think it's fair to say, vaguely New-Agey and relatively superficial work that goes on in Analytical Psychology, and I was always annoyed by it because of my background in philosophy. The philosophical naiveté of it was so staggering and embarrassing, that it made me feel somewhat alienated from the field for a number of years. So, of course I was relieved to find Giegerich. I thought, thank God, at least somebody understands that a lot of this is just (as he puts it, and I concur) amateurish. That was a great relief to me, to find Giegerich. So, I went and read Giegerich, and I think he is probably, to my mind, the most important analytical psychologist alive today.

SC: Did he provide additional structure, in addition to what you found in Jung?

PK: To some extent yes, but also, he replaced some of the structure found in Jung, because he is absolutely correct that certain aspects of Jung's conception of things, even if you take into consideration the changing conceptions that Jung had over time, are just not quite right. And I don't say that in any sense that there were mistakes made. I mean, everybody's work that they do in life is unfinished business. So, it's not the case that one can judge anybody for not having said the right thing entirely, because no one has enough time to do that. But given the fact that in Jungian studies in general a lot of Jung's pronouncements are considered almost as finished products that can now be applied, that's a terrible mistake to make about absolutely anybody's thought on anything. There is a tremendous tendency, though not particular to Analytical Psychology or any field at all, to take people's views as final. Then the job of the next generation is simply to apply them and appreciate them. That's a thoroughly incorrect view to take of just about anything. And everybody agrees when you say that, but that's not what they do. The amount of times you can sit in a lecture at an institute, where people will say there are certain things Jung wasn't quite right about, and people sort of nod and say "yes, of course, of course"; but no. People generally on the whole don't really believe that. When they actually talk about things and consider their own views and particularly do clinical workshops, that's not how they actually act. There is a lot of "What would Jung say?" going on in the background. So, talk is cheap. When people nod their heads and say, "Yes we acknowledge that Jung wasn't the last word in his views of the psyche," that's not how people actually behave a lot of the time. Giegerich is one of the few people who actually explicitly says, "We need to take that seriously, and we need to see what the problems were." It is not a personal attack. Again, this goes back to this difference between Jung the man and Jung the thinker. One isn't criticizing the person to say that some of the things they actually thought were incorrect. They are totally separate. It's not related, but they get confused together, so that people become rather protective of Jung the figure. That is just a mistake, I mean, it's simply a mistake.

And so, Giegerich was one of the best proponents, originally, of saying, how do we actually take what Jung did and actually move it further, and critique it, and put it into a framework that respects the best of what he did, while trying to better some of the worst of what he did? The irony is, that's not a really unique thing, because a lot of people try to do that. There have been attempts to put Jung in a phenomenological framework, and there are attempts to put Jung in the archetypal school framework, and various ways of reconfiguring the view of Jung so that it fits the theory that somebody else is excited about. But this is where the crucial difference between normative and descriptive theory comes in. A big problem in philosophy, and one of the things that I certainly took from it, is that if you don't keep the distinction between normative and descriptive theory clear, you are risking terrible, terrible confusions all the time. There is a big difference between saying "this is what somebody actually said," versus "this is what somebody should have said." There is a huge difference, and very often misunderstandings in academic discourse and psychological discourse can be put down to not keeping those two things straight and switching between them during a conversation. There are lots of books written about how you can see Jung was, for example, a phenomenologist, or this or that particular theoretical bent, or perhaps trying to prompt a Wittgensteinian interpretation of Jung. But very often in those books it is not kept clear whether they are making the point that Jung actually was a phenomenologist, secretly or implicitly or whatever; or that Jung should be thought of as a phenomenologist, could be thought further to be a phenomenologist, or a Wittgensteinian, or whatever. This makes it almost impossible to make any sense of that kind of work. At least Giegerich understood that distinction and was very careful in his books to say, I'm now going to describe what I think Jung was saying, and now I'm going to talk about what I think he should be saying in terms of psychology. He keeps those two things very separate. That's a rare thing, and it's a skill one learns from philosophy, because it's explicit in philosophy. In fact, there has been a whole slew of research from the '70s or '80s in epistemology, precisely about just that distinction, you know, the prescriptive versus descriptive, normative versus descriptive theories, and how they interrelate or don't. He keeps that clear; and if you don't keep that clear you can't do anything.

SC: Can we examine certain concepts? For example, Giegerich's concept of soul, or what he calls the logic life of soul; or even the difference between conscious and unconscious ... or, does he believe in the unconscious? Is there something called the unconscious? Meaning, matter, mind ... and we could go on, looking at God and ego. There is a difference between Jung and Giegerich on all these aspects.

PK: Oh, yes. Well, it depends on which part of Jung you are talking about; but the difference is quite subtle in places, and not so subtle in others. In fact, that's been the thrust of a lot of Giegerich's work, to point out the places where the differences are large and where the differences are small, and he is quite exact on that. The answer you give as to what Jung's notion of the unconscious was depends on where in the Collected Works you look. I mean, the original version in the Freudian days, which is covered in the Collected Works around Volume 5, is a rather Freudian view of repressed contents and somewhat reified pseudo-empiricist conceptualizations. After *Symbols of Transformation*, though, it starts to be more sophisticated, and Jung is really wrestling with the problem—which he does to some extent get from Kant—of: What is the status of transcendental concepts like the unconscious? Because he has somewhat given up this idea that it's kind a reified level of something somewhere. But he's not quite sure what to do with it at that point, and it's understandable to have to fight with this issue, because of the term, "the unconscious"—that's what we all call it, we all talk about "the unconscious." Now, the problem with Romance languages is the definite articles, like "the," are followed by noun roles as a general rule. And as a noun, it's very difficult to get out of one's mind that "the unconscious" is some sort of thing or some sort of place. Now of course, again, as I said earlier regarding the difference between how people speak and what they actually do when they practice: if you say intellectually, for example, "Well, the unconscious is obviously not a place; it's not somewhere that things go," everyone will nod and say, "Yes of course, of course, of course." But that's exactly how we actually operate when we use the concept to do anything, or when we are not nodding in agreement to such a sentence. It is very difficult not to think like that. Now, when pushed, we don't think "the unconscious" is a real place, but the concept of place is not just a physical thing. I mean, with the concept of a location: we can quite easily and vividly talk about Narnia, the location of Narnia, as being a place where this happens and that happens, and so the edges of Narnia are not physical edges but there are edges, there are semantic edges to it somewhere (famously, the wardrobe—which isn't a real object either, but it's a concept in that particular world). So, the edges of a place don't have to be actual GPS coordinates, but if you have a concept of the edges of something, then you have a place, whether or not it's a physical place. It's not really that relevant psychological whether the place is physical. And so, we drift into this idea of an unconscious, although it's not really a physical place but it's sort of a place where contents (whatever they are—that's another whole topic!) go when they disappear from consciousness, or that sort of thing.

So, we have this very reified and what Giegerich would call positivistic notion of the concept of unconscious as a type of abstract species of noun. And Jung was wrestling with that a lot, in the early- to middle-period Works, about what this was, the unconscious, being a location. But as his work progresses, he moves more towards the idea of the unconscious being more like an adjective rather than a noun. It's a characteristic of something rather than the place where it is. It's some kind of property that contents have that makes them unconscious or not; whether it's something like being "well defined," or the categories under which they fall are accurate, or blurred, or meld into one another, this sort of thing. But it still has this distinction between the contents that have this property, and the property itself.

Giegerich's notion is much more radical than that. It's a fully Hegelian model, where the notion of unconscious is not a positive—in Hegelian sense—entity at all, so there is no object-subject distinction with the unconscious. There's no contents/container distinction with the unconscious, so it's much more like a process. It's the name given to a process by which something is moving into consciousness or leaving consciousness. Which, of course, begs the question about what consciousness is, which is a negative definition, as well. So, it's a very, very difficult concept to master properly unless you have a certain philosophical background, because you have to give up this idea of a natural way of thinking. This is one thing that Giegerich tries to do a great deal, particularly in *The Soul's Logical Life*. He tries to demonstrate this way of thinking about concepts like unconscious and soul and meaning in an unnatural way. He will talk about the unconscious being the process by which unconsciousness is made and dissolved, and this sort of thing, where there is this recursive definition; and it's this kind of recursive and reflexive definition which is indicative of a kind of Hegelian dialectic. It is so alien to our natural way of thinking, and it requires so much effort to actually get a sense of what that means, that it's one of the reasons why I think Giegerich's work raises such heckles in people. There is an idea that it's sort of a certain type of obfuscation, or it's a way of getting around being clear about things. But it's not at all, it just requires a certain amount of philosophical background and work.

...And of course it does! I mean you're talking about the deepest, most difficult concepts imaginable. You're talking about the relationship of consciousness to itself, its self-reflexive behavior, and the fact that it can actually be its own metatheory, which are all astoundingly subtle and complicated ideas. The notion that you could understand such ideas just by thinking about them on the same terms with which you think about chairs and tables and things that you learned when you were five years old is ridiculous. It is incredible that we think that to be a physicist you have to learn higher mathematics and geometry and do a lot of hard preliminary work in order to understand the concepts required to do nuclear physics, but we think of psychology as just a sort of amateurish occupation; that we have just heard of a few philosophical ideas and we can just discuss them over coffee and that's enough to understand these things. It is astounding how insulting that is to psychology, how little one thinks of the subject one is supposed to be involved in, that one thinks that it doesn't require anywhere near the effort to become an atomic physicist. It is ridiculous. It is absolutely unbelievable that you could think so little of the subject to which you devoted your life; that all it requires is reading the odd Wikipedia article and reading some kind of small secondary text on Kant or something like this. There's no reverence for the subject. Reverence for a subject means work; that is the form that reverence takes. You can't just have this sort of sentimental feeling, "Oh, I love psychology, I love Analytical Psychology." Someone will say, "Well, prove it. Demonstrate that. How does that manifest?" And if you say, "Well I just love it," well, I just love chocolate cake—so what? You need to prove that by actually doing something, and the thing you have to do is understand certain things, understand the fundamental geometry of the philosophy and the concepts that everything rests on in the subject. And if you're not prepared to do that, why are you even bothering with this subject? Why do you value it? I mean, something that's easily obtained and you can just get from a couple of books and then chat about, and get all excited about quantum physics and archetypes and Self and individuation and just get a great feeling from it—I mean, where is the reverence for the subject, where is the duty to the subject? It has a long philosophical history. Are you saying that Jung's wide reading in philosophy, history, and mythology was just his personality, he didn't really need to do that? Of course, he needed to do it! Today we just don't think that's necessary; we think we can just absorb some lectures and a few lecture notes and secondary texts. Giegerich is correct about this. You can see I get quite annoyed by this, because I've always been annoyed about this, and I was very pleased to see Giegerich say the same thing, which is: there is an amateurism in Analytical Psychology, given the fact that psychology is supposed to be, as Nietzsche said, the "Queen of the sciences." The reverence which people claim to hold for it is not reflected in the amount of work they are prepared to humble themselves under in order to actually understand the concepts which are central to it. That I find tragic, and terrifying.

SC: Another aspect of the amateur approach, not only to psychology but to any discipline right now, is the transformation and changes in the universities around Europe with the Bologna approach. It was very interesting for me to read, at the beginning of *The End of Meaning and the Birth of Man,* when Giegerich quotes Berkeley in saying it is one thing is to have an opinion; it is another thing to think. To me, one possible reading of *The End of Meaning* parallels Fukuyama's *The End of History...*—also very Hegelian, and actually tries to contrast the naiveté of a certain view of liberal democracy spreading around the globe. And again, it comes back to meaning: what is the meaning of what is happening right now? With this I might sound a little bit like an activist, but I cannot stop thinking of George Bush Senior's speech in front of the Congress on the 11th of September 1989, a few months before the Berlin Wall collapsed, where he said that there would be a new order based on mutuality and equality. But actually, what happened was the invasion of Iraq, and so on and so forth, leading to the IS. I wonder whether the 2010, *End of Meaning...* work by Giegerich, is also looking to this concept that goes beyond the meaning, goes beyond the end of history, and actually challenges being naïve, and being approximative.

PK: Yes. This is something that's actually critical to understand Giegerich—and it's a conversation I have had with quite a lot of analysts that claim to not really understand or like this approach—and that is the fact that part of what Giegerich is doing is redefining terms. Take his notion of psychology: when he says "real psychology" or "authentic psychology," he doesn't mean what most people mean by psychology. And that is critical. You can't have a sophisticated view of a concept while retaining the validity of every single other view of that concept that there has ever been. You can't do that, it's not possible, because they are mutually contradictory and some of them are just so superficial, they can't even stand up under their own weight, so you can't do that.

The concept of meaning: I think Giegerich has a very particular view about meaning. He is very against this idea of individual meanings, which I completely agree with. I think this is partly a cultural and sociological, political phenomenon, that we are obsessed with having our own individual meaning. The problem with this is that it's terribly fragmenting. Individual meanings, unfortunately, don't have enough structure to carry anything beyond the individual. But of course, that's precisely what meaning as a vehicle is supposed to do. It's supposed to provide a transindividual structure that you can use in order to interpret other people and larger events and how your own future is going to play out, and the way you act in the future. I mean, it's not just a temporally isolated or a spatially isolated thing; it has to project spatially and temporally in order for the concept of meaning to have any sense at all. And the notion of individual meaning has a very hard time doing that. Giegerich's most extreme pronouncements on meaning, which I've heard in some of his lectures, are expressing the idea that you don't need it. You just don't need it. What do you need it for? There's being reasonable to people and...

SC: Actually, the search for meaning is the problem.

PK: Right. But that's the problem. The problem, in a lot of the modern senses of meaning, is that what is meant by meaning is the search for meaning. The meaning of meaning is a striving for meaning. And Giegerich correctly characterizes this as the zero point of meaning. It's such a tight circle, that the striving for meaning is little more than an empty form at this point. Because it is irrelevant what meaning it is. And this is why he gets so angry about that sentence in Jung, about "what's your truth?" he really doesn't like that sentence, quite rightly, because it trivializes the notion of truth to such a degree. Because what you're supposed to be doing is saying, we've got this notion of truth that we have had since the pre-Socratics, in the Western Hemisphere, anyway, and in Eastern philosophy you have these big notions of truth which do a lot of work and the machinery of truth is a cosmological machinery; in many respects it governs the movements of everything, the gods and the Earth. And these ideas of meaning are supposed to do a huge amount of work, they are everything. And then you say, wouldn't it be great if we all personally had that; we all personally had access to this huge machinery? But of course, what you do when you say I'm going to appropriate this cosmological truth and it's going to be mine, now all you have done is, not taken the cosmological truths and made it yours; what you have done is redefined the notion of truth and brought it down to something so tightly coupled, and so tightly reflexive, it basically isn't anything anymore. It's just empty content. It's an empty desire to have it. The zero point of individual truth is just the desire to have truth. There is no content left. And you can see that nowadays. And so, then you get an explosion of everybody and any truth is equal. This is my truth, this is your truth, this is their truth—they're all as good as anything else because the content is irrelevant now. It doesn't matter what particular thing you're pursuing, it's irrelevant. The only thing that matters is the desire for it. That's all that's left. That's what Giegerich calls the zero point of the concept. It's this strange, modern idea that you can take something that's intrinsically not personal and make it personal, and it retains all the characteristics it had when it wasn't personal; but it doesn't. It collapses and disappears. It is redefined.

This is because there is this tremendous connection between form and content, which is another one of the reasons why I really like Giegerich. This is something that I wrote my thesis on before I had even heard of Giegerich. It was something I was very keen on because of Kant, because in his concept of Ideas, expounded towards the end of the second critique, is this very beautiful idea about structure. Kant really does understand something about the notion of structure in the *Critique of Pure Reason* towards the end. That form and content are not separate. They are not separate things; there is not a form into which you pour content. And, when you change the form of things, it changes the content sometimes. And if you change the content of a thing, you change the form. So if you take truth, the form of truth, as it was historically, for example, mythologically, and you condense it down into the individual and say, "Now I have truth just like it was there," changing the form of that truth from this whole interconnecting, complicated, geometrical cosmological system into this utterly trivial desire for whatever you particularly desire to give you meaning, you don't keep the same content. It's not truth anymore by the same name. You have changed the content of it fundamentally by changing the form, because form and content are not separate.

Now that sentence, "Form and content are not separate," that requires fleshing out a great deal, because it's a very difficult thing, and this is where we get back to the concept of amateurism in the field. This comes in again, because I think the way I came to an appreciation of that was through forcing myself to read books on mathematical topology, and things like this. Because without sophisticating one's idea of what form can be, you can't really see how form and content can be connected. You have to look at certain types of geometrical systems where the relationships between the elements of the system are so complicated and so interrelated that it's not like in our intuitive Cartesian coordinate systems where you have an X and a Y axis; when you move along the X axis that's totally independent of when you move along the Y axis. When you start to look at certain types of geometries where the axes are not orthogonal; things like this where it means moving in one direction means you also move along another direction to a certain extent. When you expand this to multiple dimensions, you start to get a sense of what the words "form" and "shape" mean outside of the simplistic notions fostered by the narrow range of human perceptual experience. Structures can have very, very, complicated forms and one has to educate oneself about this in order to free oneself from the extremely limiting consequences of retaining a naturalistic sense of form. After all, Jung said that psychology is *contra naturam* and nowhere is nature more dangerous than in forming an untenably narrow conceptual basis for thought about psychology. In psychology, we are involved with structures that are complicated beyond our natural comprehension. We are talking about the fundamental connections between form and content all the time. Yet our views about what constitutes form are on the level of a fourteen-year-old's mathematical understanding. Our understanding of the concepts of form and content are like a teenager, but we are dabbling in a subject where it requires the sophistication of a postdoctoral math student, metaphorically speaking. Which is why Jung said you have to have read—it's mandatory, and he's absolutely correct.

In this day and age, if you're studying psychology and things like this, it is mandatory to know Hegel for the structural education in reflexive and recursive dialectics. And not just Hegel. Also, the precursors to Hegel, and it's mandatory to know what the postmodernists have said. It's mandatory to know something about Phenomenology, because the concepts being used in psychology are so embedded in these philosophical histories, they are so complicated. You have to be a bit of an expert. You have to be, otherwise you are just talking like a teenager, you don't know anything. It is absolutely painful when you see the discussions that go on about God and the ego and Self. They require all of us, every part of us, to be engaged in those discussions, because they are, I believe, some of the deepest concepts that there are. And yet we have this idea that we can discuss the deepest concepts with almost no knowledge about anything. We can just intuit and feel and be very amateurish in our reading, and again I go back to this, there is no reverence for the field. There is no, "I need to humble myself before the requirements of this field." I mean, if you walked into a nuclear physics lab and said, "I'd like to be a nuclear physicist, please," and they said, "Certainly, what are your qualifications?" and you said, "Well, you know, I don't really like mathematics much, I didn't do any differential calculus, it's kind of boring, and you know I've read a bit but it's not that exciting, but you know I really like quantum physics," they would just laugh you out of the room. However, in our field we feel that anybody can come in and say, "I really love it, it's marvelous," and we effectively say, "Come in. Welcome." Do you understand what that will do to the field over time? Like a lot of fields in modern times, it will—already has—degenerated into a sort of amateurish mishmash of bits and pieces; of people with bits and fragments of information they get from various places getting very excited about them. Which is all fine, because it's all part and parcel of becoming engaged with a subject, but if it's not coupled with an actual humility and desire to put in the miserable long hours of actually understanding what's required, then it's just chatter. And Giegerich is fighting a good battle in that respect. He doesn't just complain about it; he takes great pains to try and explain precisely how the concepts that are required lead in, connect up to Jung, take it further in places, reconstrue some of the central ideas, and more importantly, make a rigorous, coherent whole out of it. And that's terribly important, because what you often get in Analytical Psychology is no coherent whole. I might have this sort of attitude towards the Self, and this sort of attitude towards the unconscious, and this sort of attitude towards complexes. There's no coherence. It's just, "I sort of feel this about this and this about this," but there's no sort of coherent feeling that brings it together. The coherent feeling that brings it together is the product of having absorbed theory and structure and information and then having let it go so that it can become part of you.

And that takes us right back to Jung. That's exactly what Jung said. When I first became interested in Jung, that was what he said: you absorb all this theory, and you read all this stuff, and you do the work, and then when a patient walks into the room you forget all of it, because if you've done it correctly it just becomes part of you. It is structurally part of the feeling tone of what you will do. And that's where it all bottoms out for me, in practice anyway. All of this thought, and all of the supposedly theoretical work—because people have this sneering idea about theoretical work—if it's done honestly, if it's done enough, quite frankly, enough quantity of it, it saturates you, and that becomes the feeling tone of how you work with people. That's where it's supposed to be. It is not supposed to be just a piece of paper you read off and say the theory says this, I now do this. You have to have eaten the piece of paper and swallowed it and digested it, and then it becomes part of you. That is the feeling tone of how you work, and that's the truth of what Jung used to say: what matters mostly when you work with the patient is not what you know or what you think, but who you are. And your theoretical knowledge is not separate from that. It's not. That's intrinsically part of who you are, if you do it in any credible way.

SC: Thank you Dr. Kime. It was a pleasure to listen to you.

PK: Thank you.

C.G. Jung, Individuation, and Painting the Unconscious

Marianne Meister-Notter

PART I: C.G. Jung, Individuation and Dreams

SC: Marianne, thank you very much for accepting the invitation to take part in the series called "Breakfast at Küsnacht." Could you share the central steps in your intellectual biography/journey? Also, who are the authors and the research areas you consider essential for your own development and work? Which other areas do you consider fundamental in your own intellectual biography (also beyond psychoanalysis)? Last, when did you realize (and decide) you wanted to become a Jungian analyst?

MM: My intellectual biography started as a child since my father had quite a big library in which I was interested even before I could read. My fascination for books has its roots there. First, I had to wait to read those books but got instead of them many kinds of children's books, and in my most vivid memory are the fairy tales of the brothers Grimm which fascinated me a lot. From my 12th year on my father guided me very carefully through literary, psychological, and historical topics which were waiting for me in the shelves. "Carefully" means he tried to take into consideration my age and maturity state to recommend specific books, such as Swiss authors like Gottfried Keller and Jeremias Gotthelf or Russian authors like Fyodor Dostoyevsky and Leo Tolstoy.

Also the whole realm of music was constellated in my childhood—be it operas by Guiseppe Verdi or Wolfgang Amadeus Mozart and others, as well as singing in the family.

All kinds of music are until nowadays an important resource for my work as an analyst, not least my own engagement in the Oratory Choir Zurich, which gives me great pleasure.

When I was between 16 and 17 years old, school became quite important for my further development. Especially one sophisticated and widely read teacher influenced my intellectual and psychological interests greatly. She brought me into contact with many important men. Especially interesting for my thirst for knowledge were authors who were related to the psychoanalytic fields like Sigmund Freud, Alfred Adler, and Carl Gustav Jung. She made me also familiar with some philosophers, and at that time I was especially interested in Immanuel Kant's pre-critical Essay "Was ist Aufklärung?" My first lecture I gave to my classmates, about the Enlightenment appeal of Kant, "Have the Courage to Use Your Own Understanding" ("Habe Mut, dich deines eigenen Verstandes zu bedienen"), which should encourage people—and explicitly women, who in those times existentially depended much more on men than nowadays—to use their own minds and to develop their own standpoints instead of following blindly and obediently the public opinion, which was mainly dictated by the church and by the rulers as princes and kings—and last but not least by their fathers and husbands!

At the same time, i.e., from my 17th year on, I started reading on my own the collected works of Freud and Jung. I also visited lectures held by a Jungian analyst about "Psychologie und Erziehung," an essay written by Jung. In parallel, I began my own first analysis in order to gain a practical knowledge of the appearance of the unconscious mind, and so experienced how I came closer to myself. At the age of 18, I made the decision to become a Jungian analyst later in my life, after having built up my private life, having finished my studies at University and also after having performed as a professional woman (first as primary school-teacher and later as a high-school teacher of literature, philosophy, and art).

My first studies at the University of Zürich were related to German literature, philosophy, and art. I was deeply interested in German literature of the Middle Ages, the epic poetry around the mythological figure of King Arthur (the Arthurian legends), and Wolfram von Eschenbach's "Parzival" exerted a high fascination on my conscious and unconscious mind. Of course, German authors of the 17th, 18th, 19th and 20th century, as Andreas Gryphius, Johann Wolfgang von Goethe, Friedrich von Schiller, Heinrich von Kleist, Heinrich Heine, Hugo von Hofmannsthal, Arthur Schnitzler, Robert Musil, Max Frisch, Bertolt Brecht, Thomas Mann, Adalbert Stifter, Ingeborg Bachmann, Günter Grass, and many others also had a strong influence on my holistic development as a young woman. In the fields of philosophy, I was especially interested in Ethics and Theory of Cognition, and became acquainted with René Descartes, Gottfried Wilhelm Leibniz, John Locke, David Hume, Immanuel Kant, Willard van Orman Quine, Gottlob Frege, Otto Friedrich Bollnow, Karl Otto Apel, Jürgen Habermas, Benjamin Lee Whorf, Hans Wagner and some further authors. My studies in art (painting and architecture), as well as my own practical experience in doing artwork (which has its roots in my childhood, since I have always painted), support my creative approach in my analytic work and in my teaching concerning the understanding of paintings and drawings at C.G. Jung Institute Zürich, in Küsnacht, and internationally.

In addition, the studies in psychology and psychopathology I did later in my life are not to be forgotten: The clinical skills I acquired at the University of Zürich and in different psychiatric hospitals. Under the guidance of the gifted schizophrenic specialist Christian Scharfetter at the famous "Burghölzli" (where C.G. Jung developed the association experiment and his thoughts regarding the collective unconscious and the archetypes which brought him the rejection of S. Freud) I learned to recognize pathological traits in a person and so to find an adequate diagnosis which is a crucial precondition for every fitting psychological treatment. In particular Otto F. Kernberg, a U.S. psychoanalyst with roots in Austria, gave me a lot of useful advice with his differentiations regarding the ego strengths (neurotic, borderline, and psychotic level) since each of those levels demands a specific approach to the patient or analysand.

SC: When did your interest in depth psychology, astrology, and Analytical Psychology begin?

MM: My interest in Jungian typology coincides with my interest in astrology which took its beginning when I was in high school, at the age of 16. Thomas Ring was the most profound astrologer in German-speaking countries who integrated modern psychological knowledge into an astrology rooted in ancient times. So, I owe my astrological basis mainly to the oeuvre of Thomas Ring, but also read Dane Rhudyar, Liz Greene and others. All of them have an affinity to Jung, and Jung on the other hand held astrology in high esteem "as the older sister of psychology." This quotation is in my book *Schlüssel zum Ich*, which is edited by Patmos 2015, and which has been translated into English with the title *The Key to the Self* but has not been published yet. Such a birth chart symbolizes the archetypal structure of an individual that can be understood as a conversation between gods, and on this archetypal structure the complex-structure of a human being is based. The horoscope makes it possible to capture the typological attachment of a human being in an extraordinarily differentiated way. Also, the Jungian terms "introversion" and "extraversion" can be combined with the astrological structure, and such a typological landscape can help a great deal to gain an overview over the main topics waiting to become conscious.

Regarding my developmental psychology approach, which I combine with the Jungian theory and practice, I owe a lot to Norbert Bischof and Doris Bischof Köhler who taught at the University of Zürich, and to Donald W. Winnicott and Erich Neuman, whose works I got to know during my training at the C.G. Jung Institute Zürich in Küsnacht. In my training as a Jungian analyst for adults as well as for children and young people I became acquainted with many analysts who taught—and some of them still teach—in all the fields of Jungian psychology: Urs Mehlin, Helmut und Elinor Barz, Verena Kast, Ruth Ammann, Peter Ammann, John Hill, Paul Brutsche, Brigitte Spillmann, Ernst Spengler, and many others. In 2002, I got my diploma as a Jungian Analyst for Children and Adults. Since 2004, I myself have been teaching, and will continue teaching at the C.G. Jung Institute and internationally with great joy.

There are three other fields of activity in which I gained important experience and which shaped my professional and private personality: First, my many years as a primary teacher (1974–1980) and high school teacher for German literature, philosophy, and art history (1982–1988). This pedagogical and teaching activity is of great value for my current teaching as an analytical psychologist as well as for my psychotherapeutic work with children, adolescents, and their parents, as well as with adults. Secondly, I learned a lot during my seven years as President of the Ethics Committee of the Swiss Association for Psychologists (2010–2017). And thirdly, I have gained valuable strategic experience over the past eight years as a member of the Curatorium of the C.G. Jung Institute in Küsnacht, Switzerland, where I was responsible at the strategic level for professional policy and teaching. I was successfully involved in the Federal Accreditation (BAG) of the C.G. Jung

Institute as well as in direct membership in the International Association of Analytical Psychology IAAP, both of which were indispensable for the further development of our institute as a Swiss- and International Training Center for Jungian Therapists and Psychoanalysts (2010–2018; 2016–2018 as vice president). Experience in these three fields directly raises the understanding of the situation of analysands such as teachers, medical doctors, or managers on all levels, of people who have a great deal of responsibility and are under increased performance requirements and pressure.

Not to forget is a fourth point: the private life! This forms the anchor for my professional life. To be brief, I would like to mention that my life as a wife, mother, and grandmother, as well as my embedding in a large circle of good friends from all professional and social areas at home and abroad is so enriching that I am able to resume my varied and interesting work daily with renewed energy.

SC: Marianne, who was Carl Gustav Jung?

MM: I think he was a very talented and courageous man who dared to have his own ideas. His ideas were based on his experiences with psychopathological patients at the Burghölzli, the famous psychiatric clinic in Zürich where he worked as a medical doctor and psychiatrist. He had to sacrifice his friendship with Freud, who was a kind of father for him and with whom he had a kind of son status. When he was developing his own material (I am thinking of the collective unconscious), he knew that Freud would never accept it, and so he was initially very anxious to go public with his thoughts, because he had the fear that Freud would break with him. And it was like this, so he was very courageous at the end. Fortunately for us, he published his thoughts about the collective unconscious and the archetypes. These are the resource for creative energy and new life, which gives such a lot of hope and possibility for people who perhaps were not so lucky in their private lives with their concrete personal parents. Not only the parents but perhaps the whole environment was not very lucky for this person, and when they make an analysis later, new possibilities can be found that were hidden, that the person never experienced before. So, very new aspects can come into the life of a person so that the person can overcome wounds, for example of childhood or also from later times—of puberty, especially, it's a very vulnerable phase.

SC: Who is your own Jung? When did you meet Jung? (Obviously, not in person!) And when did you decide to become a Jungian analyst?

MM: This I decided rather young. When I was 17, I struggled with a teacher, and I was the class speaker. We had a very difficult literature teacher who was not nice with my classmates, and as class speaker I had to defend them. I had to make the bridge between this difficult teacher and my classmates. I wanted to resolve the tensions and understand what was happening, so I went to a lecture of a Jungian analyst that was given for teachers and parents in the school. I thought this is an opportunity for me to learn more. It was about psychology and education. I thought this sounds very interesting; I will go. I was the only young person there, and I was so interested in it that I asked the lecturer, how can I know more about this interesting man? And he said the simplest thing is to undergo your own analysis, because then you can experience it from inside. I immediately did it. Of course, I had to ask my parents if they would pay it for me, and they agreed, fortunately; they said if it's important for me they would pay it. And so, I gave the only free afternoon I had. Wednesday afternoons I went to another city where this therapist (Jungian analyst) had his own private practice. This I did for a whole year. I was very enthusiastic, and I also began to change a lot. At first, I went out of curiosity, but then I really began to deal with my unconscious and I already began to experience the difference between the personal unconscious and the collective. And so, I was caught by Jung. Of course, I spoke then about the idea of becoming a Jungian analyst later when I was more mature and adult, and this Jungian analyst encouraged me. He said that he had the impression that I correspond very positively with this kind of psychology. I also had this impression. So I knew when I got older and more mature I would go to the Jung Institute, but first I studied German literature, philosophy, and art. Fortunately, at the time when I went to this lecture at 17 and was so new to Jung, at the same time I got to know Jung through one of our teachers who was a very good woman. She taught us pedagogic and philosophy, and she familiarized us with Jung, Freud, Adler, Kant, and other famous people. And so, I began to read these philosophers and psychologists at a very young age, while simultaneously having the concrete personal experience in analysis.

SC: I am very happy that you mentioned Adler, because he is not often mentioned nowadays. But it is fundamental, I think, the three of them.

MM: It is very important also. You see it in the whole world when you look at people with an inferiority complex: They have a tendency to strive for power in order to compensate for their feelings of inferiority. This was the main thought of Adler. He was also originally a pupil of Freud, and then he had his own ideas and Freud had unfortunately the tendency to cut off his best people, because he wanted to have a kind of family, which was very close to him in their thoughts. But these students of Freud—Adler, Jung and others—began to distance themselves from him, to go their own way; and this is what they had to do because of individuation. Everybody has to become what he is meant for.

SC: Sure. Can you say something more about *individuation*, which is a terminology very important for Jung, the process of individuation. Jung didn't invent the term, it did not come from Jung; but he adopted it from others. What is Jung's concept, or process, of *individuation*?

MM: Individuation in a Jungian sense is to become as whole as possible, but in the right sense. Wholeness is connected to the real life. We all have a kind of false self we develop growing up, because we have to adapt to parents, to siblings, to school, and to university life, and later when we have a job to the boss and the professional environment. So, we have to adapt a lot, and this can lead us away from ourselves. We have a term, which is well known from Winnicott, the real self, and Jung meant the same. He had other terms for it, not these very famous terms like from Winnicott, but he meant the same thing: that we should come to ourselves more and more and find our real talents and real personality, and this needs courage. He somewhere says that people want to begin an analysis to learn more about themselves, but very often they are too anxious. He used the image of a dog who wants to become clean but doesn't like the water. So, it takes courage to meet yourself, to meet your unknown features and parts of personality which are partly repressed when they belong to the personal unconscious. These are experiences which were hurtful, painful, or sometimes also very positive but you don't think that they belong to you. The darker and lighter aspects belong to the shadow, this means our unconscious. When you don't have these aspects in your life, in your conscious life, you are very rigid.

SC: What is the shadow?

MM: The shadow? It is in the personal unconscious on one hand, but it can also be the collective shadow, at the collective level. So, the personal shadow is a result of personal experiences, and when we want to individuate ourselves, we have to confront our personal shadow, which we can see very nicely in our dreams. But it comes also out in paintings and in sand play, of course. When we begin to deal with this shadow aspect, we begin to integrate the shadow. We take back our projections on other persons. These projections of the shadow can be that we have very bad thoughts about others, think this is a bad person, or not a talented person, or something like this. But perhaps we are these things ourselves, and when we know this, we are much more relaxed. Also, however, when we project very idealistic features—for example, courage, creativity, and these kinds of traits—when we project these onto others, then we forget that we can do this ourselves. And when we begin to take back these projections, and dare to be courageous ourselves, and become creative ourselves, this means we trust ourselves more, and then we become more whole.

SC: Jung said the first step in individuation, or the first part of analysis, is to come to know your shadow. What is the second step?

MM: These are a little bit artificial steps, because they are interchanging, in a way, but the shadow is always important. Of course, very often you are firstly confronted with it, but also in the very beginning many of my clients quickly come in contact with something which looks like the Self. Very quickly there is some collective level already there, which gives hope. In many initial dreams I find this, also in initial sand trays, which have a similar quality to initial dreams, indicating that close to the shadow aspects are also hopeful images, which give hope for aims in the development.

SC: Jung talked about *anima* and *animus*. What are those? What is the anima? What is the animus?

MM: I think this is also something for which we can be very thankful to Jung nowadays, because when he lived there were very rigid roles for females and males. These are very important archetypes. Perhaps I will first say what he thought anima is, and then what animus is. Jung came into contact with his own anima. He was forced to come into contact, it was not like playing or a thought or so; he was forced because of his unconscious material and because of the very important experiences he had with female figures, such as Emma Jung, Toni Wolff, and Sabine Spielrein. He felt the power of the feminine. He already felt this power when he was a child; we can read it in this famous book *Memories, Dreams, Reflections,* written when he was an old man. And so, he began to explore this phenomena, and he began to detect that the anima is an important autonomous kind of energy in him. It is an archetype with which he began to come into contact, speaking with her, asking her what do you want? Who are you? What do you mean? And so on. He began to build up a real relationship inside of his psyche, and he detected that when a man like him and others, also his clients, began to deal with the inner female figures they came closer to themselves. So, he began to see that when you deal with the inner anima you come closer to your own self. Returning to your other question from before, this is what is meant by individuation. Furthermore, the effect of such a cultivation of one's own anima is very positive in relationships, regarding the relationship with females in the outer world. So, he began to detect and experience that he could deal much better with women. He began to understand women better, so his ability to put himself into relationships was growing. This also applies to relationship with men, of course, because when you deal with your anima you also deal with all other unconscious aspects. So, when a man deals with his anima seriously, then he becomes more feminine. He is no longer the one-sided man, this patriarchal man, or sometimes like you find in southern cultures, Italian or Spanish cultures or so, where the man can be a kind of "macho." A macho is quite one-sided, but inside often very insecure, particularly regarding emotions and females. Therefore, he has to pretend to be very male and very strong. Many men are so, also in Switzerland and Germany and in all countries, before they begin really to detect their feminine aspects. It is not easy for a man to develop his feminine attitudes, because the collective roles dictate that a man has to be strong, cool, and so on. He has to be a good fighter and so on, typical masculine features. But a man is not only this, and when he gets stuck in this role or in these features, then he is one-sided and he can fall in a very deep depression, especially when he is dealing with relationships. He has his crisis, he isn't able to deal with it. The same happens with females. When women don't develop their inner masculine aspects...

SC: It doesn't only mean they develop aggressivity. Which is an additional question for you: How about the other way around? What is the animus for women, especially in a 21st century society where, finally, women don't have to stay home, as in a patriarchal society? (Although, we are actually still living in a patriarchal society; but women can have a job, can study and learn.) How do emotions work in this new negotiation of roles in the couple?

Let me give you an example. I had a patient, about 30 years old, who came to me reporting nightmares. She said, "I am a lesbian, I have a female partner, but every night I dream of having sex with a man." Her question, her anxiety, was, am I heterosexual? What is going on? For me it was a very interesting example of how the initial dream can indicate the way the therapy should proceed in order to investigate what was behind it.

MM: I think these anima and animus aspects are very important not only for heterosexual people but also for homosexual people. It doesn't matter if you are homosexual or heterosexual. That has to do with being one-sided in one attitude, i.e., when you are either too feminine, that is, too emotional and so on, or when you are one-sidedly masculine (and you can be both; it hasn't anything to do with the gender, gender and sex are not the same). So, the question I would ask regarding your example would be: is this woman too strongly identified with the mother complex, and is the masculine aspect too far away? And in what kind of relationship is she? Is her partner also very strongly feminine, or is she very masculine? If she is very masculine, then she is searching for the masculine aspects and perhaps a woman who is very masculine, because she is very strongly like this because of her nature or by too strong identification with the father. But it can be both. She can be really more masculine as a personality. We have a lot of different shades within the genders. We can look like a woman but can be very masculine; and of course, there is the whole transgender issue, also. But in the case of your patient, it's very important to look at what she is missing. What is her psyche missing? When she needs intimate contact, in the image, with men, it means she needs to come in contact with her animus; at least, the inner animus. And of course, we don't know about the development of this woman. Perhaps she only thinks she is homosexual, but in fact she will develop as a heterosexual woman as soon as she begins to become more whole and develops her own masculine aspects. And so perhaps in this case, it is the case, as you noted when I asked what type is this female partner, you said she is really quite masculine.

SC: I would even say patriarchal. The partner was the breadwinner, was very demanding, always away for her job, and the patient was asked to do tasks of a woman in a patriarchal society. This is the first part of the struggle; the second part of the struggle was the lack of communication, the lack of conversation. Third, shall we say, she was identified with the father, a weak father who possibly had a history of repressed homosexuality; while up against a strong, over-controlling mother.

MM: Yes, dominant. Animus-possessed, perhaps. Perhaps the weak father was anima-possessed. So, it's very difficult sometimes to develop all aspects and perhaps this partner now (I can't really more closely discuss about this concrete example, but perhaps, I can imagine, because I had such cases too in analysis) is a transitional partner. Perhaps she begins to develop, when she becomes more whole. She may begin to change her choices for partnership. Perhaps it will be a man. Perhaps not, we don't know how she will develop. Perhaps she is a real lesbian woman and then she prefers women really, but perhaps she will change the partner—if she is a real lesbian and needs a good relationship, where emotions have enough space—and then either she will have a feminine male partner who is very well connected with his emotions, or she will have a nicer, warmer, more feminine lesbian partner.

SC: Yes, perhaps the point is to get in contact with oneself, with herself, which is portrayed in the dream, making love with a man. It is not about what sex your partner is going to be, a man, a woman, bisexual. I'm not interested in this, but it is really to find a space for her comfort, where she could develop both personally and professionally. It is interesting, you know I am interested in contemporary sociology about post-gender, post-Biblical, post-class society; but also, where do we put the emotion? I remember she said, "I struggle with my partner who is so demanding, so controlling, so patriarchal somehow, and at the same time ... I miss my kitchen. I feel good in my kitchen. I want to cook. I want to cook the specialties from my country. But at the same time, I struggle, because my identity is not just being in the kitchen." So, it is really a request for development, from, as you said, the collective society; from what society has, for thousands of years, said a man and a woman should be, towards new categories. I truly think that we're still in transition. It's too easy, too fast, too quick, to say, "new women are like this, new men are like this." I think Andrew Samuels is very good at portraying the new father. But again, there needs to be a conversation within the couple—of whatever sex, as he says.

MM: Yes, of course. And I think sex is related to the feelings also, very strongly, and when the feelings, when this is connected, then the problems are also connected. And I think the personal development is very important in every kind of partnership. As soon as it's no longer possible to develop in a way that you leave behind all features, that you can open new possibilities and become richer in your whole personality, as soon as this is no longer possible, we should ask ourselves, why is it? Is my partner blocking me? How can we deal with it, or am I myself blocking me? And at the end we can use this anima/animus concept very creatively to develop our missing aspects, and to become more strongly autonomous. Whether we are male or female we have to develop our missing aspects. And women, collectively seen, have the tendency to lack strong masculinity, and have to develop these animus aspects. But not all women. It depends which of your parents you identify more with. So, when you have a very weak father, like this patient in your case, perhaps he is a nice father, and perhaps he is closer with her feelings to him. Perhaps she identified more with him because she did not have nice feelings with her mother, who was so dominant and animus-possessed. But I could imagine in this case (it's only a hypothesis), if she was more identified with a feminine, weak father, as she describes him—who is closer to feelings, to feminine attitudes, to feminine talents like cooking, perhaps—then she is searching for the other aspects: for the masculine aspects, but in the figure of a woman. And then she is dominated by this very negative mother complex.

SC: This is a good point to perhaps also transition to a discussion of what Jung called the persona. Because while the anima, the animus, and the shadow are inner figures, remaining somehow unconscious until we meet them in our dreams, our persona, as Jung says, is the mask we put on towards the outer world, to cope with society.

MM: This mask, the persona, is our social face, in a way. It is the way we deal with the outer world as soon as we are in contact with it. So, this is also our professional face. As a Jungian analyst we behave a little bit differently than, for example, a priest or a pastor. They also behave differently, the pastor and priest, collectively seen; or a lawyer, for example. It is a very different kind of persona. It is very important to have a persona, to be perceived as reliable, because we can't change our persona and enjoy ourselves one day like this and another day totally differently. Then we are not trustworthy in our attitudes and kind of thinking and saying. But there is also a danger that people can become too rigid in their persona, and then they get stuck in the persona and lose contact with their real life and with the real self. This means that they don't feel alive anymore really; they perhaps fall into a depression. I have an example of a friend who was a pastor, and he had a very interesting dream. He was in a very bad state. He also had conflicts with his wife, and he was very unhappy. He was between 50 and 60 and was a very talented man in his profession, but he felt more and more depressed. I observed him and had the impression he was depressed because he was too strongly caught in the particular role of being the pastor. Then he told me (privately, he was not my client) a dream: He is standing in the kitchen with his wife, he is weeping, and his wife is standing there with a very apathetic face. He is weeping and says to her, "I am so hungry, I'm so hungry, please give me something to eat," and she is standing there without making contact with him, very apathetic. So, he begins to look in his cupboards. In the cupboards in the kitchen, in the fridge, everything is empty. He doesn't find anything to eat. This is a very impressive image for having no more nourishment of any kind in this relationship, nor in himself of course—the dream is his dream, so his wife is an image in the dream of his inner wife. Of course, then he has to ask, what is my concrete relationship with outer life? How good is the nourishment between us? So, I recommended that he enter analysis in order to come in contact again with himself, with his resources, to find a vivid anima; to come in contact not only with his personal unconscious but also with his collective unconscious, to find new resources also.

SC: When men (and women) go through a difficult time, their relationship to the partner—like in this case, the case of a priest, a pastor—many men get busy by over-working, some drink, some take drugs, some spend all of their time doing sport, some find a lover. (The same could be said for women.) What is your suggestion, from a psychoanalytic or Jungian point of view, with regard to seeking your anima or animus?

MM: So, do you still link this question with the persona?

SC: Yes, but also to the anima, because on the surface you have a man or a woman who is well adapted to society.

MM: So, when a man attempts to reach his anima, like in my example, he is at the same time too far away from his anima, and from his shadow figures, his masculine aspects; because anima, animus, and shadow can be in contrast with the persona. Because the persona tries to hide all kinds of shadows. You want to be good, to seem a good analyst, to seem a good or even a perfect pastor, and so you try to hide your shadow parts, even from yourself. And so, you lose contact with your life and fall into a depression. When you fall into a depression you can very often begin to develop a kind of compulsiveness which helps you to deal with your duties...

SC: A state of rigidity also?

MM: Yes, a lot of rigidity. This is not the good kind of persona, of course. We need a persona, but when the persona is too rigid, we don't feel the person through the persona. The person should be seen, or the real person should be present, seen through the persona; and when this doesn't happen anymore, this indicates that the person has lost contact with his or her own roots and his or her own emotional side. Such people try sometimes to help themselves by working more and more. They can develop a kind of compulsiveness, and addiction, also. You can become alcoholic. Sometimes it is combined with drinking whiskey already in the morning to help yourself to create energy you don't have when you aren't in good contact with your emotions. There is the whole strength for life you need. When you are no longer in contact with yourself you can begin to help yourself by drinking alcohol.

As in the case of a certain manager I met in a clinic who had a breakdown. He was a very talented man, but throughout his life, he lacked contact with his emotions. He was also divorced; he didn't have a partner anymore. He had an adult son, but he wasn't in contact with females. He only worked. He worked very hard and was very good in his job, but nobody saw that he was a very severe alcoholic. He began to drink whiskey already in the morning and drank a whole bottle during the day, every day. He was a very severe alcoholic, and then he was found by his son in the living room with a Korsakoff syndrome. He suffered from permanent brain damage. It was a very sad story. If this man would have found another means, for example Jungian analysis, he could have found himself again and would have been a healthy man in the end, rather than a man who lost a part of his brain for the rest of his life. This is a very sad story, but these things happen. And when a person, for example, identifies only with his or her career and with being the best and improving more and more, and leaves all the natural needs behind him or her, then it doesn't work anymore. So, they very often begin to take drugs. Very often it is cocaine, because this works better than alcohol. Sometimes it is a mixture. Then, at night, they take medication to help them to sleep and to relax, and so it's a kind of vicious cycle. When these persons find a way out on their own, then they are very lucky. Sometimes they are forced by the family, when they have a family and the wife wants a divorce, for example, because the man is never seen and she is no longer in a relationship. So, they fall into crisis sometimes. Or, they lose their job and they fall in this way into a crisis. Sometimes it takes a big crisis to detect that there are unseen and unlived parts.

SC: Hopefully in such cases it will lead to a development and not more depression. Often people don't find the courage to stand up or to go to a therapist, to get help. I remember when I was in a very difficult moment when I was at Cambridge University, and I contacted someone I trusted, Dr. Albizzati who then became my analyst. He said to me, it takes a lot of courage to sit in the patient chair, to make the first call and ask for help. But it needs, or requires, even much more courage to stay there, to go through therapy, to look at your shadow, and to let transformation happen. It takes a long, long time.

MM: That is my experience, as well.

PART II: Painting the Unconscious

SC: Marianne, now I would like to look at the unconscious through the enlarging lens of paintings and drawings, starting with the fact that Carl Gustav Jung painted his journey into the unconscious in what is known as *The Red Book*. Why is it important for us Jungian psychoanalysts/psychotherapists to work with drawings and paintings with our patients?

MM: It is very important because we can give a chance to our analysands and patients to express themselves not by speaking but in a different way. Many issues, topics, and feelings are very difficult to express verbally, so when I invite them to try to express certain very difficult feelings of course they are often very hesitant. But when I convince them to accept the invitation to use colors, they are very happy at the end of a session when they succeeded in putting some color related to a feeling onto paper, because they feel a kind of relaxation. A tension transforms into relaxation, and these are small steps. People usually paint a lot—when they start to paint they don't stop usually. And then you can see a development.

Image 1

SC: Tell me about the painting beside you on the flip chart (Image 1).

MM: This painting is from a child from whom I have some other pictures. It was a very short therapy, because they had a long way to come from another city. This girl was about 10 and she didn't want to go to school because she had anxiety, a kind of phobia. I tried to encourage her to express how she feels when she is so anxious; she wants to stay home and doesn't dare to put a foot outside the door. I asked her, when she wants to remain at home, how does she feel? And then she painted this image on the flip chart. You can see it's a very impressive painting, because she doesn't have feet. Only with feet can you go to school; you need feet. Here the feet are missing, so this means she doesn't have any stance, she doesn't have the tools to walk somewhere, for example to school. When you see the whole body it looks very strange, because while she was painting, she also described how she feels inside of the body, and you see some kind of black, inner, psychosomatic feelings. It's like a black worm or something, something black. She is filled with this fear and not with nourishment; only with something black. Of course, this child was also depressed. Behind this anxiety was also depression. And you can see something interesting again when you look at the hands. The color of the right hand where the will is located is much more intense and darker than the color of the left hand. And the lips are painted in a strong red; but it looks as if blood ran down the throat. It looks a little scary, this image, but very strong. And the eyes are blue, although this child didn't have blue eyes.

SC: Was this the first painting she made?

MM: It was not quite the first. The first one was this (Image 2), when she tried to show how she feels when she stays at home and doesn't dare to go outside. Then she feels like being here pointing at the black square in the lower left corner, like imprisoned. The school and the outside world are symbolized by the colorful squares, which are empty

Image 2

but their shapes are colorful. She would like to go there, because they are colorful, but she is stuck in this black prison. She isn't able to. The blackness, the anxiety, and the depression behind it, are too strong.

SC: What was your prognosis, or what was your therapeutic approach with this girl?

MM: So, in this case, the problem was in the mother and in the grandmother (the mother of the mother), because both of them had this anxiety disorder. Both of them tried to go outside and to be social beings, but both of them had the same problem when they were children and continued to have a lot of problems with anxiety still, and they infected the child with their own anxiety. And the father wasn't present enough. The father was a totally different type of human being. He was very confident, he was simple, he was strong and vital, but the mother and the grandmother were different, and the child was similar to them in character. I invited the mother to discuss this. I invited also the father. But with regard to the mother, I couldn't do very much. She was a little defensive against this, because her adult ego, her adult part, had become quite competent in the meantime; and the hidden part, the disliked part, was this anxiety, and she didn't want to be confronted with it. That is why she would not accept my proposal to enter her own process of analysis with a colleague of mine.

SC: Why do you think there is this defensive attitude, as if to say, "I'm not sick, I'm not mad, I can do it on my own"?

MM: I think it is as Jung said: it needs a certain courage to deal with oneself, to look at the shadowy parts. "The dog can't be cleaned without getting into the water." This is a corresponding expression of Jung, he said something similar. You can't get into the water without getting wet.
SC: This is interesting, what you just said—let's talk about that for just a moment, then we will go back to the painting—when a parent, regardless whether it's a male or female, has a transgenerational trauma or a syndrome but is not able to recognize it, nevertheless has a responsibility to the children.

MM: Yes of course parents should be responsible, or have, or develop, this responsibility when they know "my child is suffering" —

SC: —Emotional responsibility.

MM: Yes, emotional responsibility. When a parent knows "my child is suffering because of a conflict or a problem I have emotionally, and if I don't treat myself, my child is a symptom bearer and has to suffer because of me," this causes feelings of guilt, and then they quickly fall into a defense mechanism and then they repress and deny it.

But in this case, the child made also other very interesting small paintings because she had an important dream. In that case she didn't have enough male energy. The father wasn't present enough, but the father was the healthy one in the

Image 3

family. In this case, then, I tried to explain to the parents how important the father is, and that he should spend more time together with his girl. He should show her how interesting the world is and how nice it is to discover new areas in the world and so on, but that she can't do it by herself because she is prevented by the anxiety of the mother and grandmother. So, we need the father.

Then she had an interesting dream. She said it was a nightmare, and it was as follows: She was at home and a very evil wolf was following her with a sword and she had the impression he wanted to kill her. Then the nightmare ended because she woke up, crying and shouting and so on. Then I told her she could paint that wolf and herself (Image 3). Now you can see something interesting: The wolf looks very nice. Not scary, nothing; but it's a male wolf. She needs the male energy in her psyche, and the sword is related to the aggressive potential, which she needs as well. But because she is so far away from it, it appears to be evil. The sword is important, as well as the wolf as an animus on the level of

Image 4

an animal that looks very friendly, almost romantic; the expression in his eyes isn't evil at all. I tried to explain to her that she needs this energy. On the other hand, you see, in the picture her shirt is orange. This is remarkable, because the color orange is a combination of red and yellow; and red is passion, is also aggression, is suffering perhaps, but it's related to an emotional, very strong color. It has a lot to do with suffering, in her case. In other circumstances the meaning is different, for example, love. For love you also take red, or also for hate sometimes. Really strong emotions. And yellow symbolizes the color of light since it's related to the light of the sun, and it is related to consciousness, to the conscious mind. So, she captures a mixture of both these emotions, and this means she is on the way towards healing. It's the first step, of course, but this color orange appears often as a first step of healing after the biggest crisis.

I tried to tell her how important the wolf is, and she understood because she was very intelligent, but she felt it also, emotionally. I asked her, "Do you really think this wolf looks so evil and wants to eat you or wants to kill you? Because he looks as if he is hesitating, the way he is holding the sword in his hands looks quite hesitating and not at all like a murderer." She replied, "It's true, perhaps he isn't as evil as I thought," and then she made a second painting in the same session (Image 4). She said, "The wolf is quite kind, and he gives me his sword I need to defend myself if I meet somebody evil on my way to school." That is, he is giving her a present, and interestingly, the wolf now has this color red, he is no longer only black, as before.

SC: And interestingly, what I see, is that her feet are blue, like the eyes on the first painting on the flip chart that we saw.

MM: And the shirt has turned blue and the skirt has now the color of the shirt before, you see? Something meaningful has happened. Her feet now have shoes, so they are protected by rationality, by mindfulness, and also her heart is protected by this, while the skirt has this warm color of orange. The wolf also has blue eyes now. And he has red ears, so they are emphasized as something very important. It has to do with listening in an alert and careful way, with being prepared for the outer world. Also, the smelling is there, because the nose is red now, and he has blue trousers. By painting, then, she made a certain development in her animus, who turned out to be more vivid, more lively, more present. Isn't it interesting?

SC: Yes, the development is very interesting.

MM: A certain development, and this wolf has the same blue eyes as this girl, this self image comparing to Image 1, although in fact she didn't have blue eyes. Perhaps this blue symbolizes, similar to the blue shoes and blue skirt, some consciousness. She gains here some consciousness about her anxiety and her helplessness when she is in this state of anxiety, when she is caught by the emotion of anxiety and panic.

SC: What does the color blue mean, or what *could* it mean?

MM: Blue can mean a lot, but it has a lot to do with heaven, it's the color of heaven; but also of the water when the water is clear. So, it has to do with emotions, but also with the mind. When you think about Mary, the mother of God, in our region very often there's a dress in red which symbolizes the love and the passion and suffering when she was living on Earth; but with this blue coat over it, which symbolizes the color of heaven and eternity. It is a stable kind of emotion. Under this coat she covers the whole of humanity, which she is able to do because she suffered herself, which is symbolized by the red dress under the blue coat. She knows about the suffering of humans because she was a human too first, which is mirrored in this red dress.

SC: I'm really interested in, even stuck on, these blue eyes. I have a fantasy which I want to share with you. The wolf has blue eyes, and in the first picture she has blue eyes; but you also have blue eyes. Could it be that those blue eyes, and the sword: is the help of the therapist to learn how to use the sword? Also, this wolf has a red band that usually is worn by helpers in public events to indicate they are something like staff members, or helpers. So, my fantasy is that the passing of the blue eyes from one image to the other of course could be related to the masculine, as you said; but also to *you*, as a helper. To introject your blue eyes and be able to cure herself.

MM: Yes. But I also have an animus! Perhaps in the transference of the child, she took the helpful part of my

Image 5

animus and my blue eyes, which are mirrored in this gentle wolf with the blue eyes. And you are right, this wolf here (Image 4) has the colors of a medical doctor with the white coat and the red cross, and so it was white and red, yes.

SC: Symbols are very important for Jungians. The tree is usually a very positive symbol. There is one behind you in the sand tray. And I see there is also one in the paintings. Shall we look at this tree, the paintings of the tree?

MM: I had a child whose first painting was like this (Image 5)—it wasn't a tree, but a flower and bees. She didn't explain anything, but it is a kind of self image. And the next picture (Image 6) she painted in the same session was a tree with leaves that are falling, like in autumn. It was a tree which is losing its leaves. This child was suicidal at the beginning of analysis and this painting was in the very beginning. You see also in the form of the tree that she is closed up in herself. It's a very unnatural tree, because it has very strong lines; a shape which is closed up. The child seems to be very introverted. The tree will reoccur, but you see now

(Image 7) a large bee, which looks friendly with her open eyes and smiling. This is the bee from the first session (Image 5). So, the bee seems to be very important. We didn't speak about it, but she felt very alone, and bees usually are...

SC: ...Never alone, they are never alone.

MM: They are not alone, except the queen in her special position. But she didn't speak about the queen; usually bees are in a big group, and perhaps this explains why the bee is so

Image 6

Image 7

Image 8

important, why she painted the bee. She felt alone and was suicidal, although she had gracious parents, and an amiable sister, and pleasing friends. She wasn't alone at all, socially seen. And she is also in very good circumstances, financially, and everything; but nevertheless, she has this feeling. In the next painting, we can see what the problem is (Image 8).

SC: There is a change.

MM: It is again a tree, and now there is also a ladder which leads to a house in the tree. Here we have the archetype of the great mother, symbolized by the tree. It is a kind of protecting space, a protected space also, because it is round. It is an abstract kind of tree, and it could be the analytical setting, the vessel, which is protected, and she can build a house up there, a hut, for herself. There is a mother bird which is feeding the small birds in the nest with a worm, she says.

SC: So, here is the problem.

MM: Yes, so I asked myself, what is the matter with the mother? What about the mother relationship? It turned out that this girl has a very nice and intelligent mother, very cultivated. But also, professionally and socially occupied, and the child missed her mother very much.

SC: The warmth and the closeness.

MM: The warmth, the closeness, time—because a very busy mother doesn't have so much time. I had to discuss that with the mother of course. I always talk about that topic to the parents when I have a child in therapy. Afterwards, the mother changed her behavior and now does a lot to find time with her child, with her girl.

SC: And what about the father?

MM: The father is the second topic. You see, she painted her house. Now the topic of the father will come up. First, she said she had a dream of her house, but it looked different from the real house, and she painted this (Image 9). It looks a little sad, doesn't it? Very dark, especially the upper part is very dark.

SC: With a little light inside.

Image 9

Image 10

MM: A little light, yes there is a little light, this gives hope. And then I asked her: "How does your real-life house look like, what kind of color does it have?" Then she painted her real house (Image 10), which is pink, and she painted also the studio. There is a kind of special small house which is a kind of studio where the father does his artwork. He is not an artist, he has a totally different kind of profession—he is working with his brain a lot. But he needs to do something with his hands. It's a hobby, and on the weekend, he likes to relax there by pursuing his hobby. My little patient enjoys being with her father in his studio. But I asked her: "Why is it black? Is it really black?" but she only shrugged her shoulders.

Then I asked the parents in the next session when I could speak with them—the father was also there—and I asked what color this studio actually has, because his studio is very important also in the story as told by the child, because she is there together with the father. I asked if it was really black. And they were very astonished and said no, it's not at all black. It's quite a light color and not at all black! So, this blackness in the painting symbolizes the emotional state of the child regarding this studio. We discovered together that the father was very concentrated in the studio. Although he was together with his child, he wasn't really present and open for the child. He was totally concentrated on his hobby, on his own creation, while the child was creating her own artwork, but at the same time she missed

Image 11

the father. In this way we were able to speak about these things. These paintings are so important because the information they convey is different from that which we would have got if we had only talked to each other. I was allowed to show these to the parents, which was very helpful to show them the problem, and thus they could see immediately that there is a problem, you see.

SC: It seems the parents were there and ready to support the child in this case, as opposed to the first patient.

MM: Yes, they are really very good parents; but the mother and child don't fit very well, because they are very different types. The mother is a thinking type, and very extraverted, while the child is introverted and feeling. She has a lot of imagination, is very vivid, and is very similar to the father.

Then, she made a step in her development (Image 11). The next painting showed that there are snowflakes in the sky, and they fall down to earth. These blue balls are snowflakes,

Image 12

and they are inhabited by very helpful little dwarf-like men who are working a lot and doing a lot of everyday life and work. Snow is usually cold, isn't it? But here the snow is coming from the sky, so it's symbolizing some ideas or mental gifts, in a way, which are full of life. They are full of little male figures which symbolize certain animus aspects. This has to do with the development of the father complex, and, of course, of the animus.

And then the other painting is this (Image 12). I asked her about her feelings when she stays at home and is sad and she also doesn't want to go to school sometimes. Then the mother can't go to work, which makes her very angry and stressed, of course, because she has her appointments. Then she said she feels like the figure in this painting, that she also doesn't have hands or feet. Her feelings are very mixed, but most of them are expressed in grey and black, and some of them are blue; but they are held in a grey cloud, a kind of cloud which dominates these other colors. Every color expresses a certain feeling, and the child said the grey color is anxiety about being rejected or not being seen at school. Then she said only that the blue color is anger. She didn't

Image 13

say anything about the other colors, but you see there are a lot of colors, which are there already but all closed in by this main emotion of anxiety.

SC: Could it also show her inability to separate the emotions, and instead making everything into a big snowball? I mean, there are many emotions in this cloud, but they are intermingled, are not differentiated from one another. So, perhaps she has to learn to differentiate the emotions. As you said, when mom goes out it is because she's busy, it's not because she doesn't love you, it's because she has to go out and she will come back.

MM: Yes. And there is great hope, because there is a lot of blue, which also represents the thinking function. That is, she is able to reflect. In another session, a little later, she painted this: (Image 13). She painted a very nice picture of making music, although the colors are not very nice.
SC: Yes, my first impression is very dark, very sad.

MM: It looks very depressed, doesn't it? And everybody is playing. She is playing xylophone; and a friend of hers, a girl of the same age, is playing harp. This girl on the piano is also another friend, the sister of the one on the harp. Her own sister is singing and dancing on the piano, standing on the piano. You see here that the resource is music. There are a lot of resources. Especially these two instruments have a kind of golden color, a very nice color; but they are all female figures. These we can see as shadow figures, and the ego complex, herself—she symbolizes the ego complex—they look very thin and black and bodiless. So, it is really a hint for depression. This girl was suicidal in the beginning, we shouldn't forget. Here she has only been in therapy for about three months, so the depression is still there. But there is also hope.

SC: From the music.

MM: Yes. Music means balancing the two parts of the brain.

SC: And she is not alone now. The problem was loneliness, and now she is not alone.

MM: She is in a very close contact; but the images of these three girls are also shadowy. They are much darker than they are in reality, because I know them. They are flourishing girls. It's the inner image of my patient. And then she had an anxiety dream. I want to show you this girl's last two paintings (Image 14). She had a nightmare. She was in the kitchen with a robot who tried to kill her with a kind of instrument, a tool, which you usually kill flies with. This robot tried to kill her family and herself in the kitchen. The question is, what does this robot mean? It is a kind of inhuman functioning which is killing life. It could have something to do with her suicidality.

SC: Especially because I think now of the bees, of the initial bees. This kind of thing that the robot used could be used not only to kill mosquitoes, but also the bees.

Image 14

MM: Yes, bees, who are living in a society, in a well-functioning society so that they succeed in nourishing the new bees and so on. But this is a killing animus. A very bad animus; a kind of functioning that perhaps has to do with the animus of the mother, who is very organized and very clear, and so...

SC: ...Rational.

MM: Very rational, very clear, and which doesn't fit to the mind of the child, which is full of imagination and has kind of being which is different from that of an adult. And so she feels as if this animus of the mother would kill her. And when he is trying to kill her family, he is killing the mother image, the father image, the sister, herself. So, symbolically seen, at the end the whole family, she herself, will be killed. There is no life left.

But she succeeds in fleeing. And she flees through the forest, totally alone (Image 15). She is fleeing through a forest from the robot, and she is fleeing for a whole year, she says. For a whole year. This is a very nice image, also for

Image 15

doing analysis, being on the journey for a whole year. I think she really needs...

SC: Her space, and time.

MM: ...at least a year of dealing with the unconscious. She should be in contact with her own unconscious, in a relationship with her own lively emotional side, so to speak, because in the unconscious is new life. We find our new life. And she is protected there from this robot, from this super-ego. This robot also symbolizes the super-ego but a very inhuman one which kills life. But when she is in this safe forest, she is in contact with her own emotions which she can express in numerous sand trays and paintings. By expressing these emotions in further sand trays and paintings she may eventually come to herself and thus overcome her suicidality.

SC: Thank you, Marianne. It's been a great pleasure to listen to you.

MM: You're welcome. Thank you.

How Are Women Today?
Feminism, Love, and Revolution

Susie Orbach

SC: Susie, thank you so much for your time today. I'm delighted to be here with you. You are the first non-Jungian psychoanalyst I'm having a conversation with. I usually call this conversation "Breakfast at Küsnacht." I will call this one "Breakfast Beyond Küsnacht."

You are considered one of the most important and influential psychoanalysts. Can you share with us the central steps in your intellectual biography/journey?

SO: I came to psychoanalysis out of a desire to understand the persistence of our impediments to change: most specifically, at a time of enormous political upheaval, why did women, why did people who were disadvantaged feel unable to move forward beyond a certain point. The questions that emerged for me were to do with how we had internalized patriarchy and capitalism and how our psyches were not a thing apart from that but were constituted by it. That is why I turned to psychoanalytic ways of thinking. Feminism could show the collective mind, psychoanalysis could show through a deeper study, the individual mind which of course is also a collective mind.

SC: Who are the authors (and the research areas) that you consider essential for your own development and work? Which other areas do you consider fundamental in your own intellectual biography (also beyond psychoanalysis)?

SO: I come from the left so Marx was important, the Frankfurt school to some extent, anthropology, within psychoanalysis, Freud obviously, Balint, Fairbairn (for his accurate dissection of the operations of the psyche), Winnicott for his profound understanding, Guntrip for his humanity, Karen Horney, Ethel Person, Clara Thompson, Freda Fromm Reichman, the Sandlers. I could go on forever...

SC: You are one of the first and most convincing voices that challenge patriarchal psychoanalysis: On May 17th 2018, you tweeted the photo of a manifest of the first and second feminist mass meeting in London, 1914. The title of the meeting was "What is Feminism?" Susie, let me ask you now. What is feminism?

SO: Well, what the hell isn't it? It's so many different things. It's a political movement; it's a way of understanding the world, which pertains to how we construct psychologies of femininity and masculinity; it's a critique of those gendered binaries; it's a way of putting the light on patriarchy.

There are many feminisms, but I'm a political feminist; and in that sense I am not that interested in reproducing the system while simply putting women in power. I'm more interested in what feminism has to tell us about how the world as it is currently constructed hurts all of us. How it hurts women, how it hurts boys, how it hurts men—how patriarchy is a model, if you like, for forms of social control. What's interesting about feminism is that it goes in and out of being considered something that people want to support. At the moment, because of "#Me Too" and "#Time's Up" it's fine for people to call themselves feminists. But for a long period in the 1990s and the beginning of this century it was considered very sad if you mentioned feminism. So, there were all sorts of different conversations that happened around gender-conscious psychoanalysis, or attacks on the binary ways of trying to talk about the same material but not with the use of the f-word.

SC: Yes. In a tweet you wrote, "We are still at it." More than 100 years after such a conference, 50 years after the '68, forty years after your book, *Fat is a Feminist Issue*, what is the relevance of feminism today?

SO: Well, the relevance is everywhere. It's from who cleans the toilet bowl in a household, to how we look after the Earth, to what we mean by relationship, to critiques of hyper-capitalism, to rape as a weapon of war, to who has rights: the mother carrying a baby who has cancer and requires treatment or the unborn child. Feminism has really profound things to say about how we organize society; and from a psychoanalytic perspective, how that organizes our internal world and our relationship to it. So, it's like a permanent revolution, I suppose. And as soon as we think we've understood something it throws up new things which allows us to deepen our analysis, and it spreads light on things we haven't thought of before. So, the relevance is enormous, and I think what's interesting is this "#me too" moment—it exists in 196 countries. We are not talking about this being something that only happens in advanced capitalism. It wasn't started by movie stars, it was started by farm workers. I think it is also important to recognize that when women come together to highlight a problem it also affects men—they can begin to think, too. So, "we're still at it" means we are still making trouble and trying to make a society that has some humanity in it, and it isn't all caught up with brutality. And I don't mean by that we don't have conflict, that we should all be sweet and soft and lovely, because that's not what the human being is. Rather, ways of understanding conflict or why aggression comes instead of vulnerability, or how we protect ourselves—those are psychoanalytic concerns, but they are also feminist concerns.

SC: For my next question I will use your book, *The Impossibility of Sex*. I'm thinking of Carol and Maria. You wrote, "They were women of their time, free to work, to enter social territories that had previously been off-limits, to be more or less open about their sexuality, to map their own lives." You also add, "they loved their work and found it very meaningful, but they did not want it to overtake them." And then you write, "They struggled between dependency, independence, nurturing one another and being nurtured." How are women today?

SO: Exactly the same. I think the whole issue of dependency, and attachment, and autonomy, and work is still very much on the agenda. I come across young women who feel it's very bad to have any dependency needs. They feel very ashamed of them. They don't know whether their work should occupy a huge amount of their life, or where it should sit. That's particularly women in their 20s and 30s. They have a judgment that what feminism means, or what the doors that we opened mean, is that they should be okay—whereas the world isn't okay. They needed to have been brought up to know that the world is full of struggle, and there are psychological struggles as well; to manifest themselves, to dare to express their longings, to dare to connect with others in a way that is both separate and connected. Because that's really what the struggle is, I think, both within feminism and within psychoanalysis: How do you do a separated attachment, so you're not cut-off, but you're not merged? And in that case from *The Impossibility of Sex* (or that imagined case, because they don't exist, those women) they brought a third party into it in order to deal with the problems of not knowing how to take up their own space (as I remember, anyway—I wrote it a long time ago, that's got to be 20 years ago).

SC: Yes, they brought in a third party. I am very interested in these issues, especially starting my practice. It is interesting to work with, especially, women that really duel between their work (they love it), perhaps their family, their partner, their kids; and not being overwhelmed by all these—let's call it in Giddens' terms, "self-reflexivity"—in this freedom of being able to really live a life, but then to have to tick the mark. I have a patient who says, "and I tick the Excel chart." It is very interesting to work this way.

SO: I don't know. I've had the experience with some young women, that they have ticked all the boxes, but they don't exist. I've got the boyfriend, I've got the body, I've got the job, but I don't—it's not even that I'm not happy. It's: I have achieved, but those things are not integrated, they are not part of me, they are just ... and I think that is partly because of feminism or their mothers. It's not to blame their mothers, but it was the historical moment in which they were raised, which tended to project onto those girls and foster ambition without actually underpinning it with, "actually it's very hard to do all these things." So, they feel a bit empty, I think. That's just my experience. There is an example of it in my most recent book, *In Therapy*, in which the character, Helen, is in that situation. She is a lawyer, she's got everything going for her, but she doesn't exist in an alive way for herself.

SC: Missing substance. Well, my generation—I will be 40 very soon, in one month—but I remember my mother telling me: You will be part of the household, you will do things. So, she was not a feminist *de jure*, she was a feminist *de facto*. And it's very interesting that perhaps some boys grow up and become part, much more active and, as Erickson would say, equals, and equivalents. But—and this is my bias against sociology—it is not because people are individualized (as Beck says), or self-reflexive (as Giddens says), that everything is much easier, that the emotions within the family are not there anymore, yet there is equality and equivalence. I think we are very, very far from this point of view. What do you think?

SO: Well, my children grew up with two very active parents, a male and a female. But my son still wants to characterize everything as what daddies do and what mommies do. Nothing to do with the cooking or the housework, but daddies play tennis, mommies write books. The fact that daddy had also written books was a hard thing, a hard concept because he saw my physical books more frequently. On the other hand, he is involved with his children because he didn't see and thus couldn't attribute a big division there. And children do grow up absorbing what is; that is their normality. Does it make them more able to enter into wider forms of masculinity and femininity? In some cases, yes, in some cases, no, not at all, because the culture says, "Oh, you should be doing this, you should be doing that," and you want to join your peer group. I don't think I've answered your question, but I think it's the emotional ground that they grow up with. But I think they can be rejecting of it, too.

SC: From feminism to relational psychoanalysis. You joined relational psychoanalysis, you are a strong voice there. I really like it, not only because Andrew Samuels is my Ph.D. supervisor (and obviously I am very close to it), but because I find that in relational psychoanalysis, the different voices of psychoanalysis from the beginning, from Freud up to you, to Jessica Benjamin, can be included as a big family. What is relational psychoanalysis?

SO: Well, it's so interesting because it brings together different strands, but for Luise Eichenbaum and I, who wrote together in the early '80s, we didn't yet have the word "relational psychoanalysis." What we thought we were doing, not at the level of the intimate relationship but at the level of the theory, was what we would have described as "social object relations." In other words, we understood that the internal world was intricately constructed in relation to the way of the world that the parents grew up in, and that the parents were culture. Indeed, our first book together was *Outside In, Inside Out*. So, when relational psychoanalysis erupted, it was pretty much what we were doing; except I don't think it acknowledged its debt to feminists, who had said, "We're going to be psychoanalysts, but we're not going to just be the object of the patient. We're not just going to be the better object, we're also going to be a subject in the analysis. We are going to look at this as a practice in which there are two subjects struggling; obviously not bringing our struggles to the therapy room, but where we are processing everything. We are thinking, we are engaged in a way that is not from a surgical position, but it's from a subject position." So, when Stephen Mitchell and other people started to write about that, it seemed to echo everything we had been saying, except they didn't pick up gender as an issue. I remember going to a psychoanalytic conference in Peru with Luise, and we gave a paper on relational psychoanalysis's unacknowledged debt to feminist psychoanalysis. But I think it was understanding both the here and now relationality, the struggle for connection, the fear of connection, the being on the side of the person you're working with at the same time as being in what I would call a third position. (I would say more inside of myself and holding the therapeutic couple, but that's fine.) I think that's what we found, and what was developed. It was the struggle for recognition inside of the therapy relationship, which mirrored the struggle for recognition outside; but in the therapy you could deal with all the defenses against it and all the difficulties around recognition and attachment, and of course, dependency. Because in a way recognition is another way of talking about the dual needs of dependency and autonomy. Is that the kind of answer you're looking for?

SC: Well, I'm not looking for any specific answer. It's really a conversation. But, while you were talking, I was fantasizing about your therapy room, and I was asking myself, is she using a couch? Is she not? Is she sitting face-to-face? And, you know, as a Jungian, or candidate in training at the Jung Institute in Zürich, we don't use couches, or at least we don't use them much. If we do, it is positioned so that we can look at each other. And that leads to the question: Could Jung be taken as a pioneer of relational psychoanalysis?

SO: Of course! Definitely! I think—look, within Jungian thought, within Balint's thought, (there are so many strands for this, aren't there?) the geography of the consulting room is really interesting to me, or the architecture; in whatever ways you want to think about it. I couldn't possibly have a couch for people to lie on in the conventional psychoanalytic way because I'm too interested in bodies. And, somebody doesn't have to look at me, but I don't want them floating off. I want them in the room! I have never found people unable to either free-associate or ignore me, or do anything they want with chairs, it's fine. I have a couch, but nobody lies on it. I mean, it's a sitting-up couch, not a lying-down couch. And I don't like the implicit inequality of the couch; it doesn't work for me.

SC: You just mentioned Balint, and he asked, "What is the aim of therapy?" According to him, it was about elaboration. What is the aim of therapy at the beginning of the 21st century, more than 100 years after the beginning of psychoanalysis?

SO: Well, I could be very superficial and say I go along with Freud, that the aim of therapy is to transform neurosis (but by that we don't mean neurosis, we mean really troubled minds and bodies), into ordinary unhappiness. I could say that. I still feel that is true. It is about the capacity to feel a range of feelings in a non-hystericized form; the ability to have a history that is alive and reworked at different points in your life—it's history, but you reflect upon it differently at different points; the ability to situate yourself inside of yourself instead of always in projections; the ability to surrender and be vulnerable, and to connect but also to feel that there are bits of you that are private and perhaps impermeable. It's a way to join up different aspects of self. It's about encouraging the person to keep a curiosity about life, and about themselves. It's about expanding your emotional and literal vocabulary, I think.

SC: Revolution?

SO: Not therapy, no. Therapy is not a political practice to me. Politics is a political practice.

SC: Ulrich Beck, in his last book (*Metamorphosis of the World,* 2016—published posthumously) wrote that "the world is out of joint"; that there are no more Hegelian categories that could explain the world. My claim is that this sociology—the traditional sociology of Beck, Giddens, Bauman—failed to understand the unconscious. And if they did so, they went looking into the Freudian dogma, as the Frankfurt school did. Is the world out of joint?

SO: I think that's where relational, or contemporary, psychoanalysis helps us. Because contemporary Jungians, contemporary Freudians, contemporary relationals, contemporary intra-subjectives, don't look for specific interpretations of the unconscious. In fact, I don't even think we believe there is a place called the unconscious. I think we believe in unconscious processes, which we can never be fully aware of, and yet they motivate, enrich, get in our way, do all sorts of things. So, I don't think we're looking for the specificity of anything, and I think that the psychoanalytic way of thinking—or my psychoanalytic way of thinking—is very capacious, it can go very wide, and it can go very tiny and intricate. So, it doesn't feel to me that it's out of step. But it isn't a theory of the world, it's a theory and a practice of human interaction and human subjectivity, just like physics is a theory about elementary particles. And we're still very, very much at the beginning of understanding what it means to be human and how humans operate. I tend to think of myself as an anthropologist of the mind, really, and I meet more and more tribes every day, or different people every day, who have lots in common, but have idiosyncratic personal specialist things inside of them. Of course, if I look at them, I can see social relations embedded in them, I can understand exactly what Karl Marx was talking about, but not the specificity that the Frankfurt School would have given them. If that makes sense.

SC: Looks like you're reading my mind, quoting Balint first, and now Marx, because the next question is about love, actually. Sociologist Eva Illouz claims that, "I believe emotional suffering is connected, albeit in complex ways, to the organization of economic and political power." She continues, "It is the fact that the feminist revolution, which was necessary, salutary, and is unfinished, has not fulfilled men's and women's deep longing for love and passion." Would you agree?

SO: I don't know who she's writing about. The whole world? Yes, she's right. But specific enclaves? No, she's wrong. It's too big a question for me.

SC: She also claimed that the grand ambition of the book she published recently, called *Why Love Hurts*, has to do with emotion—at least romantic love. She claims that she did something similar to Marx; what Marx did to commodities. That is, to show that they are shaped by social relations, that they do not circulate in a free and unconstrained way, that their magic is social, and that they contain and condense institutions of modernity. I personally claim this is wrong. Because, if we don't look into the emotion, while the emotions are social, the social without the emotion will bring us to a dead corner. What do you think?

SO: I would have to read it and absorb it and think it. I don't want to elevate love above everything else, and I don't know that love is a commodity, although it becomes commoditized. And—I don't know—if it is an exchange, although historically and in the present, many sexual relationships would fit that. We see the commodification of desire, of relationship, on online dating sites for sure. I would need to think about it; it's not how I would be conceptualizing it.

SC: Let me then ask you a very, very simple question. What is love?

SO: Well, I don't think it is a simple question, because love is about what—if I think about it for myself—love is about what moves me. Love is about what I care about. Love is also very connected to the things that I could also hate for the things that I care about. So, love might be about an offering that you make. But love is relational, in some sense. It isn't only about me; it's provoked by my understanding of myself as a therapist, as somebody who looks at a flower, as somebody who cooks a meal, as somebody who's a grandmother. I mean ... it's a chord with a lot of different notes in it, and it's not reducible in some simplistic way for me.

SC: Why does love hurt?

SO: Why do I think it hurts? Because we have longings, and we have fears, and we're quite scared to reveal ourselves or to hope that love will last, that when we have love we sometimes get lazy and close down, we don't stay open. I don't think love always does hurt, actually. I think it does hurt, but I don't think it only hurts. It can be bloody annoying, I understand why love is hard to sustain for people, but I think that's different than why it hurts. And I think it's hard to sustain because I think we can get very... It's very interesting. in the beginning when you love, whether it's a new friend or it's a lover, it doesn't mean that you can stay open and alive in the way that you are in the beginning. You close down. And then you get disappointed, and then you get too merged, or you know, for all sorts of reasons, some of which are in that chapter in *Impossibility...*

SC: Therefore, love ends, or love could end, if we lose the ability for curiosity, perhaps? As you tried to write, I think, about Carol and Maria?

SO: Yes, I think the thing is, love could end. But sometimes love ends because it needs to end. Sometimes love has actually cured you, given you something, and that's enough. Not everybody has to be in a relationship for 100 years! The relationship could last six years, it could last ten years; I don't want to be prescriptive. Of course, love can end, if you can't allow the other person to thrive and to be in the world; if you have to control them because you're so scared of seeing them as an "other." But I also don't think there's only one formula for having love. I just don't. A love at 25 is not the same as late love. They are completely different propositions. You know, if you were in the same relationship from 25 to 60, at 60 you've lived through a lot of disappointments with each other, but your love has survived. But supposing you meet somebody—you come out of a relationship, then you're no longer trying to build a life with somebody as though you're 25, because you already know who you are, right? So, it's just too hard to say love is this, love fails for this reason, love hurts for this reason. It's too complex.

SC: Thank you, Susie.

SO: My pleasure.

C.G. Jung, von Franz, and Alchemy

Alfred Ribi

SC: Thank you very much for inviting me here. I have a question. It seems to be a small question, but it's a rich question: Who was Carl Gustav Jung?[16]

AR: I think he was a pioneer, the pioneer who discovered the psyche. I say a "pioneer," because Freud is usually taken as the pioneer who discovered the psyche; but he was still in the area of enlightenment, so he missed the irrational side of the psyche, which Jung took into account. So, the whole of the psyche is, to my understanding, understood by Jung only. Of course, then this is his message to his followers: the necessity to integrate the rational side of the psyche and the irrational side. To my understanding the irrational side is, for instance, synchronicity (meaningful coincidences), and a lot of happenings which are connected to the psyche, such as the meaning of diseases. For example, I recently was ill and then was cured again, and then I told my practitioner, "Now, I see the meaning of the illness," and he was very surprised. Meaning of the illness? For most of the doctors, it is important they diagnose you, and they know what you need. But, that illness has a *meaning* is, for them, quite irrational. So, this is, for instance, a part where Jung is not yet understood. And it will take 100 years, at least, to understand also this side—the irrational—of the psyche, because the body and the psyche are in one's personality together and they respond to each other. There is never an

[16] This interview is missing my usual first question about his intellectual biography/journey; fundamental authors and the research areas; and when he realizes he wanted to become a Jungian analyst, because Dr. Ribi answer those question throughout the interview.

illness without a psychic reaction; and there is never—and this is my hypothesis—an illness without psychic meaning. So, often, also, when a doctor admits somebody to the hospital with a broken leg, for instance, then he should ask, "And *why* did it happen at *this* moment? What was the *meaning*?" The doctor treats the broken leg, and when the broken leg is functioning again then his task is done; but for the person, it's not finished with that. The person should understand, "Why did I break the leg at *this very moment*?" So, the *kairos*, the moment in which something happens, is so important. The significance of this is not yet understood.

So, you see, Jung's psychology is very vast, very comprehensive, in different respects. It's not just a medical affair, a medical question; the psyche is the *whole world*. We can never step out of the psyche. We can never look at the psyche from outside. We are bound in this world of the psyche, but we don't understand that the psychic world is immense. It is the All, it is the universe; and this is not yet understood. We cannot know, do not know, human activity, know human sides in any respect without the psyche. And therefore, I think Jung did a lot which has not yet been understood by his followers, which has to be elaborated in different ways. And the interesting thing, I think, is that the new acceptance of Jung comes not from the psychiatry—actually, the psychiatrists are more resistant, they never mention Jung—but, for instance, comes from art. I heard from art historians that they speak about the *"archetype,"* or the images from the beginning—*"Urbild"* (primordial images)—and that they take it up; and already the linguists have taken it up for a long time before Jung, but in a different way. When they have many manuscripts from an old writer, then they collect it to find the *archetype*, the initial manuscript. So, they speak about the archetype without knowing what Jung meant by it. Thus, I think it will be discovered not from the specialists, but from anyone who meets this experience; because Jung is important from his *experience*. His so-called "theory" is not something which he had in his head—although he was a very intelligent person, of course a genius—but he experienced it in his life, and therefore he then collected his *experiences* and put them in a system. This is called the "theory" of Jung, but not like with a philosopher—from his head, from an idea which he had. No, it was first the *experience*. And this appears also to the people who meet Jung in very different respects and very different areas; and they will be the ones who discover Jung again in 50 or 100 years, I think.

SC: And what is the relevance of Jung today?

AR: Yes, I think—well, this is also my idea: every institution is like a kingdom. So, for instance, the EU, the idea of a union of European states, is like a kingdom. In the beginning, it's a wonderful new idea. We collect all the people in Europe and they have a common history, and so they have to be together, and they make a union. This is the original idea. And then the kingdom is established. It is wonderful, new; but with time it becomes old. It functions, and people think, "Well, it's good, yes, we must improve it even," and more and more it becomes the old king. And then it petrifies. Then, more and more rules are made. There is an abuse in this respect: so, we have to make a rule so that there are no more abuses possible. And there is a difficulty here: we have to make a rule!—and so they fence themselves in with rules and with laws against these misuses. So, this gradually becomes the old king. So, every kingdom is, in the long run, becoming the old king, because the old king cannot renew himself. The old king has to be killed. This was the case in what Jung referred to as "primitive" states, such as the former colony of Rhodesia in Africa, (now Zimbabwe), where the old king was killed when he was no longer a factor of welfare and fertility. And then he becomes petrified, he becomes stiff, he becomes corrupt. He is only looking to keep his power—he must keep his power!—and so on. As soon as somebody has to try to keep his power, then one knows, this is the old king. This is no longer something alive, and then he has to die, to be killed, so that the new king can come. And, therefore, in France for instance, it was said, "the king has died, *es lebe der König*"—the new king should live. This is exactly—there should be no interregnum. This is the most difficult time. It was also like that in old Egypt. When the old king died, immediately one had to know to install the new king, because [having] no king is awful. One can see it now (in 2017) in Brazil: when they have no police, people are killed. The police are going on strike, and they have no police. So, the king is a very important installation, a very important archetype! But he is becoming old when, in the long run, he cannot renew himself; and so, a new king has to come. I think in many, many respects in institutions, it's always like that. Also, in the Jung Institute, one has to look: when everything is fine and very well-organized and so on, this is dangerous. Then, it becomes a rule and then it will not change; one cannot make any exception, and so on. And so, the people are used to things going very well, and so on; yet, this is also the time of decay. New ideas, new people, new experiences, optimism, and so on have to come, and to bring a new spirit into it. This is the new king. And often the old institution doesn't want to be dissolved and renovated, because it has a long tradition, and one is fond of this tradition, and this is very dangerous... It always has to change, because: *Life. Is. Transformation.* This is also in the individual's life. If a person cannot transform anymore, is not creative anymore, then he is dead.

SC: Or provokes that into others, and therefore becomes the devil.

AR: Yes, yes. The old Adam, the old king. So, I think this is a problem of our time.

SC: I understand you are full of hope because you know that with transformation, things will continue transforming.

AR: Yes, yes, yes, and therefore I have the idea that when Jung will be discovered really, not just made into Jung Institutes here, there, and so on, everywhere in the world—No! That people are gripped, taken, by this vision of the psyche—that then something happens. Because I was Director of Studies in 1969 to 1971, and I got many letters from all over the world from people who told me they had read *Memories, Dreams, Reflections,* and they were struck by this book! This is where something happens in an individual that appeals to it, and every single person who has this experience is the carrier of the spark of Jung, into the future.

SC: What are dreams?

AR: Ha! This is a very difficult question! Because—easy and difficult at the same time—easy, as it's a message from the unconscious. Or, you can put it into religious terms: a message from the angels. There is a book about it. But the question is to understand this message; what are we doing? How can we understand the message, the dreams? And this is—looked at from this angle—difficult, because there is no recipe to understand dreams. I cannot give you a schedule and say, "Here, you can understand your dreams. Now, this is very simple." No, every dream is a unique message. One has to know the person, one has to know their circumstances, one has to know the associations of the dream, and so on. So, this is difficult. Marie-Louise was interpreting some archetypal dreams where she said (for instance from historical persons), she couldn't know the person—she knew perhaps a book about the person, biography and so on—but these dreams she could interpret just because they were collective motifs of the dreams, and this is proving what Jung said, that there are archetypal dreams. Archetypal, meaning collective, understandable for everybody in the world, whether Chinese, or Negroes, or Eskimos, or Europeans, it doesn't matter. Something in the human being is producing these archetypal images. But this is also the reason why Jungian psychology is the psychology *for the world*. It can be understood in every culture. But the dream is, nevertheless, always beside the collective individual from the moment in which the dreamer was having his dream. It belongs to the very *kairos*, the moment. Only in this moment, this dream could happen. And therefore, she was interpreting archetypal dreams, which is very interesting to see. But, for me, it is a sign also that Jungian psychology is worldwide, not restricted to a certain civilisation, Christian, Jewish civilisation. No, it's worldwide.

SC: Who was Marie-Louise von Franz?

AR: She was a very nice lady, but very strict also. I am very grateful to her, because when I entered my training analysis in 1963 I had a huge, negative mother complex, with huge feelings of inferiority; but I had already read Jung's books. She told somebody she had never met somebody who had already read all the books of Jung. Of course, I had not read all; but a big amount of Jung's books! And then I interpreted my dreams from my knowledge of Jungian psychology. I said, "Here is this archetype, and this archetype, the shadow, and the anima." When a dark figure was coming, then it was the shadow; when a light figure, a feminine, then it was the anima, and so on. And so, I brought my dreams to her and my interpretation too, and she never said, "No, this is bullshit, this is not right." Never. I would have gone *out immediately* of her room if she would have reacted in this way. No, she gently took it, and said, "Perhaps one could see it also from this side, on this perspective." And so, she slowly, slowly, brought it down to the bottom. Because my interpretation was up in the air of course! And she brought it down to the floor. And this, I could accept. And after some years, I realised one has to undergo one's own training analysis; I understood from Jung's writings. But I thought, of course, "I have no problems, I'm a normal person, I'm not ill, I'm not crazy," and so on—"I don't need analysis." But after some years I realized, I have this and that problem, and so I'm the most poor patient myself. And this was a very important experience, because then I was no more the psychiatrist who could tell the people, "Look, here you have a problem, you are diagnosed like that and that." No. I knew I, myself, need the analysis, and to see my problems. And then, only, the dreams became meaningful, to help me find my own way out of the problems. And this helped me also—because as I said, I am grateful for Marie-Louise von Franz, that she was so tactful—to become very tactful with my own clients and patients; because I knew what had happened to me, how it happened to me ... that they are poor. And this is also the big resistance, again, in Jungian psychology. One has to face one's own shadow, one's own dark side, which one doesn't like to know—the people, the community, the general, and so on, which one puts behind the chair and into the corner that nobody sees. When I'm so bright and wonderful, then I want everybody to know, but my dark side I'm carefully hiding because I'm ashamed. And so, only those who can accept their own inferior side can accept Jungian psychology. And this is why there is a general resistance against Jungian psychology. This is exactly what we don't want to know of ourselves.

SC: What is your suggestion, perhaps even wish, for those students, training candidates, diploma candidates at the Institute here in Zürich; but also for Jungian institutes around the world? You are a wise man; you are in the lineage of Jung, von Franz, Hillman, and a few others. But there are students that are coming to train here and that train around the world; what would be your suggestion to them?

AR: I always saw those people here—as you mentioned, there are many other Jung Institutes in the world—so I asked them, "Why are you coming for [such] a long trip?" For instance, on Saturday there was a lady from Hong Kong who is studying here. "Why are you coming for such a long trip?" and then they said, "Because here, Jungian psychology is alive." It is people who have still this spark from Jung, which makes Jungian psychology alive. It's an experience. It's not the theory which you get here from the Institute and from the people who are teaching you. This is so important; this is worth the long trip to come here. And I must say, among the pupils of von Franz, we often discussed it; it's also like somebody said, we can't prove it, but it seems that Jungian psychology could only originate in Switzerland. Because you have to think, in the Second World War, Switzerland was the only island that was not involved in this worldwide war; an island where Jung was isolated often. He complained in the letters—you can read, that he was so isolated from his friends in England, in America, and everywhere—but it enabled him to write his work. Because Switzerland was prevented from being attacked by all these states in war, in keeping the peace here, Jung was able to write. This was the important place in Bollingen where he was writing his work. And perhaps, at least symbolically, it is meaningful that a man who lived in isolation, in peace, put his ideas into this work which could help the world—the world caught in war—to become more peaceful, and to find a way out of this awful, destructive attitude. And perhaps also the landscape of Switzerland, with the Alps, played a role. It is the highest point of Europe where Jung was living (and he liked to walk in the mountains), and where all the rivers flow in the four directions to the sea. So, this is also the symbolic centre of Europe, where his psychology was originating.

SC: It seems as though Jung and von Franz trusted each other unconditionally and they were linked by their shared interest in alchemy. You are also very interested in alchemy. There are many ways to see alchemy and the alchemists. What is alchemy, and what could alchemy do in the 21st century?

AR: Yes, you know that von Franz had a dream when she had to decide what she would study. Because she was gifted in mathematics—she was an extraordinary pupil in mathematics—but in languages too, in old languages, she didn't know whether she should study mathematics or old languages. And then she had a dream: She dreamt that the gods of Greece were coming and asking her for a gift. And then she knew, this is the old languages, Greek and Latin, which she had to study. But during her studies, she got acquainted with Jung, and Jung was then gripped by *Aurora Consurgens* and told her this, and so on, and then she did a critical edition of the text of *Aurora Consurgens,* and wanted to have it accepted by her teacher for her thesis to end her Latin studies. But the teacher said, "I don't deal with rubbish." So, for him, alchemy was rubbish. He didn't want anything to do with that, and this shows also how the attitude in general was before Jung. Now many people speak about alchemy, and alchemy has become favorable; but before, it was nothing. Rubbish. Because somebody had to see the meaning of alchemy, and this was not seen before. One thought alchemy is a forerunner of chemistry because they dealt with different substances, though they had no idea of chemistry and so they had huge fantasies about their substances; but chemistry was a real science which developed out of alchemy. "No, no," Jung said, "this is not right," because in alchemy the irrational side, the mythical, the symbolic is still there; and they didn't know much about the real chemistry, the rational side, but both sides are together in alchemy. Later on, the mystical side was rejected as something unnecessary, and chemistry could take off. But interesting enough, if you read Jung's *Memories, Dreams, Reflections,* he had ideas, on his way to school, of alchemical things, namely that there was a big ocean and a little island in which somebody was doing alchemical experiments and had a long chimney out of which substances were coming and substances were going in to be distilled, and so on. So, he, as a pupil already, when he couldn't understand anything of alchemy really, had this fantasy. Von Franz did too. As a girl in the gymnasium (high school), she experienced making experiments with tar from the trees, from pine trees. Because she had heard that *Bernstein* [amber] is a fossilised tar from pine trees, and she wanted to produce this. Of course, this is also an idea from the alchemists. It takes millions of years until it's fossilised, but the alchemist can do this in a much shorter time by heating it up. So, she took the tar and put it into a vessel and put salt also in it because it needed it, and then it had to be heated. And then she told the tar, "Now, you have to suffer the heat; it's not agreeable for you, but undergo this and then after a while you will be a wonderful jewel," and this was her idea. But, one day, the whole thing exploded and she was burned in the face, and her mother said "What did you do?!" Then she had to admit that she had done this, and she was forbidden to do it anymore. The same thing happened to me. I was always, as a student, experimenting. I had a room, a laboratory, where I could do this, and once, suddenly the whole thing exploded and I was full of glass in my face. And my mother saw it, because I had to walk across past her room. She said, "What on earth were you doing?!" So, I said, "No, no, nothing," because I was bleeding, and so on. But, apparently, there is an old strain in people which goes with the alchemical idea, which is not coming from outside but it's in people, some people; and apparently Jung was dreaming, von Franz was dreaming the same dream, and me too, without knowing each other. And so, it is something in man which is in this way, and therefore the mystical part belongs to it. It's a loss that this mystical part is no more in chemistry; but I have to say the chemists which I met in my life were all gripped by this mystical part too. They were doing scientific chemistry, but in the background—I saw it from their dreams—the mystical part is still present. So, it belongs to it.

SC: Once, you said the following, of alchemy: "At night, a stranger knocks at your door. Alchemy suggests to open the door and to allow a conversation to begin. If you don't do this, there will be stagnation." In a time when walls are being built again, divisions are arising, what is your take?

AR: Yes, I think you are quite right; this is perhaps a way where alchemy is coming back, because I see now that a lot of people are interested in alchemy, but only because of their irrational side, so it becomes a little bit esoteric. The esoteric people are drawn to alchemy, but this is not the right aspect of alchemy; it is another. As I told you from these experiments of Jung and von Franz as children or grown-ups, as adolescents in the time of puberty. It is a dream of mankind, a dream of transformation; and you know, in the Mass you have the transformation too. This was always the danger—that the Church couldn't forbid alchemists to do their work, because they themselves spoke about transformation in the Mass: of the bread into the body, of the wine into the blood. And so, it was lucky for alchemy that it was never forbidden. It was, only once, not from the Pope, but ... but this was only for a short time. Generally, it was not forbidden, probably also because the alchemists didn't have followers. They didn't make a community. This would be a rivalry to the church. They exterminated all these Cathars and Albigensians and all that, but the alchemists were never dangerous for the church, because of the comparison of the transubstantiation in the Mass.

SC: Thank you. It's been very, very interesting to listen to you.

AR: You are welcome. It's a long life experience.

SC: It is indeed, and it's worth it. Perhaps, this is the suggestion for our patients: It's worth it. Never give up.

AR: No, no, and this I see always: When I can tell them a personal experience, then they get it. When I tell them a theory, it's boring. It's not the same.

C.G. Jung, Individuation, and *The Red Book*

Murray Stein

SC: Dear Murray, thank you very much for your time and for joining "Breakfast at Küsnacht." You are considered one of the most important, influential post-Jungian psychoanalysts. Can you share with us the central steps in your intellectual biography/journey? Which are the authors (and the research areas) that you consider essential for your own development and work? In particular, what role did Jung have? Why Jung, and not Freud, or Adler, or Klein, et cetera? Which other areas do you consider fundamental in your own intellectual biography (also beyond psychoanalysis)? When did you realize (and decide) you wanted to become a Jungian analyst? In short, how did you become a psychoanalyst?

MS: I will say at the outset that this journey has been a long one and with many twists and turns along the way. Like many people, I read Freud before Jung. As a teenager I was interested in science and pretty good at mathematics, and I thought I'd like to become a medical doctor. Then my interests changed and I took a turn toward history, philosophy, and literature and with my high school friends would spend long hours discussing these topics. Entering university, I didn't know exactly what to study but chose to major in English because of the brilliant professors in that department, notably Harold Bloom; and otherwise I took courses in languages (Greek, German, French), religious studies (with the inspiring professor, Hans Frei) and history. Because it was in my blood, I guess, and my father was a Protestant minister, upon graduation I decided to go to graduate school at Yale Divinity School and study for the ministry. I was not enthusiastic about this option, but it kept me out of the U.S. military during the Vietnam War, and besides that, the studies were interesting and the professors (among them the great Jaroslav Pelikan) were exceptionally magnetic. (Eventually I was ordained as a minister in the Presbyterian church.) I had never taken a single course in psychology in college—the courses in psychology were referred to as "rats and cats" in my day, because it was mostly experimental psych that was being offered in the department at Yale—and aside from reading Freud's *Interpretation of Dreams* as a teenager I had read no psychoanalytic literature.

Then, suddenly and out of the blue—it was between my second and third years of divinity studies and while taking a year out to work in the war on poverty in Washington, D.C.—I discovered Jung. It was something like a numinous experience. On a friend's advice, I bought *Memories, Dreams, Reflections*, and I was totally gripped when I read it in 1968 with a fascination that continues to this day (2019). I guess I fell in love with Jung. He was unlike anyone I'd ever read before, and I soaked up every word on the page. I return to MDR again and again to this day, and each time I find some new gem in this timeless text. I can say that this is a book that changed the direction of my life.

After that it was only a year until I arrived in Zürich to study at the Jung Institute. James Hillman, who was then Director of Studies, was my first contact, and in time, he became an important mentor and guiding figure as he re-invented himself after a personal crisis. With Patricia Berry at his side and Raphael Lopez-Pedraza looking over his shoulder, he began creating archetypal psychology. I fell somewhat under his spell—he was an irresistibly charming personality and most generous to me as a young beginner in this field—and I became a member of the very informal group that surrounded him at Spring House in Zürich and met in the evenings to discuss the exciting new directions his thinking was taking him. While I was a student at the Zürich Institute, too, there were quite a number of other important figures who played a part in my formation as an analyst—M.-L. von Franz, Barbara Hannah, Heinrich Fierz, Jolande Jacobi, and Adolf Guggenbühl-Craig were the most significant ones. My personal analysts, Richard Pope and Hilde Binswanger, also of course left deep imprints in my formation.

Following my return to the United States, first to Houston, Texas, in 1973, and then on to Chicago in 1976, I entered gradually into a new phase. I was accepted into a doctoral program at the University of Chicago in "Religion and Psychological Studies," where Peter Homans was my primary professor and dissertation advisor. At the time, he was working on his book, *Jung in Context*, in which he took a sociological approach to Jung's oeuvre, which was new to me and stemmed from the "social construction of reality" philosophy that was dominant at the university in those years. Eugene Gendlin and David Tracy were mentors as well, and they introduced me to humanistic psychology (Gendlin) and the philosophy of William James (Tracy). Mihaly Csikszentmihali was developing his idea of "flow" at that time, and I took his course and wrote a paper on "ethical genius," which he found of interest. Mircea Eliade was still teaching there at the time, as was Paul Ricoeur, from whom I took a course on Kant. On the psychoanalytic front, Heinz Kohut was the big name in Chicago because he lived there and had recently published his first book on Self Psychology, and his influence was felt at the university and among the Jungian analysts in Chicago. While working on my dissertation, which would become the book, *Jung's Treatment of Christianity*, I also wrote *In MidLife*, a kind of personal account of transformation based on Jung's autobiography, Arnold van Gennep's and Victor Turner's work on liminality and initiation rites, and a somewhat

Hillmanian reading of Greek myth. I loved studying at the U of C because of its totally open and liberal attitude toward every possible point of view. All of these teachers left their marks on me as I was evolving at midlife myself.

The early 1980s was also a time when British object relations theory was being strongly streamed into the Jungian community in America, and Michael Fordham's contribution to Analytical Psychology was being taken on board seriously for the first time in the States. All of these influences together moved me to abandon Hillman's archetypalist approach, for the most part, and to focus more intently on clinical work. With my friend, Nathan Schwarz-Salant, I launched Chiron Publications in 1983, through which we published a series of collections of papers by many prominent Jungian analysts of the day, titled the Chiron Clinical Series. For these collections, which came out of the Ghost Ranch Conferences that Nathan and I organized between 1983 and 1992, I wrote a number of clinical papers that show this second wave of influences. For me, this was a period of assimilation of foreign bodies, if you will, with an attempt to integrate them with my Jungian training from Zürich.

After that—this would be in the early 1990s—I took a turn back to classical Jungian psychology in my teaching and writing. The Chicago Society of Jungian Analysts was founded in 1980 and immediately began training Jungian analysts, and after some years of experimentation, a decision was made to require training candidates to read Jung's entire *Collected Works* over the course of four years in a reading seminar. Students were actually grateful for this opportunity, because the other brands of psychology and psychoanalysis were readily available in the universities in the area and they wanted to learn Jung. I felt a similar need after having delved into so many new and different schools by then.

On another front, I was becoming deeply engaged in Jungian organizational work. After getting involved with the IAAP and joining the Executive Committee in 1989 as Thomas Kirsch's Honorary Secretary and then going on in the IAAP to become President in 2001, my institutional activities were complemented by many invitations to give lectures and write papers. Increasingly, these became focused on Jung's later work, and I found myself writing more and more about the individuation process. *Transformation—Emergence of the Self* is the title of the book I wrote for the Fay Lecture Series at Texas A & M University in 1998, and this can be seen as an extension of the earlier work, *In MidLife*, now with the accent on psychological development in the second half of life. To this topic, I have since then added works in what I call "late stage individuation," which is about spiritual development in the later years of life. In addition, the publication of *The Red Book* in 2009 added a lot of material on the topic of individuation and inspired some of my most recent work.

I should say that I continue to read widely, not so much now in psychology as in philosophy, literary works, biography, and history. And in recent years I have been active with a group of talented colleagues at ISAP (Paul Brutsche, John Hill, Dariane Pictet, and Heike Weis) in creating and staging performances of Jung's correspondence with Victor White and Erich Neumann, seven scenes from *The Red Book*, and a play, "The Analyst and the Rabbi," written with my friend and colleague from Jerusalem, Henry Abramovitch.

SC: We are in your praxis, in Zürich, in a beautiful room. You told me a little bit of the story of this room and this building. Would you like to share this story with our audience?

MS: Of course, I'd be glad to. I was fortunate to get this room when my wife and I moved to Switzerland in 2003 from

Chicago. Walking down the street outside this building one day I saw a sign advertising an apartment here, so I inquired and soon enough we had moved into a lovely historic apartment on the ground floor with access to an interior garden. In addition, they offered me this room on the second floor. We have since moved out of the apartment and out of the city into the Bernese Oberland, but I kept this room. I'll never give this space up as long as I can keep on using it as a consulting room.

This building's origins go back to Roman times in Zürich (2,000 years). The owners of the building (*Neue Zürcher Zeitung*, the newspaper) commissioned a complete renovation in 2001-3—it was also a restoration, I should say—and discovered Roman elements in the foundation. In the Middle Ages, the building became a dwelling for what I suppose was a large family. It is just down the street from the Grossmunster Church, founded by Charlemagne in 800 C.E. Parades would pass by the house in the Middle Ages, flags flying, riders on horseback. It is a very colorful area of Zürich and is called "the old town." In the 18th century, a quite famous (in his day) artist and writer named Solomon Gessner owned this building. He founded the *Neue Zürcher Zeitung* (NZZ) and had a bookstore downstairs. Because he was well known as an artist and poet, he became acquainted with Goethe. Goethe had a good friend in Zürich named Johann Kaspar Lavater, who was a phrenologist and the minister at St. Peter's Church across the river. When Goethe visited Zürich to see Lavater, he also came over here to meet with Gesner. Sitting here, I often think to myself: Goethe actually walked into this building and spent some time here, perhaps in this very room. That's why I have placed a bust of Goethe on the tile stove next to you. And another special thing to mention about this building is that when Mozart was travelling through Switzerland with his father as a young boy, he spent some time in Zürich on his way from Geneva to Salzburg. And he came to this house, again because Solomon Gessner lived here. There is a picture of him (a drawing) playing his violin for Gessner here. I don't know if it was in this room, but it was somewhere in this building.

SC: I find it interesting that Goethe was here in this building where you have your practice, keeping in mind the legend that Jung might have been the great-grandson of Goethe. And this leads me to my first question about Jung. Who was Carl Gustav Jung? Or—to frame this question more personally—who is *your own* Carl Gustav Jung?

MS: Well, these are two different "Jungs," of course. The one is the historic Jung who was, in his time, extremely well known throughout the Western world and even beyond. He was on the cover of *Time* magazine, in other words a famous man, and people came from all over the world to work with him. He was considered one of the founders of psychoanalysis with Freud. He was Freud's crown prince, a gifted student who parted company and left the master in order to go his own way at midlife, then found his myth through active imagination, and became "Jung." So, I think of him as a historically important figure of the 20th century who created a body of work that will be studied, I believe, as long as people can read and are interested in psychology and questions of meaning. I've studied Jung's works since the late 1960s, and I still read him with great interest and pleasure. I think that Jung will be seen historically as one of the contributors to the *Aurea Catena*, the golden chain of thinkers and interpreters extending through history, like his fictional ancestor Goethe (though in a different genre). This Jung I never met and did not know personally.

Then, I have my own Jung, a second Jung. To me, he is as a sort of uncle or grandfather. I can relate to him easily. I grew up in a pastor's household like he did. We also moved several times in my childhood like he did. It has a special quality to grow up in that kind of family environment. It is a very political situation, like living in a glass bowl. You feel that people are always looking at you and judging your behavior. I was the elder of two children and have a much younger sister, as Jung did. When I learned a few things about Jung's life, I could immediately relate to him. I guess you could call this "kinship libido." He appears in my dreams once in a while, too. I think I have recognized most of his flaws and foibles, and I have had to work on forgiving him for them, or on putting them into the context of his life and times. I don't judge him, maybe because I realize I could have done the same things in his circumstances. For me, he remains the great elder, a sage not always wise but always true to himself. I use him as a reference point, like a North Star. Then I go my own way. But he is always hovering somewhere in my associations and especially in my work as an analyst. His writings offer a pathway for life—a good one for me.

SC: And is this what you also do with your analysands, or patients? Obviously not quoting Jung directly, but using him as an inspiration, through his teaching, to overcome, or look at, their problems?

MS: I've always got Jungian theory in the back of my mind. I gave lectures some years ago called "The Four Pillars of Jungian Analysis." The first pillar is the concept of individuation. When I sit down with somebody in initial sessions, I place them in my mind somewhere on the road to individuation. Where are they? Does their chronological age match their psychological development, or is it way off? Or are there blocks? Jung's concept of individuation speaks of a lifelong psychological process of development. It is very present in the back of my mind, and I use it as a kind of assessment tool. And then, of course, when it comes to interpreting dreams and working with them in analysis, Jung is a reference, especially for interpretations on the subjective level. Then there is the analytic relationship—transference-countertransference—that Jung writes about in his essay "The Psychology of the Transference." I use his diagram of the analytic relationship a lot to think about what's going on at various levels of the relationship with patients. For Jung, I think that the main part of analysis happens invisibly. You don't see it on the surface—it's at another level—but you can feel a relationship becoming established and deepening, gaining intimacy, its comings together, its separations, its life, its death. These states are portrayed in the alchemical pictures that Jung uses to discuss the analytical process. And then, if I feel that active imagination is an appropriate method to use, I will introduce it as a further means for contacting and working with the unconscious.

When I trained to become an analyst—this was from 1969 to 1973 at the original Jung Institute on Gemeindestrasse in Zürich—we had courses in active imagination and were encouraged to do it in our own analysis. I heard Barbara Hannah and Marie-Louise von Franz talk about active imagination, and nearly all the lecturers would bring it in at some point. I caught these teachers at their peak in those years. The late 1960s through the early 1980s was a real high point in that first generation after Jung as they came into their full maturity and offered what they had learned from Jung himself. The view was that active imagination is central to individuation and is absolutely critical if a person is going to develop further (in the second half of life especially, but anytime) what's deeply implanted within. I think that conviction has been largely lost among later Jungians, unfortunately. I'm trying to bring it back whenever I can. It is catching on somewhat since *The Red Book* was published, because it's so obvious that Jung would never have become what he was without using this method for following the spirit of the depths, going inward, listening to the voices, interacting with them, and developing a sense of the inner world. And after all, that is his greatest contribution to our culture, to put it in big terms. I once had a conversation with Michael Fordham while he was in the States on a visit, and I remember—this is Michael Fordham, mind you, the great developmental analyst!—saying in total seriousness and without any irony: "Jung's greatest contribution was the discovery of the inner world." I think that puts it in a nutshell. Culturally, in the West we are extroverted. Everything that's real is out there, and to take the other direction and look inward is something that's not much appreciated. In the cultures of the East, on the other hand, introversion traditionally held a place of respect. In Buddhism, for instance, the student is required to observe the workings of the mind instead of attending to the outer world. This is also what Jung advocates.

SC: I remember my first interview of this series, with Dr. Alfred Ribi. He said Jung discovered the irrational side of the psyche, while Freud was working more with the rational side of the psyche. This is why they separated. You have written a lot about *individuation*. What is individuation?

MS: I published a book with the title *The Principle of Individuation*, and I keep thinking and writing about the topic. In the *Seven Sermons to the Dead*, which Jung claims he wrote down in a sort trance as though by dictation, he says he heard Philemon speak (in *The Red Book* it's Philemon, but in the earlier published version of the *Septem Sermones ad Mortuos* the speaker is Basilides of Alexandria). In the first Sermon, the teacher speaks of two essences. One is the *Pleroma*, which is the All, everything mixed together, a *massa confusa* of everything without distinction, a primordial soup. The other essence is named *Creatura*, and *Creatura* promotes distinctness. In the one there is no distinct qualities such as male and female, good and bad; with the other differences, distinctions become evident. The one is timeless; the other is temporal and spatial. Both essences are within us, but as conscious individuals we are identified with Creatura. Consciousness is the principle of Creatura. A part of Creatura's distinction-making function involves separating yourself from your surroundings. On a sensate level, this is very important or you would bump into things all the time. It's a distinction between self and other. You have to be able to tell the difference between your own body and this table. But it is much more subtle on a psychological level, and that's because of what Jung calls *participation mystique,* that is, unconscious identification with our surroundings. You are not aware of this, and so it takes a long time and hard work to actually get psychologically separated from your surroundings: from your parents, from your brothers and sisters, from your peer group, from your culture and so forth. To an extent, this sense of being separate comes about naturally, of course: I'm not like my mother because I'm a boy, I'm not like my father because I'm a thinking type and he is a feeling type, et cetera. You start individuating like that. But at other less obvious levels it takes a lifetime to become conscious of identification with family values and attitudes and cultural stereotypes. And this increasing consciousness of your own distinct, unique existence as an individual is a major feature of the individuation process. You might come to it through a personal crisis like betrayal. This creates distance and triggers reflection. Or you get sick and you realize you have to die alone: You were born alone and you have to die alone. In a sense you are never alone, of course, but in another sense, you are very alone; you are an individual and unique speck of consciousness in the universe. So that's an important feature of individuation: coming to yourself, in your uniqueness.

But there is another aspect to it that is, I think, equally important, a spiritual aspect. And that is finding within yourself what in the Biblical tradition is called the *imago dei*—finding the image of God within. In Buddhist cultures it's the Buddha within. This is also you. It's something divine and related more to Pleroma than to Creatura. Making the connection between the ego part that's functioning in time and space and in history (you are born, you live, you die, you have your problems, et cetera) and this other part that's eternal is also essential in the individuation process: Getting to know *what* you are and not only *who* you are. Jung writes about this in *Mysterium Coniunctionis*, quoting his favorite alchemical author, Gerhard Dorn. Dorn advocates getting to know *what* you are, on whom you depend, *whose* you are, and so on. This level of inner knowing (*gnosis*) that's beyond ego and persona identity and personal history usually develops in the second half of life. It can happen at any time, of course, and there are many famous exceptions such as Jacob Boehme.

At that stage, you become conscious of these two levels: an ego life and an eternal life. At one point in his 1939 lecture at Eranos titled "Concerning Rebirth," Jung suddenly looks at his audience and declares: "*We* are the Dioscuri!" (twin brothers one of whom is mortal the other immortal). If we are, each one of us, in fact, Dioscuri, the discovery of this is a most important moment in the process of individuation. Of course, discovering all the more or less unconscious pieces that belong to you—complexes, shadow, anima, et cetera—and becoming conscious of these things is also all part of individuation. It takes a long time, and you have to go over this same ground many times. You lose it, you find it. The British analyst and good friend of Michael Fordham, Fred Plaut, wrote a moving autobiography along these lines titled *Between Losing and Finding*. As you get older, you start losing a lot of things and then you have to find them. He was reflecting on how we lose ourselves so often and then have to find ourselves again, and it is a constant process. Individuation is not a stable and predictable process, it is topsy-turvy. Jung said the path is serpentine—it isn't a direct line of development. We continually keep discovering and re-discovering parts of ourselves until we are no more.

SC: You mentioned the key to individuation is active imagination. But before we talk about active imagination and *The Red Book*, I would like to ask you: What are dreams?

MS: Well, it seems the brain is busy when you're sleeping, and at certain points in the sleep cycle it "dreams." This was discovered and defined by Kleitman and Aserinsky in the 1950s. It was named REM ("rapid eye movement") sleep. Your brain is more active when dreaming than at other times while you're sleeping. While you're dreaming your brain is active in a way quite similar to when you are awake, but the connections to motor behavior and activity are turned off. The sleeping mind is thinking when you are dreaming. And it thinks quite different thoughts and from different perspectives than it does when awake. The dream represents those thoughts. In my experience, the waking mind seems to be more restricted and limited than what I sometimes call the "lunar mind." It's very much taken up with immediate concerns, projects, obsessions, easy associations, and so forth. We have shutters on the windows of our waking minds and we live in a restricted space. In the dreaming mind space, the shutters open and let in what's out there in what we call the unconscious. That's why dreams usually surprise you—"Why was I doing that?" "Why was I there?" "Why these people?"—we ask ourselves. These questions are the beginning of *Traumdeutung*, dream interpretation. Why are we thinking about that when we sleep, when we're thinking other things while awake? Jung had a theory about that. He calls it compensation. The dream brings us something from outside the shuttered room of consciousness that, if we can understand the language and add the meaning to our consciousness, our conscious knowledge of ourselves will increase and maybe even of the world around us. We use this perspective to interpret dreams in Jungian analysis.

Dreams don't just tell us about ourselves, moreover. They can tell us a great deal about other people and our relations to them, about the times we live in, and even about the past and the future. Jung speculated about all of this, and his theories are interesting to think about: he claimed that the unconscious, i.e., the dreaming mind, doesn't live within the same time and space constraints that the waking mind does. It can enter into the past as though it were the present; it can enter into the future as though it were the present or the past, and so forth. It moves around in a realm beyond our familiar time-space restrictions. You can have precognitive dreams that take you into the future, for instance. You can have dreams in which you are living in another age and have another name and identity. On a more personal level, it frequently happens that you dream about somebody you haven't thought of for years, some school friend or somebody you knew a long time ago, and that memory comes back into your conscious life in a dream. It had dropped out, but now it's back. Sometimes these are repressed memories of trauma that you'd rather not think about but need to work through.

SC: Your latest book published last August—correct me if the title is wrong, but it is something like *Bible is a Dream...*

MS: Yes, that's right. It's titled *The Bible as Dream*, and it's my interpretation of the Bible as an individuation story. It's not specifically about dreams in the biblical narrative, although I do take some of those into account. The main theme concerns God. The principal character in the story is Yahweh, a divine character, and the second major character is "the chosen people," the human or ego character. The Bible is the story of an archetype's incarnation in the temporal world through various means. The archetype enters into the historical process in dreams, in visions, in revelations, in teachings of the prophets. And at the same time, the historical process takes on a divine nature. This is similar to what happens to individuals who individuate according to the Jungian program, if you want to call it that. The ego develops an identity and then becomes a representative of the Self.

SC: A Jungian perspective on the Bible. Dreams are there since the early beginning...

MS: Yes! Dreams have been with us from the beginning.

SC: ...and it is interesting to me when I sit in front of a patient or even with friends, who say, "I don't dream." Someone even said to me, "I don't dream, I think." How can we work with our patients when there are no dreams? And what does it even mean when they come in and say, "I have no dreams"?

MS: Well, I've learned to be patient, because most people normally don't pay attention to dreams, so they will say they have no dreams because they aren't looking for them. But if they start thinking, well maybe I did have a dream, and they start trying to attend to their dreams, they will usually remember some. In fact, everybody dreams. Some people remember dreams very easily. If I see them in analysis on a weekly basis, they will bring me many sheets of paper and announce: "Here are my dreams from the week!" From others I might get one dream a month or less. I think a lot of it has to do with tending to dreams and thinking of them as having importance. Then you will train yourself to pay attention: first thing when you wake up, not to jump immediately into the day ahead but rather staying in this in-between state as you wake up and pulling a dream back, maybe just a couple of images, and writing them down. Or if you wake up in the middle of the night you might think to have a small light handy and a pad of paper and make a few notes. If you have some images in the morning, you can often remember more of the dream and it doesn't just vanish totally. Probably we are constructed biologically not to spend too much time on dreams because we have to pay attention to the world around us, so there's an evolutionary reason that we don't just remain in a dream world. We wouldn't have survived in the material world if we stayed in dreams all day long. So, I think we have to train ourselves to stay with dreams a bit more than might be natural. It is an *opus contra naturam* to record your dreams and go on thinking about them during the day.

Failure to produce dreams for analysis might also indicate resistance. Patients are sometimes afraid of what their dreams will reveal about them. In the case of no dreams coming into analysis, I just work with whatever the patient may bring. I try to get us both into a kind of space that's somewhat open to random thoughts, associations, intuitions, and allow all that material into the dialogue. This also creates a dynamic in the relationship and opens the door to the larger psyche.

SC: It's not easy in this materialistic, fast world where we are connected 24/7.

MS: You know, that business of Internet connectedness, when it first started out—Facebook and all that—and the ideology of it: Oh, we're going to connect the world now, it's going to be a global village, everybody's going to be related, we can all talk to each other—sounded so good. I also thought, wow! this will advance human evolution. Now we're going to really get over the terrible biases and projections that created nationalism, racism, sexism, et cetera. We're all going to get into a wonderful global conversation. Well, it didn't go that way.

SC: Actually, it's getting worse and worse.

MS: Why? Because the shadow appeared and got into the game. What did Kant say? "Out of the crooked timber of humanity, no straight thing was ever made." Human nature doesn't tend toward perfection, toward creating ideal solutions and societies. Whether on the local level of family or village or on the large scale of nations and international relations, human nature simply doesn't allow the ideals we imagine to come to pass. We have to take this into account. There is always going to be war, there is always going to be crime, there is always going to be illness. "There is no bowl of soup without a hair in it," as Jung once said. We would like to see a total individuation of all of humanity, but it's not going to happen for a long, long time, if ever.

SC: And we cannot be naïve about the fact that the world is improving and it will improve forever.

MS: For sure.

SC: For example, Fukuyama's end of history is for me one of the biggest naiveties of the late 20th century. Now the world is free, liberal democracy will spread around...

MS: It's going to automatically spread across the globe, and everybody's going to come to see the light and install liberal democracy, right?

SC: And we see the consequence.

MS: That's right. Historical process doesn't work like that. And there is no "end" to it. Isaiah Berlin picked up on this phrase of Kant's, and I think he was realistic about the dangers of idealistic ideologies because of what they turn into. Hitler was a perfectionist: he wanted to cleanse the human race of its defects and make it into an Aryan ideal.

He was an idealist. This type of perfectionistic ideological attitude always takes these unexpected turns because of the human psyche. Idealism hides the shadow but actually then enacts it. That doesn't mean we shouldn't put efforts into trying to improve things. We can and should, but I think we should not be naïve in our expectations.

SC: These three concepts you worked on and developed: lifelines, liminality, and midlife. You wrote about midlife in a very interesting book. The concept of lifelines, I think it was in a paper of yours dated 2007 and then in a book too, is very interesting. We have to understand and be open to lifelines: what is my lifeline now, how can I be aware of this lifeline? And the concept of liminality: Without liminality there is no individuation. Would you like to expand on these three concepts perhaps?

MS: "Lifelines" are quasi-fictional narratives that we create for ourselves to give us a sense of who we are, where we come from, and where we're going. The lifeline creates a prospect for a future based on your goals and ambitions, your potentials for development as you see them and want them to be. This changes with your age and over time. And what I've learned through my own experience—and from many analysands who have reported the same thing—is that for a time you're on a certain line and it seems fine and you think you know where you are going and who you are and what your life is about, and then this line begins to unravel and come apart. Things you've worked hard for and invested in start to lose meaning. Other feelings and impulses intervene and surprise you, and synchronicities occur. And then life turns in another direction, along another line. And the time period between set directions or lifelines is what I call liminality.

I learned about this term's meaning from the anthropologists Victor Turner and Arnold Van Gennep. They write about liminality in initiation rituals that sometime extend for weeks or months. It is the period between social identities or personas, when the initiand is betwixt and between. This is often experienced as a time of confusion because identity is diffuse. In the book, *In MidLife*, which I wrote in my own early midlife period, I used Odysseus' return home from Troy as the guiding thread. He wanders around the Mediterranean from island to island, and it takes him ten years to get back to Ithaca. It took Jung about fifteen years to pass through his midlife and complete it. He started in 1913 and finished in 1928, as he reports in his autobiography. With the famous Liverpool dream in 1928 he knew he had reached his goal. He had found his center. So, this passage between identities involves a period of time, and I encourage people not to foreclose it. Erik Erikson wrote about the problem of identity foreclosure in adolescence. It's the same with midlife. If you close it off too fast, it leaves out too much of yourself.

SC: You don't know yourself so fast.

MS: You don't know who or what you are going to become. You know who you've been, but you can't predict your future developments.

SC: Jung was a courageous man. Maybe (or rather, for sure) he did not know he would find what he found. But at some point, soon after separating from Freud he felt the urge to go down, deep, as you said, and started writing and painting, and this is now called *The Red Book*. What is *The Red Book*, for those that don't know what it is? *We* know what it is; we like it, we love it, we read it. But what is *The Red Book*, actually? Because it is something unique in the history of humanities. There is no other psychoanalyst that did something similar, to my knowledge.

MS: No, I don't think so.

SC: Is it something comparable to Dante's *Divine Comedy*? Or *Faust* perhaps?

MS: I think it is comparable to them, and it's also been compared to Nietzsche's *Also Sprach Zarathustra*. But of course, *The Red Book*, or *Liber Novus* as it's properly called, is different. It's unique. It's Jung. It's a personal account of his inner journey and his dialogues with the figures he discovered on this journey. Like those other works of imaginative literature, it may go down in history as a classic account of a spiritual journey.

When I trained in Zürich in the early 1970s, and in Jungian circles generally as well after *Memories, Dreams, Reflections* was published, *The Red Book* was known *about*, and we had some inkling of what was in it. It was known to be the story of a confrontation with the unconscious, as told in Chapter Six of *Memories, Dreams, Reflections*. I used that chapter a lot in my teaching, and I used it in my book, *In MidLife*. Of the whole autobiography, I found this chapter to be the deepest and most interesting. But nobody—or I should say very few people—knew what was in *The Red Book*, really. It was kept under lock and key. There were rumors that Jung had disclosed things in there that he didn't want anybody to know about, so it was a great mystery, a secret. Then, when it was published in 2009, suddenly here it was, a facsimile, a transcription, and with many footnotes. Now we could read it, and we could see for ourselves what was in there. Immediately, many people bought it and some even read in it; a few scholars began studying it more deeply. I was fascinated and gave a number of webinars about it through the Asheville Jung Center. I was pleasantly surprised that it sold so many copies—over 100,000 in English alone in the first couple of years and by now I'm sure many more. It has been translated into many languages, including Japanese, Chinese, Russian, and all the European languages. Many people bought it as an art book. I think very few people actually read it at the beginning. I called it the "unread Red Book." One must admit, it is hard to read and easy to put down. I think a lot of people only look at the pictures. They are astonishing, for sure. Jung was quite an accomplished amateur artist, and the paintings are brilliant.

Then in 2016, Thomas Arzt, who was a student at ISAP at the time, suggested we have lunch. He wanted to propose something to me. "Why don't we offer people the opportunity to write essays about *The Red Book*?" he asked at a certain moment. At first, I thought: Hasn't enough has been said about *The Red Book* by now? Aren't people getting bored with it? But as we talked further, the prospect began to intrigue me, so I agreed: "Okay, let's give it a try. I'll write some letters, and we'll see what comes back." Well, we got a very positive response. People were excited to participate. The title we came up with was, *Jung's Red Book for Our Time: Searching for Soul Under Postmodern Conditions.* Before long, we had enough authors for a couple of volumes, and now with the third volume (just published) we have 54 contributors from a wide variety of countries and cultures, and there are two more volumes (36 new essays) in the pipeline. We are looking at *The Red Book* as a resource for people in our crazy times. Everybody says these post-modern times are topsy-turvy, confused, lacking a convincing narrative, and without direction. We don't know what's going to happen next, it's getting worse all the time. So, can we get help in coping with these times from *The Red Book*? Can it be a resource for those people who want to search for soul and find themselves in a personal way?

What you can follow in *The Red Book* is Jung's entry into the inner world and what happens when he gets there. First, he sits for many nights in the desert, and he asks himself why he's there and what's going to happen, if anything. And then he hears a woman's voice that says: "Wait, wait." And that's how Soul starts talking to him. And then he meets her face to face, and she engages him, and she argues with him, and she isn't what he thought she would be. He had set out to find his soul, but this was not what he was expecting. He quickly learns that she has a mind of her own; she is an autonomous figure. Before, what he had thought was soul was just a theory, and now he has the reality, and he has to deal with her. This is who he has to live with. Not some ideal, but *this* one. It's like marriage: you have this one, not what you thought marriage would be with an ideal woman. It's *this* one. And then other figures start appearing in the narrative. So, from *The Red Book* you get a vivid sense of what it's like to engage in this process of discovering the inner world.

SC: You read my mind, because my next question would have been: Why do we need to look into *The Red Book*, to have a suggestion about how to deal with these times? You know, my Ph.D. research is a comparative investigation about Jung's individuation and Ulrich Beck's individualization, which links to Bauman and liquidity. In 2017, Beck wrote, in a posthumous book, confessing his bankruptcy. He couldn't find a way to understand this world, even stating that the world is out of joint. As we said before, the world is not out of joint. There is progress, and regression. Why do I say this? Because in the play, *The Analyst and the Rabbi*, which you wrote with Henry Abramovitch and that I watched, both in Avignon and here in Zürich, Rabbi Baeck says something I find very, very interesting, to Jung. He is angry. And he is telling Jung, "We looked to you for psychological insights and guidance." Isn't this what our patients want from us? Isn't this what we, as psychoanalysts, could provide to the world? And then we can also discuss whether to think of *tikkun olam*[17] or not. This is perhaps why we need *The Red Book*; why, as you said, that method

[17] Repair in Hebrew. Also means to "repair the world" or to "perfection the world"

could help us to understand the world without being naïve, without being too positivistic. Fukuyama, as we said; the Democrats' years in the U.S.A.—the Obama years, which have compensated down to the Trump years.

MS: Exactly. As we have Rabbi Baeck say in the play, he looked to Jung for guidance, and Jung disappointed him in those years of the Nazi terror in Germany. Later, in his meeting with Jung in Zürich in 1946, they did have a reconciliation, and he probably could again read Jung for psychological guidance. Politically, Jung had missed the mark and "fallen off the path," as he confesses in his meeting with Baeck. He underestimated the evil that was rampant in Germany and was insensitive to the suffering of the Jews and other persecuted people, which is what we argue in the play. Reading the reality of the times that you live in is very difficult when you are in them. In retrospect, things seem so clear.

Maybe in retrospect, our age will look like the preparation for the Age of Aquarius. Many people feel that we're in a huge historical transition, globally and culturally. It was predicted long ago that these in-between times would be turbulent. At the end of his life, Jung forecast very dark times ahead. Edward Edinger, who was a significant Jungian in the United States, said the same thing toward the end of his life and wrote a book with the title *Archetype of the Apocalypse*. It's going to get much darker, and it's going to get worse according to these forecasts. Recently Peter Kingsley published a book titled *Catafalgue: Carl Jung and the End of Humanity*, which announced the immanent end of Western culture and more.

At the same time, Jung also believed that a new global archetypal dominant would emerge in the coming centuries, a new religion, a new kind of spirituality. We see some signs of that in our time, especially in the dreams of analysands. What *The Red Book* offers is a way to cope with difficult times. That is to go inward, to find "the spirit of the depths" that runs deep beneath surface of history, to discover the elements for a personal myth, and perhaps to anticipate developments that will take a long time to emerge fully into the light of collective consciousness. I think we have to be very patient and keep the faith, for ourselves and our patients. Is the human narrative going to turn out well with ever greater consciousness and sense of responsibility, or is it going to be the story of a tragic species on tiny planet Earth that became extinct by its own doing? We don't know. But I have the feeling, the belief I guess you could call it, that the positive outweighs the negative by just a little bit. Good outweighs evil by enough so that in the process of history things don't just completely fall to pieces and never recover. They fall to pieces, then they recover; and then you go on to another stage of consciousness.

SC: I would like to end our conversation with three straightforward questions. First one: what is love?

MS: Love is a word. It's a very difficult word, and a very powerful one when spoken with passion and sincerity. Of course, it's also an emotional reality that poets and composers and lovers and ordinary people express in many different ways. My view is that Love—I capitalize it to indicate its impersonal and archetypal nature—is the glue that holds the cosmos together, that connects us. It's the linking energy in the universe. (There is also the opposite—a dividing energy that people call hate. It's the dark force.) There is a universal view that everything is connected—the "unified field," "non-duality," the "All-Self"—it has many names. The medium of this unity, in which it is embedded, is Love. I think Love is what holds the pieces together. It holds humans together in couples and families, in tribes and nations, in communities large and small. It gives us a connection with nature, with animals, and with the universe. As humans we have it, but it's in all of nature too.

SC: Second question: What is freedom?

MS: Again, a difficult question. As individuals we have a little bit of it. Some people exaggerate their freedom, others underestimate it and feel needlessly confined and helpless. It's true that we are largely molded and shaped and influenced by many factors inner and outer, but this is so unconscious to us that it's easy to fall into the illusion that we have freedoms that we don't have. In a sense, we are just puppets of tribe and culture but we don't know it. On the other hand, I think there is some measure of freedom inherent in the human being or there would be no culture, no innovation or creation of new things. We would be chained to our biological instincts and cultural conditioning and there would be no change in forms of culture.

The freedom to think is the most precious freedom in my opinion, the freedom to think your own thoughts, to let your mind go where it wants and to observe it and be critical of it. This is the miracle of consciousness. We often can't act on what we feel and what we know, but we can think it. And so, to open the mind to its potential—that's what I try to do in analysis, to free the mind to float and think and entertain possibilities, and then from those maybe to choose some options to act upon after further reflection.

SC: Last question: do you believe in God, Dr. Stein?

MS: [Laughing] Jungians can't answer that question without thinking immediately of Jung's famous answer to his BBC Interviewer, John Freeman: "I know. I don't need to believe. I know." Personally, I consider myself to be a Christian. I was raised a Christian, and I remain a Christian, though not in a dogmatic or a mythological sense. And I have had a number of anomalous experiences that have given me a kind of experiential knowledge, and this is different from simply believing in received teachings and texts. I freely entertain the possibility that Love plays a decisive role in the creation and maintenance of the universe, of human communities certainly, but beyond that of nature, too, and of the whole cosmos.

Synchronicity is not only a theory; it is an experience. When one has a number of what are sometimes called "numinous experiences," as Jung called them, or "hints" of the divine in the here-and-now, it is but a small step to conclude that these strongly suggest the existence of an invisible spiritual ground of being, that our very being rests on a guiding and sustaining spirit that gives our lives meaning and direction. For me, this is Divinity, and as a person who has been formed by Christian culture it makes sense to me to call this "God," in accord with the New Testament witness to such a divine Presence. I have faith that the power of Love is stronger than the power of hate, and will prevail, ultimately.

SC: That is a nice way to finish. Thank you very much for your time. It has been a great pleasure.

MS: You're welcome. Thank you, Stefano.

C.G. Jung and Becoming a Psychoanalyst

Mark Winborn

SC: Mark, thank you for joining "Breakfast at Küsnacht." As we begin, I would like to ask a few questions about your background. When did you realize you wanted to become a Jungian analyst?

MW: That is quite a clear memory for me. That moment occurred while I was doing my doctoral internship in clinical psychology in 1986-1987. I was 28 years old at the time. The internship followed the completion of my doctoral coursework. One of the supervising psychologists at the internship, who was leading a process group for the interns, mentioned two books that had been important to him. Those books were *Memories, Dreams, Reflections,* and June Singer's (1973) *Boundaries of the Soul: The Practice of Jung's Psychology*. Naturally, I was moved by MDR, but it was Singer's intimate description of what transpires in the consulting room with her patients that was transformative for me. After finishing her book, I knew that I wanted to become a Jungian analyst. Prior to that moment, I had not had a clear vision of who I was to become as a psychologist.

SC: How did you become a psychoanalyst?

MW: I was quite fortunate in terms of the timing of my discovery. My internship was completed while I was an officer in the United States Army. Upon completion of the internship, I was assigned to be the staff psychologist at the United States Military Academy at West Point, New York, which is a short distance from New York City. After arriving at West Point, I was able to begin my first analysis and begin taking courses at the New York Jung Foundation. A short time later, I was able to participate in a year-long training program in Rye, New York, organized by Don Kalsched. That experience was formational for me in deciding to formally make an application to a Jungian training institute. In 1990, after completing my time of service in the Army, I returned to Memphis, Tennessee, where I had done my Ph.D. in clinical psychology. There is a Jungian seminar in Memphis which is affiliated with the Inter-Regional Society of Jungian Analysts [I-RSJA, an IAAP training society]. Upon returning to Memphis, I began my private practice and enrolled in the Jungian seminar. I became a matriculated candidate in October 1993 and completed my training in April 1999. While all training programs have strengths and limitations, ultimately my training experiences provided the necessary opportunities to explore in depth the areas of psychoanalysis that spoke most deeply to my psyche.

SC: Can you share with us some of the steps in your intellectual biography and journey?

MW: I grew up in an intellectually rich home. Both of my parents were avid readers, and my father was a university professor in educational psychology and counseling psychology. However, during my early school years I was a rather average student. My initial intellectual blossoming occurred during my first year of high school [equivalent to gymnasium in Europe]. My father was a Fulbright scholar providing consultation to the University of Utrecht in the Netherlands. Therefore, most of the school year was spent attending a Dutch school and traveling throughout Europe, which provided in-depth exposure to different cultures as well as new perspectives on the United States from the outside. During that time, I also began reading broadly; becoming infatuated with several Russian authors, such as Alexandr Solzhenitsyn, Tolstoy, and Chekov, as well as James Clavell, J.D. Salinger, and Trevanian. Looking back, it was through these authors, particularly Solzhenitsyn, that I became curious about how people survive psychologically under extreme or adverse circumstances; how they cope. My time living in Europe laid the foundation for my later intellectual and aesthetic development.

Upon returning to the United States, I completed high school and entered university. However, I did not discover my interest in psychology as a field until my third year of university. I realized quickly that I needed to obtain a graduate degree in psychology if I was to do anything of substance in psychology. I was accepted into the Ph.D. program in clinical psychology at the University of Memphis in 1982. While the training was useful, particularly in the practical sense of receiving significant experience with a wide variety of patient populations, I left for my doctoral internship uncertain about my direction as a psychologist. It was only after discovering Jung, while on my internship, that my intellectual development took another step. Jung's writing provided the broad education in the humanities (and psyche) that had largely been absent from my undergraduate and graduate programs. The encounter with Jung exposed me to philosophy, religion, mythology, literature, art, anthropology, and so on, in ways I had not encountered before. Eventually, my exposure to Jung led me back to various psychoanalytic authors that had not previously appealed to me.

SC: I would like to move now to the usual question I ask: Who was Carl Gustav Jung?

MW: That is an interesting question, because I think who Carl Jung was depends on where you met him and where you reside. At the Copenhagen International [IAAP Congress, 2013] there was a presentation called, "Whose Jung?" The European panelists were somewhat surprised by the American presentations on the panel in contrast to their presentations. They said they experienced the Americans as having a more personal relationship to Jung; that is, that the Americans thought of Jung in a more personal way. I am not sure about that, but for me, Jung was really the person who opened me up to the realm of the numinous. I was largely an agnostic prior to discovering Jung. There was something about the way Jung wrote about the numinous that made the numinous seem very real and helped to crystallize many of my own experiences. Jung gave me a language that I did not have before. That occurred during my doctoral clinical psychology internship, although I had some minor exposure to Jung in my doctoral studies. When I began to read Jung in more depth, he opened the doors to psyche in a way that reading Freud had never done. I had taken an undergraduate course in Freud by a well-known Freudian named Bertram Karon, yet there was something very dry about the way Freud was presented. It did not feel alive. Somehow, in Jung's work, all the notions of psyche and the interior drama really came alive for me. Eventually, I was able to go back into Freud, back into Melanie Klein, into the object relations theorists, into Self Psychology, and have a new appreciation for these other psychoanalytic perspectives.

SC: This is interesting. So, it seems the more appropriate question could be, "Who is your own Carl Gustav Jung?"

MW: Yes, I think it has to be. I think that is entirely in keeping with how Jung saw his own work and his hope for those exposed to his work. You know the famous quote, "Thank God I am Jung and not a Jungian." I think when we try to become Jungians, we do Jung a disservice. The idea is not to be able to reiterate all that Jung said and to adhere to every letter of Jung's writings. The goal is to internalize the vision that Jung had of the psyche, and then make it your own. That is part of the individuation process. And when we simply repeat what Jung has already said, we have not individuated. We have internalized something, but we have not individuated it. We have not made it our own.

SC: Well, Jung used to say, that is the *Imitatio Christi* versus becoming Christ.

MW: Yes, exactly. It is a model of a way of being, not a form to fit ourselves into.

SC: You mentioned the numinous, which is absolutely a very interesting concept coming from Otto. I just wrote a paper titled, "The Numinous and the Fall of the Berlin Wall," where I link the numinous and the development in history. What is the numinous, according to Jung?

MW: Well, I am grateful that he does not try to define it too closely, because I think it is anything that strikes us as greater than ourselves. The numinous can be something geographic; like, the Grand Canyon or the Alps—those places can be numinous. Or, it can be a moment as simple as being deeply affected by a leaf falling from a tree. It can be something very small or something very wondrous. It can be experienced through something exterior to us or something from our interior; but it is always something that creates a sense of connection to something larger than our individual selves.

SC: We touched briefly on the question, "Who was Carl Gustav Jung?" What is his relevance today, in 2018?

MW: I think he is certainly becoming more relevant than ever in the sense that the matters that he spoke of, and wrote about, with such eloquence are so pertinent to the issues we confront today. In many ways we are seeing a resurgence of some of the same issues that Jung was observing prior to World War II. We are seeing the resurgence of nationalism in the same way that he was observing, and I have the same concerns about it. Then we have additional concerns about technology and how that seems to be encroaching on our capacity to experience soul in a deep way. Of course, we also have the ongoing specter of climate change that is so vast that it is difficult to fully grasp the significance of it. Right now, we are facing a little microcosm of the climate change disaster with the impending "Day Zero" in Cape Town, South Africa, where an entire major metropolitan city is about to go dry; losing their supply of fresh water. We have never faced something quite like this at any time in the history of the world that we know. These issues are about a sensitivity to our relationship between ourselves and others, between ourselves and psyche, and between ourselves and the world. Such matters are the things that Jung wrote about so beautifully and with such sensitivity. So, Jung's message is now more relevant than ever.

SC: Jung was fond of dreams, perhaps even more than Freud. What are dreams?

MW: For me, I have come to the conclusion, most simply, that dreams are our attempt to digest our experiences in one way or another. And so, there is something about an experience, either something from the past that is unresolved, or something about an experience that is moving us forward, that we are wrestling with in some way. The dream is our way of attempting to digest that experience, and to some degree make sense of it so that we can have a relationship with it. I try not to utilize many formulas about what a dream is, or how to interpret a dream. As much as possible I attempt to let the dream speak to me. I think less and less about what is the meaning of the dream, and more and more about what is the experience of the dream, particularly the experience of the dream ego; and what does that experience bring to us that has not yet been fully digested?

SC: You teach at the Institute about cultivating the analytic attitude. Jung was the one who suggested to Freud that analysts should be trained; and because of this, analysts started to train properly. Gabbard and Ogden wrote about becoming a psychoanalyst. How does someone become a psychoanalyst? What is your point of view?

MW: Their paper [Gabbard and Ogden, 2009] on becoming a psychoanalyst is quite beautiful. Gabbard and Ogden address this essence of analytic work; that it is not about learning a set of theories, although that is necessary and essential, and it is not about learning a set of techniques, although that too is necessary and essential. It is about having a particular attitude towards the work. While this phrase first entered the psychoanalytic literature with Freud in 1915, the "analytic attitude" did not receive a fuller exploration until much later [Schafer, 1983]. While Jung wrote about several similar themes, he did not provide an overarching framework that would allow a fuller development of the concept. When Jung writes about the Opus [The Work] (taking the alchemical term for it), he is writing about an aspect of the analytic attitude. He is also writing about the analytic attitude when referring to the "symbolic attitude." But in general, when speaking of the symbolic attitude, he is speaking about something the analyst hopes to cultivate in the patient. It can be easily forgotten that the symbolic attitude is something that first must be cultivated in the analyst.

The analytic attitude takes nothing for granted; it involves always being open to the possibility of surprise, always being willing to look under the rug, and to consider what else something might be (other than what it appears to be). I think it is the holding of a tension between something known and something unknown. So, in teaching, particularly with analytic candidates (people who are eventually going to be practicing as analysts), one should beware of the tendency to latch onto formulas for analysis; for example, the formula that the analyst and patient must always confront the shadow as the first step in analysis. The analytic attitude says there are no predictable first steps in analysis other than creating the initial relationship with the patient and establishing the frame of the analysis. The analyst who holds an analytic attitude receives whatever is coming into the room, is in the "here and the now" with psyche as it is, and does not maintain preconceptions about what is to be encountered. The analytic attitude is fundamentally an attitude of trying to open oneself, as much as possible, to what is being experienced in the analytic setting.

SC: This is very interesting, because psychoanalysis is not so popular today. There are many other ways to actually get psychological support. Actually, I remember my first analyst, Dr. Alessandro Albizzati, said one has to be courageous to ask for help and knock at the door of a psychoanalyst. But one has to be much more courageous to stay on the chair or the couch and let therapy happen, let the cure happen. How do you work with your patients when they come to you and they have never been with a psychoanalyst?

MW: I provide my patients a brief introduction to the analytic process during the first session. This information is presented as suggestions or guidelines, rather than rules. I tell them, "As much as possible say everything that comes into your mind: feelings, thoughts, images; even if they include me." In a sense, I am encouraging them not to censor what is happening. They are still going to do that anyway, but they have at least heard that there is permission to speak openly, both about what is happening in them and what they might be feeling about me. So, I introduce the possibility, in non-technical language, of the transference and countertransference right from the beginning. I tell them it is often useful to record your dreams during this process, but there is no demand to bring dreams. I tell them that sometimes it is useful to keep a journal during the therapy process to reflect on things that are experiencing during therapy. I tell them that they have the choice of sitting up or lying down on the couch. There are few people I discourage from lying on the couch, and there are a few people I encourage to lie on the couch, depending on what their issues are.

SC: Can you give an example?

MW: Well, somebody who is already fairly decompensated probably should not start on the couch because it will encourage further regression, and they probably need a period of time of consolidation; a period of sitting up and monitoring the social cues that go on during a face-to-face session. If I began to see some stability emerging, particularly in their ego functioning, at some later point I might encourage them to lie on the couch. In reverse, somebody who is rather tightly wound, who seems very rigid, who has difficulty opening up to their imagination, and who seems very focused on reading my social cues (for example, whether I am smiling or frowning or look interested or bored)—for those people I will often encourage them to lie on the couch, because they are still able to see me if they choose to turn their head, but they do not have to keep me in their visual field. I am out of their natural line of sight. I find lying on the couch fosters for the patient a greater connection to the imagination, a greater connection to what is happening in their body, and a greater capacity to move into states of reverie. At the same time, when they are able to do that, it facilitates my capacity to move into deeper levels of reverie.

SC: Mark, is psychoanalysis for everyone?

MW: I do not think it is. I think the capacity to engage in psychoanalysis is a temperament as well as a psychological capacity. Jung said in one of his writings that psyche is not a democracy, it is an aristocracy; that many are called to the work, but few are chosen for the work. So, I think Jung believed there was a certain temperament that is more suited to psychoanalysis. But I think that our population has changed over the years as modernity has encroached on our symbolic capacity. As we grow more and more dependent on technology, that has resulted in a shift in the relationship with psyche. I think we see fewer patients coming prepared to do full analytic work from the beginning, and there is often a longer period of time required in order to develop those capacities within the patient. Unless somebody says something to me that disqualifies them from beginning an analysis (for example, if they insist on doing therapy in a way that is not compatible with the way I do therapy), I give everyone an opportunity to try analysis to see if it becomes possible to work analytically. Some patients have come for analysis who I did not think were very capable of analysis, yet ended up being quite capable. Other patients, who I initially thought were capable, ended up not being very capable. This is part of my analytic attitude; I do not presume to know who is going to benefit the most from psychoanalysis and therefore I give everyone who comes for analysis an opportunity to try it.

SC: Especially because many times patients come in with no idea about what psychoanalysis is, or with a fantasy about psychoanalysis from Woody Allen's movies; there are many ways. And another thing is theory in practice.

MW: I prefer to work with people who do not have an idea about psychoanalysis rather than people who have read something about it and come with preconceptions. When somebody has read some of Jung and has these ideas about anima and animus and shadow and things like this, then they push towards those ideas rather than letting those experiences happen. Often a little bit of knowledge gets in the way of the analytic process. As much as possible, I attempt to keep technical language out of the analysis, even when a patient is well educated about Analytical Psychology or psychoanalysis. One of my most memorable moments in analysis was with a patient who said, "You know, I can't really tell what we are doing. It just seems like we come in here and talk, yet when I leave, and I go home, I know something is different." For me, that was the mark of an analysis shaped by the patient's psyche, not by theory.

SC: And by the patient's consciousness.

MW: Yes, yes.

SC: When a patient comes and says, "That is my shadow, isn't it? That must be my anima or my animus," I find it very destructive, and perhaps even counterproductive.

I know you are an expert of comparative psychoanalysis, what is that?

MW: Comparative psychoanalysis is the study and comparison of various schools of psychoanalytic theory. Becoming familiar with a variety of theories permits identification of the similarities and differences with Analytical Psychology. It also allows an assessment of where those differences are significant and where they are not. Ultimately, comparative psychoanalysis facilitates cross-fertilization between the schools of psychoanalysis (including Analytical Psychology). During my analytic training, I was fortunate to be significantly influenced by a woman who trained at the Society of Analytical Psychology in London, named Mel Marshak. Mel was trained as a Jungian analyst but she also had broad exposure to the psychoanalytic community in London and she was a very wide ranging and inclusive reader. I think of myself as a wide reader, but she was always five steps ahead of me, and she was always asking me if I read the latest book from various authors. She would recommend writings of Melanie Klein and other Kleinians, object relations, traditional Freudian psychoanalysis, or works by Wilfred Bion. So, it felt to me as though there was nothing off limits conceptually, particularly during my interactions with her. Through Marshak's mentorship, I grew to appreciate that various theorists have different orientations to psyche and a different vocabulary to articulate that orientation, but that each theoretical framework is a different way of engaging psyche. I draw on the metaphor of the secret garden—there are a number of doors through which the garden (psyche) can be entered, but we each need to find a doorway into the garden that is significant to us. We need to find the Jungian door if that is where our predispositions are; but perhaps somebody else is not going to find their way into the secret garden of psyche through the Jungian door. Perhaps they are going to find it through the Kleinian door. There are many doorways into the garden, but we are all attempting to navigate the unconscious. That is the central common element of the various models of psychoanalysis. Jung, in his vast breadth of his writing, alluded to many of these areas that have been developed more fully in later schools of psychoanalysis. For example, what we now refer to as intersubjectivity is a significant element of Jung's (1946) "The Psychology of the Transference." Jung does not call it intersubjectivity, but he is describing that domain. There are so many concepts, developed through these different schools of psychoanalysis, which more fully articulate things that Jung only had time to foreshadow. Often, I find that these other theories complement my Jungian training (which I am grateful for); but Jung's voice is not the only voice that I speak with. Even Jung indicates, in *Memories, Dreams, Reflections*, that sometimes he can be heard speaking as an Adlerian, sometimes as a Freudian, and sometimes just speaking as Jung.

SC: I resonate with what you just said. Andrew Samuels, who is my Ph.D. supervisor, opened my eyes to this, for example, to relational psychoanalysis, to psychosocial studies, and to a variety of authors—like Susie Orbach (feminist psychological theory)—that I believe are relevant. Susie—or actually her book, *Fat is a Feminist Issue*—helped me, as a man, work with a male patient who had a problem with weight.

MW: Samuels' book, *The Plural Psyche*, was a very formative book for me as well. He was one of the people, along with Marshak, who really opened my eyes that there is a place for this plurality of orientations that does not take anything away from Jung at all—it adds to his work. I feel somewhat sad for people who feel the only person they are interested in reading is Jung; that is not Jung's ethos. At the Eranos conferences he was delighted to interact with physicists, anthropologists, theologians, and mythologists. Jung was hungry for knowledge beyond the psychological, and I think that we must have the same openness. Jung carried an openness to so many diverse fields, yet I think that is sometimes lost in the valorization of Jung. Most "Freudians" are already beyond Freud. Nobody refers to themselves as Freudians anymore. They are over their love affair with the personality of Freud. We are not quite there yet with Jung.

SC: In my recent interview with Professor Luigi Zoja, I asked him "Who is Jung?" and he started to laugh, and said, well first of all he is a man, not a god. And the additional point would be to take Jung as a starting point, but not as catechism. That would be, for me, very important.

MW: Lovely. I agree with that sentiment exactly. Yes.

SC: Who are the other authors and areas of research that have been essential in your development as a psychoanalyst?

MW: As I mentioned earlier, Jung was essential in opening me to the numinosity of life and the reality of the unconscious, particularly the interior drama, which is so wonderfully articulated in his theory of complexes. Following Jung, I was strongly influenced by Michael Fordham's poly-theoretical synthesis of the psychoanalytic theories of Jung, Freud, and Melanie Klein. Fordham referred to this comparative-synthesizing view of the unconscious as "the fenceless field" (Fordham, 1998). From Fordham I began to be influenced by the work of Heinz Kohut [founder of Self Psychology] as well as various authors from the object relations and intersubjective perspectives. These authors facilitated a deeper understanding of the nuance of the analytic encounter and a focus on the transference-countertransference matrix. Much of my later development as an analyst has revolved around the work of Wilfred Bion and several post-Bionian authors, such as Thomas Ogden, James Grotstein, Antonino Ferro, and Giuseppe Civitarese. I find the Bionian perspective quite compatible with Jung, while also providing significant insights into levels of experience not explicitly articulated by Jung. In addition to my interest in the Bionian perspective, I also have strong interest in music (particularly blues and jazz), aesthetics, comparative psychoanalysis (as discussed earlier), the technique of analysis, and metaphor. These are the areas I have spent the most time thinking about, lecturing, and publishing.

SC: Would you say more about metaphor?

MW: I think metaphor is an under-appreciated aspect of Analytical Psychology. Myths, fairy tales, religious motifs, and alchemical themes are typically seen as systems of symbolic material and as representations of the collective unconscious, but at the most basic level they function as metaphors. However, metaphors are not only associated with manifestations of the collective unconscious; they also manifest, and are utilized constantly, consciously and unconsciously, in everyday life and language. Metaphor is the process which allows music, art, poetry, or film to move us. It is also the process which brings imagination alive. Metaphor can be defined as the utilization of one conceptual or imaginal domain to map or articulate the characteristics and experience of a different conceptual or imaginal domain. The term metaphor derives from the Greek verb *metaphora*—to transport or transfer. In the use of a metaphor there is the juxtaposition between different domains resulting in a transfer of meaning from one to the other. Another way of thinking about metaphor is that it serves as a bridge from one realm to another realm; linking the two realms in a way not previously seen. As a result, an understanding of metaphorical processes is essential to engaging the dialectic between consciousness and unconscious processes. Analytic interpretation is essentially an art form; an artistic expression grounded in the utilization of metaphor. Metaphor creates the potential for change in the analytic process and provides the foundation for any creative experience.

SC: I would like to ask a final question. I know you have a new book out, by Routledge, titled *Interpretation in Jungian Analysis.*

MW: Yes, *Art and Technique* is the subtitle of it. I am quite proud of that. It is the culmination of my history as a psychologist and as an analyst, and I think it provides something that has not been published before in Analytical Psychology. Analytical Psychology has an ambivalent relationship with the whole issue of technique, and interpretation is the most central aspect of technique. Jung, as you know, was introverted and not comfortable with the systematization of analysis.

Yet, through experience we know that there are elements of analysis that are better done in a certain way rather than others. Not every approach works equally well and not everything done by an analyst always constitutes analysis. So, it is one thing for Jung, who was a very charismatic personality, to have a great deal of latitude in what he did. But for many people, latitude just creates a certain degree of wild analysis and sloppiness in the analysis. There are better ways of doing things in analysis, particularly better ways of saying things.

That is what my book is about, identifying the patterns that are useful to the analytic process; patterns that maximize the expression of the unconscious while also minimizing interference with the expression of the unconscious. The book surveys the history of technique and interpretation, both within psychoanalysis and Analytical Psychology. It provides a contemporary explanation for why interpretation is important in an age in which we are paying significantly more attention to relational aspects of analysis and the issue of the body in analysis. Among some analytic theorists, there a perception that language is not connected to relationality and not connected to the body. Yet, as I review the literature, both the literature from within psychoanalysis, as well as ancillary literature from neuroscience, philosophy, and cognitive studies, I find a great deal of support for the idea that what we say and how we say it in analysis does matter a great deal. There are better ways of saying things; better ways of intervening, communicating, and connecting. That is one piece of it.

Then there is the heart of interpretation; that to speak interpretively is to speak metaphorically. To speak with a poet's heart—not in the sense of trying to create or craft beautiful words. Not to say things in a pretty way, but the way the poet approaches every word used to construct a poem. They poet weighs the significance of each word; trying to get a sense—a felt sense, not an intellectual sense—of whether that is the appropriate word to capture the essence of a moment or an experience. That is the essence of what we should strive to do as analysts; weighing our words with the heart of a poet. It is essential to reflect deeply on what we are saying to our patients, why we are saying it, and when we say it to them (the issue of timing). So, the entire book is about this process of the verbal interaction; that is, where we get the words from. Not from theories often (although our word choices may be informed by theories), but through learning to work with our own interior experience; drawing from those interior experiences and our reactions to the patient: the images, feelings, sensations, and bodily experiences that we have while we are sitting with patients. Those experiences inform what we say and when we say it.

SC: Do you use clinical cases in your book?

MW: Quite extensively. I was grateful that many of my patients gave permission for me to use verbatim extracts from our sessions. I either record sessions or take extensive notes during sessions, so I was able to include long clinical examples that reflect the different ideas I develop in the book. I have a number of current patients that are in the book; as well as patients from long ago who were seen during my analytic training. I was fortunate to receive their permission to utilize the material after they read the passages I wanted to include.

SC: Can you share with us an example, maybe not only revealing, but that will drive us to buy the book?

MW: That is a good question. I have a patient in mind that from the book who was speaking about the anxiety he felt about calling his mother on the telephone. She had recently sent him a letter with some money in it. The patient was in his 30s at the time and had a very difficult relationship with his mother throughout his lifespan. He had told me in a previous session about "needing" to drink two beers before he felt able to call his mother. We were at the close of the session, and I mentioned that he had said in a previous session something about his anxiety around calling his mother and the need to drink the two beers before calling her. Looking surprised, he said, "Oh, you remembered." If I had wanted to conclude that session, I could have just said, "Yes, of course I remember," and allowed him go on his way. Instead, I said to him, "You seem surprised that I remember," and he replied, "Yes I am. I have had other therapists and they didn't seem to remember what I said from week to week." He became a somewhat tearful at this point. Then I said, "You seem surprised that I can remember you as an individual from among the other people that come to my office," and he said, "Yes, I am." I continued, "I think it surprises you that you could be important enough to me to hold a place in my mind." Then he became more tearful, and he said, "Yes. I have never experienced that before." What I helped him experience in that series of interventions was not simply support. If I had just stopped and said, "Yes of course I remember you," that would have been an adequate supportive intervention. But what I helped him experience through the interpretation is how he thinks of himself in my mind, which is not an easy psychological task for many patients. Often, they are not aware of it until it is spoken about and brought to consciousness. So, I was guided in my interpretation by what he was revealing to me through his reactions to me: that he was surprised I remembered him among my other patients. My interpretative task was to help him see that he did not experience himself as memorable. Of course, in this example, I am describing the operation of a complex without using any of the technical language of Analytical Psychology, yet the interpretation provided him with an experience of the complex and words to engage with the complex that he would not have had otherwise.

SC: Thank you, Mark. Good luck with the book. I look forward to reading it.

MW: Thank you. And thank you for the interview. I enjoyed it, and I look forward to seeing your other interviews as they continue.

References

Freud, S. (1915). Observations on transference-love. Standard Edition XII (1911-1913), pp. 157-171.

Jung, C.G. (1946). The psychology of the transference. In CW16 (pp. 163-323). NJ: Princeton University Press.

Fordham, M. (1998). Freud, Jung, Klein: The fenceless field. London: Routledge.

Gabbard, G. & Ogden, T. (2009). On becoming a psychoanalyst. *Int. J. Psycho-Anal., 90*, 311–327.

Schafer, R. (1983). *The Analytic Attitude*. New York: Basic Books.

Singer, J. (1973). *Boundaries of the Soul: The Practice of Jung's Psychology*. New York: Anchor Books.

CONTRIBUTORS

Paul Attinello, Ph.D., is a diplomate analyst of the C.G. Jung Institute Zürich, as well as a senior lecturer at Newcastle University; he received his Ph.D. at UCLA. He has published in a number of collections, journals, and reference works on contemporary music, HIV/AIDS, and cultural, philosophical, and psychological topics. He was diagnosed HIV+ in 1987, has been a member and manager for a number of HIV patient groups and projects, and has lived and worked on four continents.

John Beebe, Ph.D., is a North American Jungian analyst and author in practice in San Francisco, USA. He received degrees from Harvard College and the University of Chicago medical school. He is a past president of the C.G. Jung Institute of San Francisco, where he is currently on the teaching faculty. He is a Distinguished Life Fellow of the American Psychiatric Association.

Ursula Brasch, M.A., is a German Jungian analyst in practice in Schopfheim, Germany. She has a background in sinologym is an expert on I Ching and is a lecturer and member of the Curatorium at the C.G. Jung Institute Zürich, in Küsnacht, Switzerland.

Stefano Carpani, M.A., M.Phil., is an Italian psychoanalyst trained at the C.G. Jung Institute Zürich. He graduated in Literature and Philosophy in Milan and received his M.A. and M.Phil. in Sociology from Manchester and Cambridge Universities respectively. He is a Ph.D. candidate in Psychosocial and Psychoanalytical Studies from the University of Essex (U.K.), and works in private practice in Berlin (DE).

He is the author of "The Consequences of Freedom" (in *Jungian Perspectives on Indeterminate States: "Betwixt and Between" Borders*, Routledge, 2020) and the editor of the forthcoming books, *The Plural Turn in Jungian and Post-Jungian Studies: The Work of Andrew Samuels* (2020) and *Breakfast at Küsnacht: Conversations on C.G. Jung and Beyond* (2020).

Gottfried M. Heuer, Ph.D., is a German Jungian training analyst and supervisor, neo-Reichian body psychotherapist and independent scholar based in London. He is co-founder of the International Otto Gross Society. His previous books include *Sacral Revolutions. Reflecting on the Work of Andrew Samuels and Sexual Revolutions: Psychoanalysis, History and the Father*. His last book is titled *Freud's "Outstanding" Colleague/Jung's, Twin Brother* (2017).

George Hogenson, Ph.D., is a North American Jungian analyst. He received his Ph.D. in Philosophy from Yale University and his M.A. in clinical social work from the University of Chicago. He is a diplomate Jungian analyst in private practice in Chicago, where he works primarily with adults dealing with life transitions, dream work, and trauma. He serves on the editorial board of the Journal of Analytical Psychology, was the vice-president of the International Association for Analytical Psychology and is the author of *Jung's Struggle with Freud* (1983), as well as numerous articles on archetypal theory, synchronicity, and the nature of symbols.

Philip Kime, Ph.D., is a British Jungian Analyst in private practice in Zürich, Switzerland. He has a background in philosophy and artificial intelligence. He is a former Vice President of the C.G. Jung Institute Zürich in Küsnacht, Switzerland.

Marianne Meister-Notter, Dr. Phil., is a Swiss psychotherapist working with adults, children and adolescents in her own private practice in Zürich (CH). She is a former Vice President of the Curatorium, as well as the Head of the "Further Training & Vocational Policy" committee, and is a lecturer, training analyst and supervisor at the C.G. Jung Institute Zürich, in Küsnacht, Switzerland. She is the president of the Ethics Commission of the Association of Swiss Psychotherapists (ASP). Her most recent publication (2015) is titled *The Key to Self: Recognition of Self Through Depth-Psychology-Oriented Astrology.*

Susie Orbach, Ph.D., is a British psychotherapist, writer and a social critic. She co-founded The Women's Therapy Centre in 1976 with Luise Eichenbaum, and they co-wrote three books, including *What Do Women Want* (1983). Her interests have centered around feminism and psychoanalysis, the body, counter-transference, psychoanalysis and the public sphere, the construction of femininity and gender, globalization and body image and emotional literacy. Orbach´s first book was titled *Fat is a Feminist Issue* (1978). Her additional work on eating disorders includes: *Fat is a Feminist Issue II* (1982), *Hunger Strike* (1986), and *On Eating* (2002). She also published *The Impossibility of Sex* (2005), *Bodies* (2009), *In Therapy* (2016), and *In Therapy—The Unfolding Story* (2018). She was recently the recipient of the first Lifetime Achievement Award given by the British Psychoanalytical Society. She continues to help many individuals and couples from her practice in London.

Alfred Ribi, M.D., is a Swiss psychiatrist and psychotherapist. In 1963, he entered analysis with Marie-Louise von Franz and worked closely with her from that time. He served as Director of Studies of the C.G. Jung Institute Zürich (1969-1971), and is currently one of the most senior lecturers, examiners, supervisors, and training analysts at the Institute. He is a past President of the Foundation for Jungian Psychology, and of the Psychological Club Zürich.

Murray Stein, Ph.D., is a North American Training and Supervising Analyst at the International School of Analytical Psychology Zurich (ISAP-ZURICH). He was president of the International Association for Analytical Psychology (IAAP) from 2001 to 2004 and President of ISAP-ZURICH from 2008 to 2012. He has lectured internationally and is the author of *Jung's Treatment of Christianity, In MidLife, Jung's Map of the Soul, Minding the Self, Outside Inside and All Around,* and most recently *The Bible as Dream.* He lives in Switzerland and has a private practice in Zürich.

Mark Winborn, Ph.D., is a North American licensed clinical psychologist and Jungian psychoanalyst in practice in Memphis, Tennessee. He is a training coordinator of the Memphis Jungian Seminar, training analyst at the Inter-Regional Society of Jungian Analysts, as well as faculty member and external supervisor at the C.G. Jung Institute Zürich, Switzerland. He is a member of IAAP's ethics committee since 2016 and the author of *Interpretation in Jungian Analysis: Art and Technique* (Routledge, 2018).

www.ingramcontent.com/pod-product-compliance
Lightning Source LLC
LaVergne TN
LVHW070743240926
848802LV00005B/11/J

* 9 7 8 1 6 3 0 5 1 8 0 5 9 *